D0687475

On appraising the performance of an economic system

On appraising the performance of an economic system

What an economic system is, and the norms implied in observers' adverse reactions to the outcome of its working

RUTLEDGE VINING
University of Virginia

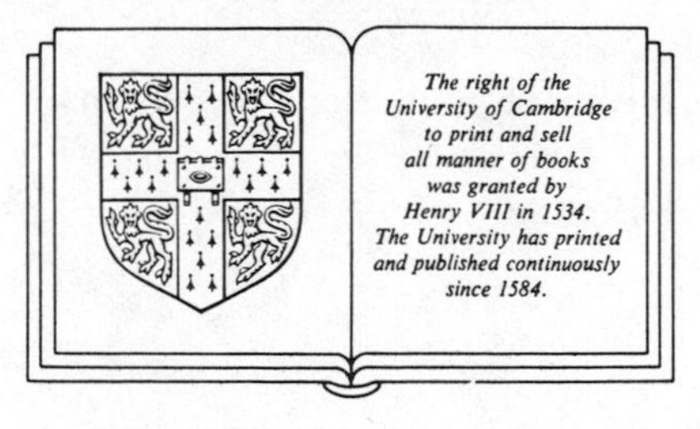

Cambridge University Press

Cambridge
London New York New Rochelle
Melbourne Sydney

Published by the Press Syndicate of the University of Cambridge
The Pitt Building, Trumpington Street, Cambridge CB2 1RP
32 East 57th Street, New York, NY 10022, USA
296 Beaconsfield Parade, Middle Park, Melbourne 3206, Australia

First published 1984

Printed in the United States of America

The author gratefully acknowledges permission to reprint material from the following: "Vilfredo Pareto (1848–1923)" by J. A. Schumpeter, *Quarterly Journal of Economics,* 63 (May 1949), pp. 155–6, © 1949 John Wiley & Sons, Inc.; "The Statistical Law of Nature" by Erwin Schrödinger, *Nature,* 153 (June 10, 1944), pp. 704–5, © 1944 Macmillan Journals Limited; *Freedom and Reform: Essays in Economics and Social Philosophy* by F. H. Knight (New York: Harper and Bros., 1947), pp. 10–11, 12–15, 182–3, 198–9, 212, 216, 217, 383, 390–3, © 1947 Harper and Bros.; "On Two Foundation Concepts of the Theory of Political Economy" by Rutledge Vining, *Journal of Political Economy* (March–April 1969), pp. 207–10, © 1969 The University of Chicago Press; "Science, Society, and the Modes of Law" by F. H. Knight, in *The State of the Social Sciences,* ed. L. D. White (Chicago: University of Chicago Press, 1956), pp. 21, 25, © 1956 The University of Chicago Press; "Virtue and Knowledge: The View of Professor Polanyi" by F. H. Knight, *Ethics,* 59 (1948–9), pp. 280–2, © The University of Chicago Press; *On the History and Method of Economics* by F. H. Knight (Chicago: University of Chicago Press, 1956), pp. 152–5, 174, © 1956 The University of Chicago Press.

Library of Congress Cataloging in Publication Data
Vining, Daniel Rutledge, 1908–
On appraising the performance of an economic system.
Includes bibliographical references.
1. Economic policy. 2. Economic history.
3. Economics. I. Title.
HD75.V56 1984 338.9 83-25236
ISBN 0 521 25656 9

The word "system" is nowhere defined. . . . I would like a discussion of the concept of "system." . . . That is one of my stumbling blocks.

Jacob Viner

We have involved ourselves in a colossal muddle, having blundered in the control of a delicate machine, the working of which we do not understand.

J. M. Keynes

Contents

Preface

The object of the inquiry that these chapters report upon is to identify and clarify the basic concepts and suppositions of the subject field in which the primary practice of economists lies; and it is our belief that we have proceeded in this inquiry along a line of thought of F. H. Knight. "It would hardly seem to call for argument," Knight remarked, "that the methodology of economic theory should be worked out in relation" to the problems that gave rise to it and that sustain an interest in it. "The first fact for emphasis," he continued, "regarding the relation between economic theory and action . . . is that the activities for which it . . . furnish[es] guidance are those of the citizen and statesman, not those of the individual as a *wirtschaftender Mensch.* Its practical problems are those of social policy. And the first requisite for 'talking sense' about social policy is to avoid the nearly universal error of regarding the problem as in any sense closely parallel in form to the scientific-technological problem of using means to realize ends. The social problem, and the only problem which should properly be called social, is that of establishing a social consensus on matters of policy. . . . The social action which the study of economics has as its function to guide, or at least to illuminate, is essentially that of making 'rules of the game,' in the shape of law, for economic relationships" (Knight 1956*a*: 174).

I shall find occasion to refer back to this observation by Knight several times later on. As an instance, the characterization in it of what our science is about contrasts radically with that given by Professor Tjalling Koopmans in the opening paragraphs of his Nobel lecture (1977: 261). In Section 1.8 (Chapter 1) I comment upon this, Koopman's characterization being on its face what Knight mentioned as "the nearly universal error." It certainly is not an error for one to hold with Professor Koopmans that the theoretical apparatus that he expounds upon is powerfully applicable to real problems that confront people who are in the act of allocating resources. The error lies in one's supposing that these have much, if anything, to do with the problems that first gave rise to and now sustain an interest in our science – which are descriptive and technical ones of a different kind that confront legislators in the act of jointly choosing changes in the law, that class of it in particular called economic legislation.

I exchanged letters with Professor Koopmans upon this matter of the contrasting problem fields, remarking, as I recall, that although I had not started out with Wesley Mitchell in mind at all, I had incidentally run into what seems to me to be the proper rationale for the emphasis that he and his early associates placed upon specifying certain frequency functions (Koopmans 1949: 89): They were describing statistical properties of the real populations and processes of really occurring events that do in fact convey to responsible persons a sense of how well or ill an economic system is working (see Sections 2.3 and 2.5 and the following Appendix); and that what really lends the impression of Mitchell's work being "Measurement without Theory" (Koopmans 1947: 161–72) is the lack in it of a formal concept of the "working" mechanism the performance of which is thus being specified and depicted; but that this key concept, in the specific form that these particular circumstances require, is no less lacking in the general body of economic and econometric theory down to the present day; and that I was now so bold as to hope that I had made a useful start upon an accurate identification of what this "working" thing really is.

In his reply, Professor Koopmans sent along a reprint of one of his articles of which I had not at that time been aware. It has a title that is right to the point of my subject: "On the Description and Comparison of Economic Systems" (Koopmans and Montias 1971). In the linguistic usage of legislators and their economist advisors, *economic system* is the name of the thing that is doing the working: "the outcome of the working of the economic system," "the performance of the economic system"–these are the familiar phrases. And had I at hand Professor Koopmans's article while drafting Section 2.4, I would have made an especial point of referring to it at that place. But I would have remarked upon it exactly the same as I remarked upon those works to which I do refer: The "mechanism" or "machine" or "engine" that Koopmans here sets forth is not the one for which we are called upon to look. The devising of it is a piece and parcel of a universe of discourse different from our own. Long ago, about the time of the early Mitchell of which we speak (see Section 2.5), Keynes was lamenting our involvement "in a colossal muddle, having blundered in the control of a delicate machine, the working of which we do not understand" (1931: 136). Koopmans's construct, along with those of the others mentioned in the later section, is not this *machine*.

But how is one to know this? How does one tell if such an assertion is true – about what is and is not accurate, is and is not required, in a description of this "working" thing? For this determination I have a simple rule, and a brief statement of it here may be an aid to a reader in alerting him to the narrowness of the focus of our study.

Our attention is to be strictly concentrated upon what specifically it is that legislators talk about when they talk about the *performance* of a currently operating *economic system;* the discourse in strict particular is among such responsible persons as they strive to reach agreement upon the reasonableness of the adverse reactions actually being experienced by some of them. The very first step is to identify precisely what kind of things these are that are being looked at and reacted to as conveying the sense of the performance for which these persons are responsible. This identification is crucial, and I can, of course, be mistaken about just what the technical character is of this that is being reacted to, that is, that carries this meaning; but as I see it, as an observer of actual cases of these strivings to reach agreement, and expressed in its most general form, it is *variation* as this is manifested in one or another population, dispersed over geographic space and developing over time, or one or another process of events occurring in space and time (see Sections 1.4 and 1.5). The properties of this variation convey sense as *performance,* and to illustrate what I am saying now I have gone through an illustrative descriptive exercise in Chapter 5, wherein the nation's population is described, dispersed as it is over the national area and developing as it did over a particular span of time when it was generally said to be in a state of full employment. What is thus described is called a *population process* in the literature in which such a matter is treated analytically; and a description of it consists of specifications of pertinent frequency functions.

If the thing whose properties are being reacted to is in fact a population process, in the technical sense of the theory of the subject, and if a main object of one's study is to discover what these properties depend upon, that is, what it is that generates in its "working" the variation that is characterized by these properties, then it is a specification of what is called a *statistical mechanism* that is being sought. And the basis for my holding that Koopmans's "mechanism" is not the one for which we are called upon to look is the fact of its not being this kind of mechanism – it is not a kind of thing that can generate in its working such shapes and forms as are descriptive of what is being reacted to (see Sections 1.6, 2.4, 5.5, and 6.1).

I have thought it appropriate to put this as a foreword to these chapters inasmuch as the principle followed – in this rejection of a tendered description as having for its subject something other than that for which we are looking – is applicable to much else. Readers of these chapters, even especially friendly ones, have expressed surprise and disappointment over my having drawn so little upon what they have come to look upon as formal economics. But my study does have this narrow focus: upon identifying, and illustratively describing, just what it is that choosers of changes in the law are looking at and reacting to when they experience adverse reactions to what they see as the performance of the economic system – then, what it is with which they are contrasting this that exists in fact and upon which they will have made observations – and, finally, what that special kind of modifiable thing really is that does in fact generate in its working this that is actually being looked at and reacted to. For these strictly descriptive problems I have found in the corpus of traditional economic theory little to draw upon, apart from what a person of moderately sound common sense would virtually take for granted. Much of what is now predominantly taught in academic departments of economics I would put under the heading of the science of management and administration, which is a new science of this century in which impressive advances have been made over the past several decades (see Section 1.8). And much of the rest of it is addressed to the problems of modeling and explaining human behavior, that particular class of it called economic – and this part of what is done and taught assumes, in my view, something of the form of a special branch of psychology. These are two distinctly different universes of discourse; and each is different from the one in which this present study falls. Choosers of changes in the law are not, in strictly being so, managers or administrators; and I am not undertakng a modeling of their behavior – as would seem to be the case among expositors of what is called the economics of politics. Mine are descriptive tasks: those that legislators are obliged to do or have done – ones that they would do for themselves but for the technical difficulties involved.

There is an almost prideful attitude among economists toward what they apparently see as marked advances in their science over the last several decades. But then, anomalously, there are also prominently expressed complaints of the poverty and ineffectualness of modern economics as an intellectual discipline for discussions of public policy. I think this anomaly is to be traced to the fact of these accomplishments being in extraneous subject fields. Let the reader try this experiment: Let him study intensively cases of Marshall, Fisher, the early Keynes, and the distinguished like, in their assumptions of the role of professional practitioner – the published records, that is, of their testimony and advising before legislative commissions and committees (see footnote 9, Chapter 1, and footnote 11, Chapter 3). And in the process, let him try to catalog to some extent the scientific knowledge and descriptive technique that these specialist practitioners of long ago had at hand to draw upon in their professional advising – beyond, of course, what naturally came of the abundant common sense and sharp perceptiveness that all possessed. And then let him do the same for the leading figures of the present day in their assumptions of this practitioner role (see Section 3.6) – being strict and fair with himself and not being fooled when he may run across an invocation of an econometric model, for example, or some mysterious reference to a welfare function (see footnotes 3 and 12, Chapter 1). If he sees what I think I see in an intensive study of actual cases of this old and ongoing professional practice, he will find that there is not much difference between what substantively applicable technical knowledge these two groups of practitioners respectively have to draw upon. The science in whose problem field this present study falls remains essentially undeveloped.

If, having said all of this, I yet have not made clear to the reader what he may expect to come upon in the chapters that are to follow, and if he would still like to be so apprised, I bid him go now to the final section of the book, Section 6.2, in which I set forth the principles to which I have tried to conform in the descriptive work that will have been presented – the Knightian principles, as I perhaps misname but nonetheless regard them, of empirical inquiry in the social studies.

Although the reader may think it odd that such would have to be the case, I have worked, off and on, for over 20 years in trying to find suitable expressions of the ideas herein presented; and during this time I have shown no mercy toward colleagues and associates, imposing upon them preliminary drafts and requesting of them comment and advice. Some fought fiercely back and thus escaped; but others, if only from goodness of heart, have been crucially and decisively helpful. I can say, with no doubt in my mind about it, that I would never have persisted so long upon this line of thought had I not had the encouraging assistance of my former academic colleague, James M. Buchanan, and my present one, John Whitaker. It may turn out to be scant credit to them, but this book could not have been brought to its present stage apart from their willingness to discuss with me, constructively and in detail, the matters treated in it. I do not mean to convey the impression that they are wholly or even mainly in agreement with me upon the interpretations I now submit. But I can see in my correspondence with Professor Buchanan, covering some 20 years and more, that quite a number of the sections of the book as it presently stands had their first appearance as letters in response to cogent points that he had made in his own.

There are many others to whom I am also much indebted. Professors Donald Dewey, Scott Gordon, Craufurd Goodwin, Geoffrey Moore, and John Parr all read early drafts of large parts of the book, and from them all I have careful and extended letters in which the very best of counsel, substantive as well as editorial, was offered. I also feel most fortunate in having whom I do as my departmental chairman, Roger Sherman, and whom I did have as the publisher's reader, whose identity I do not know. Finally, I must acknowledge the debt owed my students – James L. Butkiewicz, Geoffrey Rockliffe-King, Elizabeth W. Wogan, John Cushman, and Barry Love – the results of whose work I report upon in Chapter 5.

PART I

The circumstances in which the conceptual problems are posed: legislators deliberating upon how well an economic system is working

CHAPTER 1

Three main concepts that inhere in the circumstances cited

1.1 The three concepts introduced

The *Wealth of Nations* is said to have been the first systematic treatise upon the subject of economics, and students of that problem field should not be allowed to forget that it had its origin as a section in Adam Smith's lectures on jurisprudence. Its author referred to the subject as "the science of the legislator" (1976: 19, 428). To see the aptness of this characterization of "the science of political economy," one need only review the circumstances of its application in the actual practice of its prominent practitioners since the days of Smith. In his most characteristic role as practitioner, the economist is a specialist advisor to legislators and citizens in a legislative frame of mind. The advising of business firms and other administrative organizations or agencies with well-defined ends to attain is an altogether different activity. In the role by which he is familiarly known in the history of the subject, he has practiced his profession as counselor to legislators in their deliberations upon how well or ill an economic system is working and upon how it might be modified to improve its performance.[1]

It is in this factual setting, in which the economist will have assumed his characteristic role of legislative advisor, that we may identify the basic concepts – the categories of things and relations that the reasoning and talk are all about. Three of these classes of things may be noted immediately. There is first the something that is said to be "working," referred to in these legislative discussions as the *economic system* – or in certain of its details as the *monetary system* or the *tax system* or the *price system* or the like. It is prodigiously difficult for one to even think about the task of describing an actual instance of the operating thing for which *system* in this context is the name; but a modification of it, when proposed, assumes a fairly definite form. Real human beings, in legislative and quasi-legislative capacities, do

[1] In proceeding upon this understanding, it is our belief that we are following a line of thought of F. H. Knight. This has been indicated in the Preface, and we shall subsequently elaborate upon the conceptual and descriptive problems to which this Knightian line of thought leads. See especially Chapters 2 and 3.

in fact design modifications of currently operating tax systems, monetary systems, and price systems; they can be observed and listened to while doing so, and the specifics of what they design and propose for adoption can be laid out for anyone to see.[2]

Next, evidently distinct from this working thing that is subject to deliberately designed modification, is the *outcome* of its working. This is what the participants in such legislative discussions will have initially reacted to – observed properties of it conveying to each some sense of how well or ill the system is performing. In subsequent sections of this chapter, and in Sections 2.2 and 2.3 of the next, I think I make it clear, if there could be any doubt about the matter, that this outcome is manifested in strictly physical phenomena: populations of real elements distributed over geographic space and developing in time, and processes of real events occurring in space and time. It is this immense congeries of physical things and events that a conventional periodic census is an observation upon. When the term *economy* is used in legislative discussions of the sort that we are now contemplating, the reference seems frequently to be just these physical phenomena. But not infrequently this same term *economy* is used in such a way as to indicate that the reference is to the operating entity itself rather than to the outcome of its operation. We shall try to be consistent in our usage – understanding *economic system* to be the name of the directly modifiable mechanism that performs, and understanding *economy* to be the name of that in which the outcome of this performance is manifested. There is a modifiable something that performs, and we shall call that the *economic system;* and there is the outcome of that something's performance, and we shall call that in which this is observed the *economy.* This latter, so far as I can identify it in actual discussions among persons responsible for how well a currently operating economic system is working, is that mass of populations and processes of events upon which a census is an observation. Note definitely and keep in mind this fact, for much is to depend upon it: that it is only the former, a specific identification of which is a main objective of this inquiry,

[2] Congress, in 1908, directed the National Monetary Commission "to inquire into and report . . . at the earliest date practicable what *changes* are necessary or desirable in the *monetary system* of the United States" (emphasis added) (*Report of the National Monetary Commission of the United States*, Washington, D.C., 1912, p. 3). In due course the commission responded with a proposed alternative to the monetary system then in operation. And should one wish to see what a designed modification of a monetary system looks like, he may examine this alternative that the commission designed and submitted to Congress for its possible choice in preference to the system as it then stood.

and in truth only one of two components of that, that is subject to direct and immediate modification and choice; that the properties of this latter – this collection of real populations and real processes of events – are not directly alterable by any human agency.[3]

The third basic notion is that of a numerical specification of the stable properties of the outcome in terms of which the *performance characteristics* of an economic system are described. It seems to me no less essential to the clarity of our thought that this distinction be maintained between the physical reality whose properties convey a sense of performance and the measurements made upon this reality for numerically specifying these properties, than that the distinction be maintained between the thing that is performing and the performance of that thing. The real entities that census enumerators classify and measure and count exist independent of this classifying and measuring and counting. And it is the properties of these real

[3] It is a fact not properly taken into account, as I am led to view the matter, in the formal structuring of welfare economics – in particular, the welfare function as commonly conceived. The argument of this function typically consists of some combination of quantities defined upon this collection of populations and processes of events – e.g., an "allocation of resources" or a "distribution of income." It is some such thing as this – some combination of measurements made upon these real populations and processes – that is posited as an alternative subject to a people's choice. The function is conceived to be such as would assign a value or order to each alternative; and the choice is assumed to be of the means–end kind: the end being the maximizing of the value of the function, and the means being the function's argument, i.e., this combination of measurements. But a choice implies a chooser – and there plainly does not exist any human agency that chooses an allocation of a nation's resources or a distribution of a nation's income, or any of these other things that are specified by measurements made upon existent populations or processes (say, e.g., a spatial distribution of variously sized cities, an "optimizing" of which one may sometimes see expounded upon). These are aspects of the outcome of the "working" of what in fact is subject to being directly chosen by or on behalf of a people. The alternatives subject to direct choice are alternative designs of statutory law and administrative rule, i.e., of rules of the game. So that for a pertinent modeling of a people's choosing of what is called *social policy*, and if in this modeling the existence of such a function is to be postulated, the argument of the function, i.e., the thing to which an order is to be assigned by the function, must surely be that which is actually being chosen by the choosing agency whose behavior is the subject of the description – and this thing is a modification of statutory law, i.e., the "rules of the game."

The form assumed by the theory as it has come down to us follows along the lines of the earlier theory that purports to model, i.e., to describe in terms of its elements, the choosing behavior of an individual firm or family – and this form does not fit the reality of the supposed subject of the description. A close study of this reality of a people's choosing of its social policy – i.e., of its agents in the very act of designing and adopting changes in its economic and social legislation – leads, I think, to a distinctly different form, one that follows more or less along the lines of the yet earlier "fair game" theory. See footnote 12 of this chapter, and especially Sections 3.4, 3.5, and 3.6.

phenomena – that is, the real populations of identifiable elements and the real processes of identifiable events – to which responsible discussants will have reacted who are contemplating possible modifications of a currently operating economic system. A description of these properties is required inasmuch as the choice being exercised is a joint one: The discussants are obliged to communicate one to another what those properties are to which they are respectively reacting, what they think these properties depend upon, and why they think their reactions reasonable. This description is formed from such data as result from classifying, counting, and measuring real things and events and consists of graphic and tabular presentations of sums, ratios, averages, variances, and other numerical specifications of features of form of frequency distributions. In actual discussions among real choosers of modifications of economic systems, one may see that the statistical properties of selected populations and processes of events are submitted in these numerical terms as being descriptive of the performance characteristics of a particular economic system, the existent one that is currently operating. We shall emphasize in subsequent sections and chapters that this official talk and practice – indeed the very notion of democratic public policy choice itself – is not intelligible apart from a supposition that the statistical properties thus described are stable in some sense and also dependent upon the statutory and administrative rule and law that is subject to legislators' choice.

Conventional terminology would seem either to confuse or else to gloss over essential differences among these three basic concepts; and as an aid for keeping them distinct in one's thought, I shall propose a notation. The modifiable operating mechanism, the thing for which *economic system* is the name in the special usage here proposed, I shall denote by $\{\theta, S\}$. The θ is to represent a set of constraining and prescriptive rules – "the rules of the game," as Knight expressed it. It is this set of rules that legislators alter by their enactments of "economic legislation" and by their authorizing or acquiescing in changes of administrative rules. What the S is to represent is more difficult to put briefly. An identification of just what this S comprises is the main thing that I think this inquiry has made a start upon; and I wish to proceed circumspectly so that the reader will not too hastily pass it over and miss its peculiarity and the significance that I attach to it. In subsequent sections of this chapter, and in Sections 2.4 and 2.5, I shall consider somewhat more what the S part of this $\{\theta, S\}$ is. And in Section 5.5 and in the following Section 6.1, I submit all that I am prepared to do toward setting forth just what it is for which *economic system* is the name, conceived as an operating, working, modifiable mechanism.

The physical outcome of this thing's "working," (that is, the *economy* in our special usage, I shall denote by π_t. In later sections of this chapter and in Sections 2.2 and 2.3 I shall try to be explicit, with the aid of concrete examples, about what it is that π_t denotes. Finally, I shall denote by β_t a performance vector whose components numerically specify statistical properties of π_t that have acquired meaning as *operating characteristics,* that is, that convey to responsible persons a sense of how well or ill a currently operating economic system is working.

1.2 Rudimentary illustrations

As our notation now has it, $\{\theta, S\}$ is the system or mechanism that performs, π_t is the mass of developing populations and processes of events whose statistical properties convey a sense of performance, and β_t is a numerical specification of these statistical properties in terms of which performance characteristics are described. These distinct categories of things may be illustrated with a familiar case in which they stand forth clearly.

Think of a group of responsible persons in a diagnostic frame of mind deliberating upon the *congestion* that they will have noted in the outcome of the working of what is called a traffic or queueing system.[4] *Congestion* is a state of things that such persons observe in the motion and momentary arrangement of physical things in space and time. From a vantage point in a high building, one may look down upon a pattern of passageways and literally see congestion and sense differences in its amount at different places and at different times. A scaled-down three-dimensional model could easily be contrived so as to show placements and motions of small objects that would concretely depict what one directly perceives as greater or lesser amounts of congestion. This spatially dispersed population of real elements in motion is in fact a component of that comprehensive thing that we are denoting by π_t—and it of course exists

[4] The distinctions that we are now drawing—among a population of real elements upon which responsible persons make observations, the measurements that such persons define upon this population for specifying stable properties of it that convey sense as *performance,* and the modifiable circumstances and conditions upon which these measured properties are presumed to depend—are evident in Chapter 3 of F. A. Haight's *Mathematical Theories of Traffic Flow* (1963) and in Chapter 2 of W. D. Ashton's *Theory of Road Traffic Flow* (1966). Also see the preface of the book by Mr. Haight.

apart from any measurements that might be defined and made upon it.[5]

The next step in the group's consideration of this more or less dense spacing and more or less impeded movement of things is the counting, timing, and computing whereby the greater or lesser degree of congestion is measured. A discussant of the traffic problem typically expresses this measure of degree or amount in terms of averages and variances; and he describes the phenomena somewhat more comprehensively by referring to the relative frequencies with which certain sorts of events are observed to occur – for example, the frequency with which the time required for a "passage," or with which the number of vehicles that are waiting, exceeds some specific value. As intimated earlier, we are to bear in mind that when one submits such averages, variances, and frequency distributions as a description of the performance characteristics of a currently operating system whose modification is being deliberated upon, a stability and steadiness in time is being attributed to the values of these averages and variances and to the forms and shapes of the frequency distributions. The properties that are being described are not simply those that were in evidence during the observation period. It is an *expectation,* in the sense assigned to this term in the theory of probability, that is being estimated – a description of statistical properties of the populations and processes in question that one may expect in the future if no modifications in this currently operating system are effected. The observed averages, variances, ratios, transition rates, and frequency distributions are submitted as estimates of stable parameter values and stable frequency ratios and forms of distribution functions that are descriptive of the particular system. As such, they are instances of components of what we propose β_t to denote.

There is finally the working thing whose performance characteris-

[5] I very much hope that the reader will closely attend to the point of what now is being said – and that he will see its bearing upon matters that are of more direct concern to practicing economists. *Congestion* is the name of a quantity; and measures of its amount are provided by values of variables defined upon a population of real elements. But no less is this the case when one comes to the inequality of the distribution of a nation's income or the unemployment of a nation's labor force. These, too, are quantities whose measures are defined upon populations of really existent elements. And it is of utmost importance for the reader's understanding of the intended direction of our inquiry that he acquire a capacity for visualizing the comprehensive realities in which these quantities are manifested. All that is being said here about this more easily visualized quantity called congestion will be set forth again in later sections and chapters in our discussions of quantities that are subjects of economists' deliberations.

tics are thus specified. We may be reminded that a proposed modification of a traffic or queueing system invariably assumes the form of an alteration either of a system of rules, analogous to "rules of the game" that one may imagine an individual driver to be playing, or else of some part of the physical "layout of the game," the apparatus and arrangement of terrain that set the constraints upon the players in their respective private choices of actions.[6] An alteration of the traffic system is brought about by enactment of a statute or ordinance or by lawfully authorized administrative action – so that the choice that is exercised by real human beings in the act of choosing a modification of a system that is currently in operation is between alternative systems of statutory law and administrative rule resembling in essential respects "rules of a game." It is this modifiable system of rules and physical apparatus and terrain that we propose be represented by the θ in our notation $\{\theta, S\}$.

Bear in mind that this case of a *traffic system* and its performance characteristics, and the problem that confronts real people who are obliged to choose between a version of it that is currently operating and some proposed modification of the thing, is not being submitted here as a mere analogy. Rather, it is presented as an instance of identically the same kind of situation, involving the same classes of phenomena and the same kind of motivations. There are actual persons who are induced by the degree of congestion that they observe in the outcome of the working of a presently operating traffic system to inquire into the possibility of this system's being modified so as to reduce the expected amount of congestion and thereby

[6] Our persisting problem throughout these chapters is that of formulating a statement of what the thing is for which *system* is the name in this specific context – the context being strictly this and only this: wherein responsible persons are reacting to what they observe as properties of physically existent populations and random processes of events, and being induced by these observations to seek for some modification of the system upon which these observed statistical properties are presumed to depend. This is the task that I hope will attract the reader's attention and interest, so that he might himself help straighten out and clarify what I have been able to do. Getting at and getting clear this truly fundamental concept of an operating mechanism called by the name *system* is the main thing that I have in mind to do in presenting Sections 1.6 and 1.7 in this chapter, Section 2.4 and the Appendix in Chapter 2, Section 4.5 and the Appendix in Chapter 4, Section 5.5 in Chapter 5, and Section 6.1 in Chapter 6. In these latter two sections I think at least a beginning is made toward specifying in operational terms just what this machine or mechanism or system is that is said to generate the forms and patterns of variation that are observed and reacted to – i.e., that do in fact convey to responsible persons a sense of performance of the system. If what I have been able to come to in these final sections should seem anticlimactic to the reader, not up to what a finished mathematician and probabilist might have done, it is at least a start upon an absolutely fundamental identification and descriptive problem.

improve in this respect the system's operating characteristics. In essentially the same setting, in which identically the same categories of concepts are involved, actual persons are induced, by the degrees of *instability* of employment and prices, *inequality* of distribution of income and wealth, *concentration* of power in industry, *immobility* of families among status classes, or the *depression, inflation, stagnation, imbalance, underdevelopment,* and the like that they observe or somehow sense in the outcome of the working of what they themselves call the presently operating economic system, to inquire into the possibility of this more inclusive system being modified so as to reduce the amounts of what these names connote and thereby improve this system's operating characteristics. Congestion is the same kind of phenomenon – in a sense that we shall take especial pains to illustrate – as instability, concentration, inequality, depression, immobility, stagnation, underdevelopment, imbalance, and the rest. And it is a group of legislators, or persons who will have assumed advisory roles in a law-making or law-administering context, who are induced to make the inquiry, whether in the one or the other of the cases. To modify the system in either case, the group drafts and enacts ordinances or statutes or else stipulates some administrative alteration of rules or physical apparatus and layout.

This seems evidently to be the plain fact of the matter – readily confirmable by close examination of any actual instance of legislators, their specialist advisors at their sides, in the act of deliberating upon how well an economic system is working for whose performance they are responsible. And there is an important point to this fact for those of us who are concerned with the pedagogy of our subject. These advisors are called upon to describe, in the very special sense in which *description* is understood in the theory of probability, random variables defined upon populations of really existent elements and upon random processes of really occurring events – and *description* in this context must aspire to a finding and specifying of the critical factual cricumstances that may be said to generate the variation that is being observed and responsibly reacted to (see Section 5.5). These are demanding technical tasks upon which economic theory as familiarly conceived and taught has no analytic bearing at all – distribution functions, and what it is that generates and accounts for their analytic shapes and forms, are not what it is about. The truly cogent theory that immediately and directly bears upon these particular descriptive tasks is the theory of stochastic processes. And the typical curriculum and academic training program for authenticating economists for this characteristic advisory practice does not presently see to it that practitioners are suitably grounded in this specifically applicable theory.

1.3 Further illustrations marking the distinctions to be drawn

Having proposed a notation for the three categories of things – the operating system, the physical outcome of its operation, and the numerical specification of stable properties of this outcome in terms of which the operating characteristics of the system are defined – I shall now consider in a preliminary way illustrations of these three concepts in a context of more direct concern to economists. And as a point of departure for this consideration, I shall use a 30-odd-year-old essay by Frank H. Knight,[7] "The Sickness of Liberal Society" (1947*a*: 370–402).

There is a section in this essay of Knight's that he addresses to "the *system* as it actually works" (1947*a:* 379). This working thing, called by the author "the system," is the gamelike entity that we are denoting by $\{\theta, S\}$. In his comments, he remarks that "the system as it actually exists" has certain "mechanical imperfections" and thus "fails to work" in the way that "theory" may lead one to expect. In particular, he discusses "two major mechanical weaknesses" – "mechanical imperfections of the *system* as it actually works" (1947*a:* 379, 384): (1) a tendency for the degree of *inequality* of wealth and income to increase progressively and (2) a degree of *instability* of prices and employment rates that a people might sensibly look upon as being excessive. In these terms, Knight is referring to specific performance characteristics of a currently operating economic system $\{\theta, S\}$. The performance vector β_t, as we conceive this to be, and were it known, would consist of components some of which would numerically specify these particular operating characteristics.

It would seem evident enough on the face of things that the defects, such as they may be, are attributes of the system that is currently in operation. It is not the outcome of the working of the system that may be said to be "mechanically weak," but rather the working system itself. But a person in this role that Knight assumes will have been led to believe that such is the case by the results of certain observations made upon the outcome of the working of this system – that is, upon the economy π_t, this term and notation having

[7] I suspect that Knight would not have liked, at least on first encounter, the illustrative use that I here make of some of his expressions. In the following chapters this same essay is drawn upon again, and in ways more in keeping with the emphasis of its author.

the special meaning assigned to it in our present usage. As noted earlier, this physical reality, upon some aspect of which observations will have been made, is that vast congeries of populations and processes of events whose elements and occurrences census enumerators periodically classify and measure and count. This person, like the one concerned with the performance of the traffic system, will have devised (i.e., will have had devised for him) a classifying and counting and computing procedure that defines a variable upon some real population, or upon what probabilists call a *realization* of some process of events. It is a random variable that is so defined, no less than are the variables defined by traffic specialists in that similar context; and the person's statements about the amount of inequality – or of instability or concentration or the like – that characterizes the outcome of the working of the currently operating economic system are expressed, in effect, in terms of estimates of what in the abstract are parameter values and analytic forms of distribution functions. What will thus have been observed, as values of variables and forms of distributions, has induced in the observer some degree of belief that the system is mechanically weak – that is, is subject to being altered so as to render more nearly right the properties of the outcome of its working.

Note the implications of all of this: namely, (1) that there is a functional dependence of β_t (which is a vector whose components consist of parameter values and distribution functions of random variables) upon $\{\theta, S\}$ (the modifiable component of which is a system of constraining and prescriptive law and rule) and (2) that there is a standard or norm against which is being compared the observed properties of π_t (which is a congeries of developing populations and processes of events). The observed state of things, in which the inequality or instability or concentration or imbalance or congestion or blight or underdevelopment or unemployment or the like is manifested, is declared to be aberrant – that is, not what it would be but for the "defects" of the system. In the discussant's adverse reaction to the observed properties of the reality as it exists in fact, there is the notion of a standard or norm, an idealized state of this aspect of the economy – "what it would be" were the system suitably put in order.

These are the distinctions that we are drawing: between the thing that is performing and the performance of that thing; and between the physical reality whose statistical properties convey a sense of performance and the measurements that are made upon this reality for numerically specifying these properties. And to these we have added this third: between the actual reality that exists in an everyday sense and to certain particularities of which the person is reacting adversely, and whatever elusive kind of reality it is of which the standard or norm consists against which the actual is being compared.

1.1 The physical reality in which performance is manifested

To pursue somewhat more this third distinction, consider a legislator who will have experienced an adverse reaction to what he sees as an untoward amount of inequality in the distribution of the income of the nation's people – and who is now speaking to other responsible discussants about what this people might aspire to in the choices that are exercised on its behalf. What he will have reacted to, and is now making statements about, is patently a geographically dispersed population of real human beings, each at any moment in some distinguishable income state. In a preceding section we mentioned the possibility of one's constructing a three-dimensioned physical model of a developing population of things in which an observer perceives congestion in some degree – with the elements of this population represented by small objects located in geographic space at any moment and from moment to moment moving about from place to place. We may as readily envisage the construction of a three-dimensioned physical model of the real population in which the observer perceives inequality in some degree. Small objects would represent the elements of the population. Each would be located at any moment on a plane representing the national geographic area over which the actual population is dispersed; and each would be differentiated in some way to indicate the income class to which the represented member may be said to belong at that moment of time. There would be births and deaths of individual members occurring as a continuous process in time. There would be individual transitions from income class to income class also occurring as a continuous process. And individual members would be moving about from place to place and from occupation to occupation, and their respective capacities and responsibilities would be continuously changing with the passage of time. Ways could be contrived for showing in small scale, small enough for one to really see, such placement and motion and class transition of which the actual physical reality consists. One may at least imagine a drawing up of classification and counting instructions for clerical enumerators to use, such that he might tentatively take as being suitable for getting the requisite data. The real thing that is being reacted to and talked about does in fact exist; it lies there in time and space ready to be depicted.

I may well be overdoing this insistence upon the usefulness of such a device, but presently I do not think so. I do not have in mind, of course, any prospective actual construction of such small-scale representations. But I think it a useful mental discipline for one in the act of arranging and interpreting the data he has in hand – as he ponders, as he surely must be doing, upon their inadequacies, what might be misleading in them and what they do not disclose and just what the ideal data are for which he is using those in hand as proxies – that he go through this mental exercise of imagining himself proceeding in the construction of this physical model; for this is the true subject of his descriptive studies: the real populations and the really occurring events whose statistical properties do in fact convey to responsible persons a sense of how well or ill something else is working. If there is a numerical record of the outcome of the working of the currently operating economic system, there will have been some selection of really existent populations and collections of things and events upon which variables were defined for the forming of this numerical record. The numbers of which the record consists, marvelous instruments though these be, are yet only instruments for the description of this reality. And it would seem to me to be essential to their effective descriptive use that the user be capable of visualizing what the real particularities are that are conveying to responsible observers this sense of ill-performance.

In Chapter 4, and continuing into Chapter 5 (as I say, I may well have overdone it), I have illustratively gone through such an exercise. The task as I have put it in these chapters is that of finding a numerically specified rule for one's arranging small objects over the area of a large map so as to show, first, what the spatial distribution of a nation's population looks like at a moment in time, and then, with a sequence of such maps for a succession of moments, to show certain features of its development over time. There is a literature that can be drawn upon for this illustrative purpose; and I at least go through the motions of outlining a crude form of rule of this kind. With the population of undifferentiated elements thus depicted, there is next the matter of so distinguishing the individuals as to show the state of each at the time of the observation. The illustration that I present has to do, not with the individuals' income states of which we have been speaking, but rather with their employment statuses – and not of individual members, either, but of spatially designated subpopulations of individuals. But what I have tried to do with one set of data, to depict this one particular aspect of the economy π_t, is illustrative of what I think would be usefully done to show this other aspect – that pertaining to the incomes of individuals.

To assume that a rule of this kind may conceivably be specified, by way of observing and measuring and classifying population members over a succession of moments in time, is of course to imply that there are statistically stable characteristics of pattern and structure manifested in a human population as it develops over time. But this is precisely what is presupposed in a person's adversely reacting to what he observes in the population or events that have caught his notice and to which he is calling the other discussants' attention – and indeed is a supposition apart from which the very idea of *public policy* itself is not intelligible. It is variation among the elements of the population to which he is reacting. It seems natural that he should do so, and it certainly is the custom, that he thinks about and describes and numerically specifies the variation that he observes in terms of frequency distributions. An income distribution is literally just that – the analytic form of which is the probabilists' distribution function, which in this example would tell one the proportion of individuals whose incomes lie within any given interval of the range of variation of this variable. If the mobility of individuals among income classes has also caught the notice of this observer, it is a frequency ratio that he is thinking about, the frequency with which individuals move from one income class to another with the passage of some interval of time – and the analytic form of this naturally conceived notion is the probabilists' matrix or transition rates. Now, it is only to the extent that there is some regularity and stable uniformity in the shapes and forms and arrangements of values represented by these distributions and tabulations of ratios that it makes sense for the discussant to speak of the properties so measured as being characteristic of the outcome π_t of the working of the currently operating economic system $\{\theta, S\}$. His statements are descriptive not merely of the state of things during that limited span of time when his observations were being made. What he has seen and recorded during that time has served him as a basis for estimating measures of the properties of an outcome π_t in the abstract, the particular one corresponding to the economic system $\{\theta, S\}$ that is presently working and whose performance is being thought about and assessed. In the context of his discussion, in any public discussion at all, it is taken for granted that this system, viewed as a mechanism whose operation generates the variation that is being reacted to, is subject to designed modification by legislators acting jointly on behalf of a people; and the statements about what those properties are that induce the adverse reactions experienced by the observer essentially assert that so long as the critical components of this modifiable mechanism remain unaltered, the outcome π_t of its working will continue to be characterized by the offending statistical properties.[8] It is this consideration, I think, that gives point to the emphasis that Wesley Mitchell and his early National Bureau of Economic Research (NBER) associates put upon the discovery, in numerical records of the outcome of the working of an economic system,

[8] I take it as a fact, of fundamental importance in the conceptualizing of our subject field, that no human agency can choose or decree or fix specifically and directly the income or wealth or employment or any other of the momentary states of individual members of a nation's population. What is subject to being directly set or changed or chosen by an agency acting on behalf of a people is strictly confined to statutory law and public administrative rule – i.e., the rules of the game. The states, say income or employment, of individual members at any moment, and the individual transitions from state to state that occur with the passage of time, are among the details of "what tends to emerge" as a result of a playing of the game. This expression, "what tends to emerge," is a phrase used, I think I recall, by von Neumann and Morgenstern. These authors, following what would seem to be a natural bent, illustratively described aspects of "what tends to emerge," i.e., our *outcome,* in terms of *imputations* (which in our example would be the distribution of income) and of *coalition* or *power structure* (which corresponds in our discussion to the notion of concentration of industrial or personal power). What is aspired to in the development of the theory associated with these authors is knowledge of how to deduce *descriptions* of such features of "what tends to emerge" as implications of the rules of the game. The method of deduction in this literature is not commonly by stochastic analysis, but the phenomenon itself, the reality of "what tends to emerge" in an actual happening of it, is stochastic, and the methods that are typically hit upon seem to me to reduce to what probabilists call *deterministic methods* of analyzing essentially probabilistic phenomena. See Cox and Miller (1965: 157–9).

But whatever the method, a supposition that there exists a describable "what tends to emerge" – the description being given in terms of distribution functions, parameter values, matrices of transition rates, and the like – corresponding to any of a class of "rules of the game" is an assumption of a statistically stable outcome of the "game's being played." It is the stability of shape and form of the distribution functions of which a description of the "what tends to emerge" consists. In exactly the same way, an assumption that the distribution of income (or of employment or of commodity price relatives, or the like) can be changed by a changing of statutory law and administrative rule (i.e., by changing the rules of the game) is an assumption of a statistically stable outcome of the working of the system. A stability of the form of the thing as it stands, this supposedly being dependent upon (i.e., an implication of) modifiable statutory law, is a precondition for one's making sense in stating or assuming that it is subject to being changed.

One's doubting that such stabilities in fact exist, whatever this might mean (see Section 5.5), thus seems to me to be tantamount to a doubting of the possibility of public policy itself, i.e., of changing the statistical properties of an outcome by changing statutory law. This, of course, is not the same thing as one's doubting the efficacy of public policy. Veblen appears to have been among authors of this persuasion; see the last two chapters of *The Theory of Business Enterprise* (Veblen 1904). And Knight, at an opposite pole from Veblen, remarks somewhere upon how impervious our language seems to have been to all efforts at influencing its form and development (even those sensibly directed to the spelling of its words) and goes on to entertain a suspicion of this also being the case with the things whose forms legislators try to alter by superficial changes of statutory law.

of statistical regularities and uniformities; it was in terms of these regularities of form and shape of frequency distributions that the performance of a currently operating economic system was to be specified and described.

In Section 2.5, and especially in the Appendix attached thereto, I try to develop this interpretation of Mitchell's method and work and to identify what would seem to be the special form of the analytical problem that is posed in this early NBER emphasis – and also the subsequently developed technical theory that is specifically applicable to it. I have the feeling that Mitchell was on the right track in the 1920s and 1930s and that the basic concepts implicit in his emphasis have not been recognized for what they truly are.

1.5 The notion of a norm against which the actuality is compared

The descriptive problem that sets our science apart from natural science, however, as being distinctively *social* is the problem of identifying and specifying what those norms or standards are against which responsible observers gauge the actuality that they see in fact. I presently have in mind, as concrete instances of such norms or standards, the several states of things that are called by the familiar names: the nation's population of people, its members distributed over the national area, each at any moment in some employment state and from moment to moment subject to changes of state, and during a time when the population would be said to be in a state of *full employment;* or this same population, each of its elements being distinguished so as to show the momentary state of its income level, this being subject to change from one moment to the next, and during a time when the population would be said to be in a state of *equitable income distribution;* or the process of commodity purchase–sale transactions, these being, as they are, events occurring in time and space, and during a time when the process would be said to be in a state of *price stability;* or a nation's stock of money, the size of this at any moment being measured by a count of the elements of which it consists, the "births" and "deaths" of these countable elements occurring, as they do, as events in space and time, the existent ones at any moment being dispersed over a national or multinational area in variously sized concentrations, the size of each such substock varying from moment to moment, and during a time when this quasi-population process would be said to be in a state of *monetary stability* (see the Appendix to Section 4.5); or a nation's economy, this being the congeries of populations and processes of events for which π_t is our notation, its spatially dispersed components growing at varying rates, and during a time when the whole would be said to be in a state of *balanced regional development.*

The sense in which the states connoted by these italicized names are *norms* is evidently a different one from the natural science sense of normal structure and functioning. But the entity itself is "natural" – the population that would be said to be in a state of full employment is a real population; the said state is presumed by discussants to be realizable, that is, credible as a conceivable outcome of a real system's "working"; discussants, for the sake of the sensibleness of their talk, simply must take it as a real "what tends to emerge" that would result from a conceivably real "game's being played" (see footnote 8 of this chapter). There is thus a kind of reality about such norms, but yet a fundamentally different kind from that represented by the subjects of natural science. Whereas a natural scientist comes to know the norm of structure and functioning by repetitive studies of instances of the thing itself, one's finding out the specifics of this other kind of norm involves his finding and drawing upon sources of knowledge other than those afforded by the thing itself; and his descriptive statements about it are subject to tests of truth or falsity different from those that are applicable to descriptive statements of natural science. The best way that has occurred to me for getting a firmer feel for what these conceptual differences are is to painstakingly try to go through an exercise of describing one of these named norms, which I have done in Chapter 5. It is a character of this peculiar kind of norm, I now am led to believe, that any description of it is doubly tentative – not only would another independent doing of it show features that are different, but also the subject of the description is inherently transitory, the specifics of the thing being subject to changes over time, and any that are newly disclosed being subject to review – the *validness* of it, that is, as a characteristic of the norm. In proceeding through this descriptive exercise, I have made every effort to conform with what I have come to think of as Knightian principles of empirical inquiry in the social studies, an interpretation of which I set forth in the last section of Chapter 6.

1.6 The probabilistic character of the concepts introduced

This conceptualizing of our subject field is, of course, an empirical undertaking in itself; anyone may, and should, see for himself what the basic concepts are. In any specific instance of the practice of the profession[9] there is a characteristic sequence of operations: There is a numerical record formed from measurements made upon selected populations of things and processes of events occurring in space and time; there are computations upon and arrangements of these data that serve as descriptions of statistical properties of these developing populations and processes; reactions to these observed statistical properties are expressed, the discussions typically having been entered into as a result of responsible persons experiencing adverse reactions to what is thus connoted regarding the performance of some component of the economic system; modifications of this component of the system are designed and submitted as an alternative subject to being chosen, a proposed modification consisting of conditions and rules of action and procedure stipulated in statutory and administrative law and rule. This is an observable sequence of operations, and in any case of its occurrence one may see for himself what the real phenomena are that correspond to the concepts represented by our notation: the π_t, the β_t, the $\{\theta, S\}$. He may also confirm the supposition of a functional dependence of β_t upon $\{\theta, S\}$ implied when a people, acting through their legislators, modify the θ with the expressed intent of altering β_t in some predetermined respect–

[9] What I have in mind as cases, available for one's study of the "practice of the profession," consist of written or otherwise recorded discussions among legislators and their specialist advisors about how well or ill some component of a currently operating economic system is performing and what alterations might be made in it for improving this observed performance. Ricardo's "Speeches and Evidence" (1952) would be such a case; and the monographs and books by which he is known are largely but a systematizing of these legislative discussions. Marshall's *Official Papers* (1926) afford an instance. There is no dearth of such cases; the leading figures of our science, throughout the history of the subject, have virtually all left records of their practice either as legislators or as specialist advisors to legislators in their choosing of modifications of the economic system. Among my favorite cases of this professional practice is the one provided by the monographs sponsored by the National Monetary Commission and the final *Report of the National Monetary Commission* (1912). This was a joint committee of Congress that in 1908 was directed "to inquire into . . . what *changes* are necessary or desirable in the *monetary system* of the United States" (emphasis added). The report led to the congressional hearings that culminated in the drafting of the Federal Reserve Act as a designed modification of the currently operating monetary system. The better-known economists of today devote much of their professional time to appearances before congressional committees and to the preparation of legislative advice. Another of my favorite cases of this professional practice is provided in the monographs submitted to and the hearings before the Joint Economic Committee of the Congress in its study of employment, growth, and price levels (*Employment, Growth, and Price Levels,* Hearings before the Joint Economic Committee of the 86th Congress, Washington, D.C., 1959), organized and directed by a presently prominent economist and sponsored by a legislator who had previously pursued a distinguished career as an academic economist and had served as president of the American Economic Association.

and the further supposition of an imaginable idealized state of an aspect of π_t with which an observed state is being compared when adverse reactions are experienced.

A science of economics, with these its foundation concepts, entailed in the very circumstances of the actual practice of the profession, merits the name *statistical economics – statistical* being understood in its probabilistic sense as in statistical mechanics or statistical equilibrium. In this connection, the following remark by Erwin Schrödinger raises a point that I should like to stress:

> In the course of the last sixty or eighty years, statistical methods and the calculus of probability have entered one branch of science after another. Independently, to all appearance, they acquired more or less rapidly a central position in biology, physics, chemistry, meteorology, astronomy, let alone such political sciences as [that pertaining to] the national economy, etc. At first, that may have seemed incidental: a new theoretical device had become available and was used wherever it could be helpful, just as was the microscope, the electric current, X-rays, or integral equations. But in the case of statistics [i.e., probability], it was more than this kind of coincidence.
>
> On its first appearance the new weapon was mostly accompanied by an excuse: it was only to remedy our shortcoming, our ignorance of details or our inability to cope with vast observational material. In the study of heredity we might prefer to be able to record how the hereditary treasure of a particular individual is composed from those of its grandparents. In textbooks on gas-theory it has become a stock phrase, that statistical methods are imposed on us by our ignorance of the initial co-ordinates and velocities of the single atoms – and by the unsurmountable intricacy of integrating 10^{23} simultaneous differential equations, even if we knew the initial values.
>
> But inadvertently, as it were, the attitude changes. It dawns upon us that the individual case is entirely devoid of interest, whether detailed information about it is obtainable or not, whether the mathematical problem it sets can be coped with or not. We realize that even if it could be done, we should have to follow up thousands of individual cases and could eventually make no better use of them than compound them into one statistical enunciation. The working of the statistical mechanism itself is what we are really interested in [1944: 704].

In our subject field, probability has not yet attained to that central position to which Schrödinger alludes. Among most economists, *statistical* conveys substantially the same sense as *quantitative;* and probabilistic concepts and methods enter into their thought by way of estimation and hypothesis testing pertaining to relations that are interpreted as "deterministic" – which is a variant of Schrödinger's first stage in the introduction of the "statistical" point of view. But not among all; the process as he describes it seems under way – and a literature can be put together in which the authors do explicitly come to terms with the probabilistic nature of the basic facts of their branch of the subject field.[10]

As is intimated in the quotation, it must surely dawn upon one who would study actual cases of the practice of our profession – the aforementioned characteristic sequence of operations of which the practice consists – that what the responsible discussants and advisors are "really interested in" are stable statistical properties of populations of things and processes of events occurring in space and time. The state of any particular individual thing is never of primary interest; always the central focus is upon statistical properties of developing populations and processes. The names by which the features discussed are called are names of population phenomena: instability, inequality, concentration, depression, underdevelopment, imbalance, blight. In the preceding sections we briefly outlined what the population is that manifests congestion in some degree and then what the different but similar population of real elements is that manifests the degree of inequality that will have aroused a discussant's concern: and in Sections 2.2 and 2.3 in the following chapter we shall return to this matter of identifying the reality to which the familiar names refer. In any case that one may study, the real

[10] A reader has commented to the effect that I do not seem to be aware of how widely shared among economists this view of the importance of probability concepts is and of how much recent work has gone into the construction of "probabilistic models of the workings of the economy." But I think I am aware of what this reader is calling to mind, and I believe it to have virtually nothing to do with the problem field that I am outlining in these chapters, which field, to repeat a remark included in an earlier footnote, consists of the descriptive and analytic problems immediately and inherently posed in this specific context – the context being strictly this, no more nor less: wherein legislators, being held responsible, as they are, for the working of what they call the economic system, are reacting adversely to what in fact probabilists call *realizations* of population and other random processes, and being induced (by what they are led to believe are characteristic statistical properties of these processes) to seek for some change of law that will modify what probabilists call the *statistical mechanisms* presently in operation and upon which these properties depend, thus to make more nearly *right* the outcome of the working of the economic system. The problems are: to identify in actual cases of this factually experienced adverse reaction, specifically in concrete terms, what it is that is said to be working, and what these responsible persons are looking at and reacting to when they experience the adverse reactions to what they think they see as characteristic properties of the outcome of this working, and what standards or norms those are that are implied in this experienced sense of disapprobation.

It is true that I am not aware of a literature that is explicitly addressed to these particular identification and descriptive problems – specifically, to the very special form of analytical problem that I believe to be inherent in this context and that I discuss in some detail in the Appendix to Chapter 2.

There are certain authors, however, certain of whose works do seem to me to be such as may be fitted into the line of thought that I am presently pursuing; and in Section 2.5 I comment upon some of this work.

phenomena to which the discussants will have initially reacted will be found to consist of populations and processes of events developing in geographic space and time. And should one try, as I do in Chapters 4 and 5, to specify and visualize as scaled-down physical models the reality that is being reacted to by persons who are actually responsible for the states of these things, he would see that the problems of describing these phenomena and of discovering what their characteristic properties depend upon bear much in common with the descriptive and analytic problems posed in such natural sciences as Schrödinger cites that treat of probabilistic phenomena.

"The working of the statistical mechanism itself is what we are really interested in," he says. And so must we – in that it is this working of a mechanism that generates the variation whose properties are conveying the sense of dubious performance. Immediately following the quoted remark, Schrödinger indicates well enough what a statistical mechanism is in the natural science usage. It consists of stable relative frequencies with which specifically defined events are observed to occur. The events in question, and the relative frequencies of their occurrence, are defined upon and observed in the real phenomena that we are denoting by π_t. From these empirically established facts about certain primary statistical properties of these population processes, other statistical properties are deduced as implications. The mechanism consists of the numerically specified probabilities (i.e., relative frequencies) of the primary events. The sense of its working is conveyed in the stochastic theory that is applied to deduce the implications pertaining to the other statistical properties; and the variation that is characterized by these properties is said to be generated by the working of this mechanism. For example, certain diffusion phenomena are described by distribution functions of variables that specify some feature of the spatial arrangement of particles at successive moments of time. The forms and parameter values of these distribution functions are deduced from matrices of transition probabilities (i.e., stable frequency ratios). The statistical mechanism that generates the variation described by the distribution *is* this matrix of transition probabilities. And it is in terms of the theory of random processes that the working of this mechanism, in the generating of the variation having the predicted statistical properties, is understood and explained. All of this – the variation for which an explanation is to be found, as well as the mechanism upon which the properties of this variation will have been shown to depend – is encompassed in the two concepts that we are denoting by π_t and β_t. In the physical reality π_t, there is what is actually seen as variation among individuals at any moment, and individual transitions from moment to moment; and the components of β_t numerically specify just such variation and change. The *statistical mechanism,* in the natural science usage of this term, consists of the same kind of numerical specifications of stable statistical properties as those that comprise the *performance vector* β_t – they being interpreted as doing the generating, the latter being descriptive of this generated variation.

In proposing this notation for the fundamental concepts at the end of Section 1.1, I postponed giving an account of what the S in the $\{\theta, S\}$ is to represent. I shall now say that it stands for a collection of existent mechanisms of this particular kind.[11] Legislators are presumed to be in a position to design and jointly choose modifications of what the $\{\theta, S\}$ denotes – that is, to make changes in the economic system so as to render more nearly *right* the properties of the outcome of its working. But no human agency can directly alter a component of what it is that S connotes – that is, what a natural scientist conceives a statistical mechanism to be. The choice that legislators exercise is strictly confined to changes in the law – that is, to alternative sets of what θ represents. Yet, to change the properties of the variation to which they are reacting, the mechanisms upon which these properties depend must be altered. Thus, in this choice that legislators exercise, there is a connection presupposed between the mechanisms S, which generate the variation whose properties convey a sense of performance, and the constraining and prescriptive rules θ, to which they are restricted in their choice.

1.7 A juxtaposition: corresponding concepts in the theory of probability

If there is to be a science whose subject is the economic system – a cumulation of knowledge about how a thing of this sort works and about what happens to the outcome of its working when designed changes are effected in it – then it would seem of elementary importance that a general understanding be reached among its students regarding what this working thing is that goes by the name *economic system.* And although the reader may not at all agree with me, I think it adds to the clarity of one's thought about this matter to juxtapose the concepts for which we have proposed notations alongside of

[11] I shall note once again that the identification of what specifically this modifiable thing is that is said to be working is a primary objective of this inquiry. See Section 5.5 and especially Section 6.1; also see Section 2.4.

similar concepts discussed in familiar expositions of the theory of probability and its applications.

In an author's introduction to the theory of what is known as statistical probability, he typically begins with a consideration of the notion of a *conceptual experiment.* It seems an unappealing name to call it by, but that is the name given to it. For example: "It must be understood . . . that we are concerned not with modes of inductive reasoning but with something that might be called physical or statistical probability. . . . Our probabilities do not refer to judgments but to possible outcomes of a conceptual experiment. Before we speak of probabilities, we must agree on an idealized model of a particular conceptual experiment. . . . At the outset we must agree on the possible outcomes of this experiment, our sample space, and the probabilities associated with them" (Feller 1968: 4); ". . .we consider a determined *random experiment,* Φ, that may be repeated a large number of times under uniform conditions. . ." (Cramer 1951: 141); "The practical situation with which we are concerned involves a *random experiment.* That is, we consider an *experiment* Φ, the outcome of which. . ." (Cramer and Leadbetter 1967: 1–2).

It is this conceptual experiment Φ in this theory that corresponds to the concept that we denote by $\{\theta, S\}$ in our contemplated application of the theory. When the author submits an example to illustrate the intuitive notion that he intends his Φ to connote, it consists of a set of rules, identically as though they were the rules of a game, that stipulate physical circumstances and apparatus and that prescribe and constrain certain operations and actions. He thus tells the reader what the game is a "play" of which would constitute a trial of this instance of a Φ–that is, what he might do so as to observe a sequence of performances of the experiment. A performance of the experiment results in an outcome. This notion of an outcome is also an intuitive one. The outcome is a physical occurrence; it will have momentarily existed independent of any measurements that may have been made upon it. In its primal form it consists of real elements constituting a population at each of a succession of moments in time, or of some process of instantaneously occurring real events, each of these really existent things being in some identifiable state at any moment and (if an element of a population) moving about and making transitions from state to state from moment to moment. This is our π_t, and it is not a kind of thing (no more than is a topography or a face) that is subject to an exhaustively comprehensive specification. But when one undertakes to describe certain isolated features of it that he has an especial interest in, he makes measurements upon it and expresses the description in terms of the numbers that result from the measurements. It is in this form that the probability theorist conceives of a mathematical idealization of the outcome: as a point in a well-defined space, the point being specified by a vector whose components are these measurements.

The Φ (i.e., our $\{\theta, S\}$) and the π_t are not mathematical concepts. They represent the parts of the physical world that afford the intuitive background for the mathematician's formulation of his concepts. But the *sample space,* the space of points representing all conceivable outcomes thus idealized, each being specified by a vector of imaginable measurements made upon a π_t, is well defined in a mathematical sense; and beginning with this introduction of the mathematical concept of a sample space, the author's development of the theory is purely mathematical. His events and random variables, and his probabilities pertaining thereto, are all well-defined functions upon this space.

Now, a mathematician would show impatience with a discussion of the "nature" of a conceptual experiment, and so, too, I suspect, would a natural scientist. In his application of the theory, he has no call to go back beyond the concept of a sample space, as a suitably mathematized form of the outcome π_t upon which his variables and their probability functions are defined. It would seem to him far-fetched for one to inquire into the nature of the conceptual experiment a trial of which will have resulted in the outcome he is studying. Whatever its nature, it is fixed and unalterable and thus conveniently identifiable with the sample space implicit in it.

But, as noted earlier, the circumstances of an economist's studies are such as to preclude his assuming this attitude. The practitioners of his science act as specialist advisors to persons who are responsible for how well or ill a currently operating conceptual experiment $\{\theta, S\}$ is performing; and this professional advice is supposedly tendered for the aid of these responsible functionaries as they try to be rational in the designing and choosing of a modification of some component of this performing thing. In this context, the statistical properties of the outcome will have acquired meaning as *performance characteristics;* and their study is to the end that clues be turned up regarding how an existent conceptual experiment may be modified so as to effect certain predetermined alterations in the statistical properties of its working. It is not a sample space (with events and variables and associated probabilities defined upon it) that is subject to being designed and chosen, but only the conceptual experiment in which the sample space inheres. And hence, rather than being far-fetched as in the case of the natural scientist, an inquiry into the nature of this performing thing – how it is that observed statistical properties of an outcome are dependent upon an existent but modifiable system of rules – would seem to deserve recognition as an essential subject of inquiry of the science that is applied in this practice.

1.8 The person whose descriptive problems are the subject of our inquiry

When I think of the pedagogy of our subject field, I am reminded of the unfamiliarity of the students with whom I come in contact with this kind of analytical relationship – this that we have expressed as the functional dependence of β_t upon $\{\theta, S\}$: of the properties of random variables upon a modifiable system of rules. There is a field of application of the theory of probability, however, that affords ample illustration in rudimentary form of an analytical treatment of this relationship.

Were he of a mind to do so, one might correctly characterize a mathematical statistician as a practitioner who applies his science for the designing of conceptual experiments so that sample spaces and certain functions defined upon them will have predetermined properties. As an illustration of this, the *critical region* of Neyman–Pearson days, the crucial detail in a specification of a rule of action, is a region of a sample space. A sample survey design is a conceptual experiment in the sense of Cramer's or Feller's use of the term, as is a quality control system or an inventory control system or any other instance of a statistical decision function. Any such thing consists of a system of rules of action and exemplifies in rudimentary form the same abstract concept as is represented by the stupendously complex thing that we are denoting by $\{\theta, S\}$. In the context of this professional practice, it is an instrument so designed that there are certain known *operating characteristics* corresponding to it. These are expressed in terms of probabilities of certain kinds of events or expected values of random variables, these events or variables being defined upon a sample space of the designed experiment. Such numerical specification of operating characteristics may serve to exemplify the nature of the components of our *performance vector* β_t. And one may thus look upon the analytic theory as applied in this practice as being directed to the analysis of the functional dependence of a vector β_t, descriptive of properties of stochastic processes, upon $\{\theta, S\}$, the modifiable component of which is a system of constraining and prescriptive rules of action.

I have thought for a long while that there would be much merit to having, in a curriculum for the training and authentication of economists for their characteristic practice as expert advisors to legislators, an extensive course of study of the form and evolution of form of the theory of choice of which modern mathematical statistics and programming theory consist – not the least of this merit coming from a demonstration of a prevalent and widely familiar kind of choice that one is to avoid confusing with the peculiar legislative choice of law. One may see in the forming of this theory ingenious minds properly and effectively going about the business of conceptualizing the factual circumstances of a really observable process that culminates in the exercise of a particular class of choice: the general lineaments of the *person* who is exercising this choice; what the circumstances are that require that a choice be made; the practical matter of how to specify a concrete instance of an alternative subject to this person's choice and of the set of all known alternatives from which he is obliged to select; how a person in this situation gauges better or worse in a comparison of alternatives and the practical matter of devising an operationally applicable criterion for assigning a value or order to each known alternative measuring its worth as this person in an informed state would appraise it, thus leading to an operationally defined concept of *optimality;* and the conclusive practical matter of devising an operational technique for identifying those particular alternatives that bear a well-defined attribute of optimality among a stipulated set of alternatives of which the choosing agency will have been made aware.

There is a feature of the treatises and textbooks in this field (at least the older ones) that I find very appealing. Typically, at the outset of the exposition there is included, under some such heading as "The Person," a detailed account of the circumstances of the choice that is to be the subject of the theory. In L. B. Savage's *The Foundations of Statistics* (1954) there is an early section having this title. There is a corresponding person at the beginning of Abraham Wald's *Statistical Decision Functions* (1950); and the first chapter of that neglected but very valuable teaching aid, Jerzy Neyman's *First Course in Probability and Statistics* (1950), is devoted to a discussion of a person who is in the process of deciding upon an action in a special set of circumstances. But the chapter that, in my opinion, would be particularly useful for economists to study intensively – in its illustrating what it is to conceptualize a special class of existent and observable processes in which a particular kind of choice is exercised (thus demonstrating what economists have yet to do for their own very different person in the process of choosing a *change of law*) – is the opening chapter of Raiffa and Schlaifer's *Applied Statistical Decision Theory* (1961). The first heading in this first chapter is "Description of the Decision Problem." The first two sentences under this heading indicate the special kind of situation calling for decision and choice that their book is about. Then follows a list (under the heading "The Basic Data") of six fundamental concepts that the authors will have discerned as essential elements inherently to be found in any actual occurrence of a process in which this particular kind of choice is being exercised.

Such statements cataloging the fundamental concepts that inhere in this situation are descriptive of a factual set of circumstances that really does exist apart from and external to any describer of it. The details of such an inventory of concepts usually are highly controversial, this one of "The Basic Data" being no exception; but if there is an error in an author's account of this decision process, the error lies in his misconceiving and falsely describing what in fact goes on, what is being decided upon and by what standard, in any actual instance of the deliberations of real human beings in the act of exercising the choice in question.

Now, this person, whose decision process is being conceptualized in this literature of decision and programming theory, is the same person as is found in managerial capacities in what our textbooks in economics call a *firm;* he really is allocating resources at his disposal among competing uses and seeking optimal, or at least satisfactory, means for attaining more or less well-defined ends – and the development of techniques based upon this theory has been a great boon to him in enhancing the efficiency of his operations. The contributions of Wald and his associates and successors such as Koopmans and the inventors of programming techniques are said to have saved actual firms hundreds upon hundreds of millions of dollars worth of resources.

But it is a mistake of the very first magnitude to confuse this person, as I believe the founders and expositors of welfare theory have done and do, with the person whose descriptive and analytical problems are the subject of this present inquiry – the chooser of social policy (i.e., of statutory law), that class of it in particular called *economic legislation.* Recall Knight's remark quoted at the beginning of the Preface: "The first fact for emphasis," he said, "is that the activities for which [economic theory] furnish[es] guidance are those of the citizen and statesman, not those of the individual as a *wirt-*

schaftender Mensch. Its practical problems are those of social policy. And the first requisite for 'talking sense' about social policy is *to avoid the nearly universal error of regarding the problem as in any sense closely parallel in form to the scientific-technological problem of using means to realize ends.* The social problem, and the only problem which should properly be called social, is that of establishing a social consensus on matters of policy. . . . The social action which the study of economics has as its function to guide, or at least to illuminate, is essentially that of making 'rules of the game,' in the shape of law, for economic relationships" (italics added) (Knight 1956*a*: 174).

Let the reader now take note of the striking contrast between this statement by Knight, about what and whose problem it is that economic theory is about, and the opening paragraphs of Professor Koopmans's Nobel lecture, "Concepts of Optimality and Their Uses" (1977: 261). Koopmans's characterization of the subject field – as "the study of the 'best use of scarce resources' " – is on its face a committing of Knight's "nearly universal error," as is the same epitomizing of what the study is about that one may find in textbooks in economics. In Koopmans's case it may be looked upon not as this but rather as a mere matter of words, of what the reference of "economic theory" is understood to be; for the theory that he is expositing is a powerfully applicable theory about just those problems of a person who is in the process of rationally allocating certain resources at his disposal. The science that Koopmans discourses upon, I have thought from its inception, is the genuinely new science of this century: the science of management and administration, of decision and programming, an applied mathematical science of the highest order.

But this is not the subject treated in the general run of textbooks in the field of economics; and it is, as Knight declared, an error – devastatingly detrimental to the formation and development of a descriptive science of economics – for teachers and students of this other special field to confuse the person whose important problems Koopmans's theory is about with that many-headed person who is in the act of choosing "social policy" (i.e., changes in the law). The fascination that teachers and students of economics show for such optimizing operations as Koopmans expounds upon is a case of mistaken identity; there are no optimizing operations, none to be strictly defined and routinized, in a people's choosing of its law. The concept of an analytic criterion of optimality does not inhere in the fact of choice or selection; there are categories of choice (the choice of changes of the law being among them, other and familiar instances to be illustrated subsequently) wherein this notion, in a well-defined sense, is out of place.[12]

Knight's statement of "the first fact for emphasis" (i.e., of what the action is that the theory is to illuminate) is an identification of the person whose choice the theorizing is to be about. His statement of

[12] In saying this, I have particularly in mind the circumstances of a group of persons in the act of choosing (i.e., of reaching agreement upon) a criterion of choice – to be routinely applied, say, in actions subsequently to be taken on the group's behalf. A choice of this kind, a choice of a criterion of choice (i.e., of a definition of better or best, e.g., in the designing of a quality control or inventory control system) is in reality an event that occurs in the form of an authentically sensed meeting of minds among the members of the group in the course of their discussing alternative criteria. A refined form of the kind of discussion of which we are now speaking may be seen in textbook accounts of the pros and cons of alternative criteria proposed by theorists in their constructions of theories of choice or decision. See, for example, Luce and Raiffa, *Games and Decisions: Introduction and Critical Survey* (1957: 278–98). The notion of a well-defined objective test of optimality applicable to such an actually chosen criterion of optimality, on the basis of which an expert might authoritatively declare an agreed-upon criterion of choice to be suboptimal or not, would seem to be not an intelligible concept. The test of the "truth" of the criterion that is to be applied on behalf of the group comes only in the reactions subsequently experienced by the group's members to what the criterion will have selected out for them. The expert's declaration of the "worth" of the criterion can be no more than a fallible prediction of what these reactions will be. And I think there is a fundamental sense in which it may be truthfully said that a group's choosing of the rules of a game, or of a change in a people's existent system of statutory law, is similar in this respect: namely, that the notion of a well-defined objective test of optimality applicable to a rule of a game or to a change in a people's law is not an intelligible concept.

The term *optimum* is, of course, commonly used in a figurative sense in this context – to convey the user's judgment regarding what the reactions of actual players or citizens are likely to be. For example, von Neumann and Morgenstern, in commenting upon the rules of the game of poker, mention that the rules allow for any of a range of numbers of players: "The 'optimum' – in a sense we do not undertake to interpret – is supposed to be four or five" (1953: 197, note 2). They did, of course, undertake a rigorous interpretation of *optimality* as an attribute of a strategy subject to being chosen by a player – their expressed objective being that of elucidating the meaning of rationality in a person's strategic behavior. In doing so, they were constructing a model descriptive of a special class of human behavior, an abstract picture, so to speak, showing what this rational strategist looks at and what action he chooses to take depending upon what he sees. It is a particular class of human behavior that is being modeled, thus to elucidate what rationality is in the behavior of a person in this strategic role. But for the distinctly different behavioral situation, wherein players will have dropped for a while their player roles and assumed instead the roles of choosers of the rules, the subject of the description undertaken by the authors was not rationality per se, as manifested in the behavior of persons in this different choosing role, but rather such physical properties of the outcome of a game's being played as the ones that choosers of the rules do in fact try to find out about: what coalitions tend to be formed when the rules in question are in play, what the "power structure" is that "tends to emerge," what the distribution of "winnings" is that tends to result. The objective was to work out ways of deducing, from the conditions imposed by the rules of a game, descriptions of such properties of the outcome of the game's being played. Had these authors gone on "the error to be avoided" – and my extension of it that would exclude the concept of *optimality* from a listing of "The Basic Data" – is a factually descriptive statement about the process in which the choice in question is exercised. In Chapter 3 there are included two exhibits of real human beings in the process of deliberating upon this very choice. And if Knight's statement (and my extension of it) is itself in error, the error lies in our misconceiving and falsely describing what in fact goes on, what is being talked about and thought about and decided upon and by what standards, in any such deliberations as these that are exhibited; and it is to this observable set of factual circumstances that one must turn for checking upon the accuracy or pertinence or bearing of descriptive statements upon what the deliberations are about.

We must first reach, I think, a definite understanding upon this: that our statements reporting the results of our studies are descriptive statements about actual realities as these are to be found in any such process as the ones exhibited at the end of Chapter 3. This being mutually understood, I should then submit that the following basically elementary statements, drawn from an article by Knight (1949: 271–84),[13] are descriptively accurate and provide a basis for delineating a problem field of a descriptive science that is specifically applicable in the professional practice of economists as specialist advisors to legislators:

1. "Now in all discussion [of the problems] of society, the crucial matter is the making of law – or, more accurately, *change* in the law" (p. 280).

to speculate upon how reasonable persons combine information of this kind in reaching judgments upon which rules to choose, I should think that their modeling of this particular class of rational behavior would have followed more or less along the lines of the older theory of fair games – which, as I see it, can be taken as a simple prototype of a theory of welfare economics that would be realistic, in contrast to the one we now have. See footnote 3 of this chapter, and see especially Sections 3.4, 3.5, and 3.6.

Knight comments at several places upon what he took to be a crucial fact for our subject field – the extreme fewness, within any population, of persons who are intellectually capable of participating in a discussion of the choice of rules of the game (Knight 1947*a*: 392; 1936: 349–50). The orientations of mind of most persons placed in this role quickly lapse into either that of the player or else that of the referee or umpire, the strategist (the "scientificist") or else the judge (the "moralist"), in either of which "the rules" are being taken for granted. It was this supposed fact of the rarity of this intellectual capacity that he regarded as being the real weakness of a Liberal form of Society (i.e., a society whose members are themselves the choosers of the laws that constrain their respective private actions) (Knight 1947*a*).

[13] This article was called to my attention in correspondence with Professor J. M. Buchanan. See his commentary upon it (1967: 303–10).

2. "The latter [i.e., 'the making of *change* in the law'] centers in a relation between reality as it is and reality as it ought to be" (p. 280).
3. "The notion of a kind of reality or objectivity in what ought to be undoubtedly grows out of conflict in what different people *want* reality to be like, the incompatible ways in which they want to change reality as it is, together with the necessity of appealing to something beyond these clashing subjective desires if there is to be any *discussion* looking towards agreement" (p. 280).
4. "The root problem is the necessity – if social and hence human life is to exist – of *agreement* . . . to agree freely, rationally, peacefully . . . before resorting to arbitrary devices or to force, which are always involved more or less" (p. 280).
5. "A central issue is . . . the relation between various professional specialists ('experts') and the general public; in a society that is to be *free* [a *free society* being one whose members are themselves the choosers of the law (see Section 2.1)], the various expert functionaries [legislators and their advisors] must be 'responsible' to the general public, which must be itself a unitary body; it must reach agreement in some way" (p. 280).
6. "The problem is *free* cooperation, which means *free agreement*. . . . The social problem arises from the greatest spiritual revolution of all history. Our culture has taken the fateful step of rejecting the sanctity of tradition and established authority, and it must find norms for judging and changing previously accepted norms" (p. 281).
7. "Prima facie, the main conflicts center in the 'economic' life or aspect of conduct. . . . But the problem . . . is less that of 'satisfying wants' than of making the rules of the game, a game that covers an infinite variety of component games" (p. 281).
8. "In short, the problem is that of defining the social order, or 'justice' in the widest meaning, by describing the social order which embodies the ideal" (p. 281).
9. "The conclusions of [natural] science are . . . analytically descriptive statements . . . the 'is' versus the 'ought-to-be,' facts about the world 'out there' versus feelings in 'minds.' The latter are . . . 'mental facts' and are affected by a kind of 'validity' . . . attributed by different people to widely diverse content" (p. 282).

These numbered statements I take to be accurately descriptive of certain essential features of a class of observable situations in which a special kind of choice is in the process of being exercised; and it is my belief that in this and the following five chapters I am consistently following the lead therein given and providing concrete illustrations that may serve to elucidate the abstractions in terms of which Knight's statements are expressed. As I have intimated, my main interest is in the pedagogy of our subject field – in the working out of a curriculum for training and authenticating economists for their characteristic practice (i.e., as specialist advisors to legislators in the designing and assessing of legislation called "economic"). And these seem to me to be the factual circumstances that condition and determine what a training program specifically suited to this end would be centrally focused upon: that in any instance of responsible deliberations upon how well or ill some component of a currently operating economic system is working, the deliberators are reacting to what they think they observe as statistical properties of developing populations of really existent things and of processes of really occurring events – this is the concrete manifestation of Knight's "is" (remarks 2 and 9); that the adverse reactions actually being experienced among the deliberators imply norms, Knight's "ought to be," against which the observed properties are being compared (remarks 3, 6, and 8); that these norms are "mental facts" (remarks 8 and 9) and are existent in a special sense of *exist* – so that the task of discovering and describing what they currently are involves observational problems that are unique to our science (see Section 6.2); but that this "ought-to-be" norm is not an alternative subject to immediate and direct choice – that it is only the laws constraining and prescribing individual actions, the "rules of the game," that the deliberators can immediately and directly change – so that the crucial analytical task is that of discovering how, if at all, and the mechanisms whereby, these statistical properties of populations and processes of events are dependent upon the modifiable system of statutory law.

CHAPTER 2

On the peculiarities of economics as a descriptive science

2.1 What *free* means, as in *free society*, and the descriptive problems entailed

Apropos of our starting place in Chapter 1 – Adam Smith's characterization of economics as "the science of the legislator" – and to further relate this with the thought and writings of Knight from whom I think have come the ideas that I am trying to develop, I shall first comment upon two distinctly different meanings of *freedom* as this author used that word. My intent is to lead up to an expression of the doubt that I have come to feel for the usefulness of such terms as *free market system, free enterprise system, laissez-faire* – or their supposed contrasts or opposites, *planned, mixed, socialist, communist,* and the like – as names of alternatives subject to being chosen by or on behalf of a people. Freedom, in the sense of absence of overt constraint, does not now seem to me to be an applicable concept, in that this sense of freedom is not accurately descriptive of what human beings actually experience as freedom and constraint – whereas the actuality of a people's freedom in this other sense does inherently pose the conceptual and descriptive problems of Smith's science.

So far as I understand it, the sense of Knight's usage of the term *free society* (Knight 1946*b*: 217), in that usage that is essential to our present inquiry, is in effect the same as the sense of Karl Popper's usage of the term *open society* (Popper 1971: 173–5). In these contexts, these are the authors' names by which they designate a developed form or "species" of human society. One somehow knows when he has a *society* before him – insect, lower animal, or human.[1] A free or open society is an identifiable class of human society: one whose members are critically conscious of the laws that constrain and condition their respective private choices of actions and of the possibility of their jointly choosing modifications of this system of constraining and prescriptive rules. In the matter of identifying an in-

[1] E. O. Wilson tells how he would have this done in the cases of insects and lower animals – i.e., how to recognize (measure) *sociality* as a property of an observed population. The contrast is between a society of individuals and an aggregation of individuals (Wilson 1975: 7–31).

stance of this developed form of society, Knight makes a point of "the limited significance of political forms" (Knight 1947*c*: 184–204, especially 197–8) – who votes, the voting rules, how a choice of the laws is actually effected. The essential element is the state of awareness of the possibility of the choice and the mutual understanding that the thing being chosen is "the rules of the game" for all to play, not some individual's or coalition's or constituency's strategy or means for attaining a private end in a playing of a game whose rules are being taken for granted.

> The existence of free society – meaning a legal social order in which the ordinary individual is recognized as an end rather than treated as a means and in which issues affecting all are settled by discussion open to all – depends chiefly on the ultimate moral and intellectual capacity of the mass of individuals themselves to reach by free discussion substantial consensus on the scope and general content of their constitution and laws. It depends relatively little . . . on political forms [Knight 1947*b*: 217].

Each of these authors indulged in prehistorical, anthropological speculation about primitive forms of human society not free or open in this sense (Knight 1947*b*: 212; 1947*c*: 186–90; 1956*d*: 21; Popper 1971: 176). Popper's name for the closed form is *tribalism;* and Knight visualized an evolutionary development of that attribute or state of a society to which he gave the name *freedom:*

> At some time far back in prehistory, developing Homo became aware of the customary law to which he had previously conformed automatically . . . When custom ceases to be mere historical process and becomes compulsory, as mores, we cross the great divide into the new age of prescriptive laws, as morality. [Another] new age began when men first thought that their laws could be wrong . . . The coming of freedom to change . . . ended the sanctity of law. The idea of improvement had been impossible before, since the laws, . . . in the original sense, contained the whole meaning of right or wrong . . . At this point, man took or underwent his second great "fall," in the sense of the first; as he had then fallen from the innocence of insouciance into responsibility for obeying laws, he now took on the far more onerous responsibility for determining the content of the law itself [1956*d*: 21, 25; 1956*c*: 282 et seq.].[2]

[2] For the language used in the expressing of it, I shall record here two other authors' references to what Knight calls the second great "fall." In his enthusiasm, apparently, for the memory of the person whom he was eulogizing, Lord Brougham put the occurrence of it much later and attributed it to a single mind's urging: "The age of law reform and the age of Jeremy Bentham are one and the same. He is the father of the most important of all the branches of reform, the leading and ruling department of human improvement. No one before him had even seriously thought of exposing the defects in our English system of jurisprudence. All former students had confined themselves to learn its principles – to make themselves masters of its eminently technical and artificial rules; and all former writers had but expounded

Although I do not recall his mentioning Adam Smith's characterization of economics as the "science of the legislator," and although I suspect that were he to have done so he would have shown a dislike for the sound of the expression, Knight seems to come by this way to a delineation of a subject field that might sensibly be so regarded. Thus:

> Law, in the inclusive sense, is the essence of any social group . . . Law becomes a problem, and there come to be social problems, only when men are not merely conscious of their laws and institutions and of the imperative to conform but are also critical and more or less defiant of them . . . In free and progressive society, every social problem centers in differences as to what the law is or ought to be . . . To some extent social problems may arise out of unique situations and may have no connection with law. One thinks of war and natural catastrophes. But this . . . special problem of ad hoc action may be ignored here, and all social action viewed under the form of changing the law [Knight 1947*a*: 392; 1947*b:* 212; 1947*a:* 391; 1947*b:* 212].

Then:

> Political discussion properly so called . . . centers in the problem of what the law "ought" to be – how existing law ought to be changed, if at all [And] the great bulk of the issues discussed in modern political life . . . are economic in the broad sense of the term [1947*b:* 216; 1947*c:* 198–9].

And finally:

> The social action which the study of economics has as its function to guide, or at least to illuminate, is essentially that of making "rules of the game," in the shape of law, for economic relationships [1956*a:* 174].

the doctrines handed down from age to age . . . He it was who first made the mighty step of trying the whole provisions of our jurisprudence by the test of expediency, fearlessly examining how far each part was connected with the rest; and with a yet more undaunted courage, inquiring how far even its most consistent and symmetrical arrangements were framed according to the principle which should pervade a code of laws – their adaptation to the circumstances of society, to the wants of men, and the promotion of human happiness." [Quoted in Dicey, A. V., 1914, *Law and Public Opinion in England* (1920, reprinting of 2nd ed.). London: Macmillan, pp. 126–7.]

Lord Bryce, however, points to a public office of an ancient society whose function it was to do what Bentham would thus have had some office do: "The Praetor, therefore, . . . is a stronger personality than the English Common Law Judge . . . He has, not only a more unfettered discretion in carrying out his judicial and quasi-legislative mission, but also a clearer sense of his duty to do so . . . The English Judge is primarily a judge, appointed to pronounce a decision: The Praetor is also an executive magistrate, placed at the head of the whole judicial administration . . . with the duty of providing that the system works properly. His wider powers give him a sense of the obligation laid on him to see that justice is duly done, that wrongs for which there ought to be some remedy have some remedy provided against them; in short, that the law as a machinery for setting things right and satisfying the demands of the citizens is kept in proper order, with such improvements and extensions as the changing needs of the nation suggest. His business is not merely to declare the law but to keep the law and its machinery abreast of the time" (Bryce 694–5).

This marking out of the province of a scientific subject field is illustrative of what we have been emphasizing: Knight proceeds as a commonsensical empiricist; he sets forth what in some sense he "sees" or what from what he sees he can infer. *Freedom* is a name designating a developed state into which an existent society will have evolved: It is free if its members jointly and at will choose modifications of its law. A *social problem* is a problem confronting the members in the exercising of this choice. *Political discussion* is a communication process in the continuance of which a solution of a social problem occurs. A *solution* is an event that occurs in the form of a provisional "meeting of minds" upon "what the law ought to be." *Economics* is an intellectual discipline, a collection of facts and descriptive and analytical techniques applicable to the tasks of "revealing and clarifying the 'given conditions' " of this choice of the law. And continuing further with this thought and inquiry – that is, by examining cases of real responsible persons in the act of designing and choosing modifications of what is generally known as economic legislation – we find as the fundamental concepts and operations of a science specifically applicable to this task the ones briefly outlined in the previous chapter.

In this first sense, *freedom* is a name for the distinguishing characteristic of a class of human society. The society will have evolved, made an irreversible transition into this state, and will have had nothing to do with choosing it. The term in this first usage carries not as much as a hint of a recommendation of what a people in the state so designated would be well advised to choose as modifications of its law. But consider now the second usage: as a name for an objectively factual characteristic of a system of law subject to choice by a people who are free in the first sense. This is the sense of the term as it appears in the expressions *free enterprise system* and *free market system.*

Freedom thus understood, as a quantitative attribute of any proposed or existent system of law – as something of which there can be more or less – would be roughly measurable, say, by some kind of weighted count of the number of constraints upon individual action imposed by that system, so that a legislative repeal of certain of these constraints would be a change of the law that would increase the freedom of this system. In quite a few of his essays, Knight uses the term in this quantitative sense – for example, arguing traditionally respecting the dependence of *efficiency* of resource use, *concentration* of power, and *inequality* of income distribution, on the one hand, upon *freedom* of individual enterprise, on the other (1947*c:* 200–10;

1947*d:* 176–7; 1947*a:* 377–81). But he hems and haws and backs and fills and is evidently not comfortable with the idea.

To measure in this way the freedom of persons whose private actions are constrained by a given system of law – that is, by listing or counting the individual actions proscribed – is to miss the essence of what human beings actually experience as freedom and constraint (1947*e:* 10–15). A player of a game does not feel his freedom imposed upon by the rules of the game – unless he is brought to believe that the rules are unfair or else stupid. And it is similarly the case with the laws of a society:

Scrutiny of any typical case of unfree behavior reveals that the coercive quality rests on an ethical condemnation . . . Illustrations are at hand in the commonest business or legal relations. The ordinary citizen who sees a desired article in a store does not feel oppressed or constrained because he is not permitted to appropriate it without submitting to the condition of parting with the price – as long as he considers the price necessary or reasonable. And his standards of necessity and reasonableness, moreover, are entirely relative to the accepted economic organization at large . . . As long as everything is assumed to be in accordance with accepted standards of fairness, there is no feeling that freedom is interfered with. All taxes and legislative or administrative regulations take away property values, but they do not "confiscate" if sound social-moral reasons underlie them. We do not feel constrained in having to take the right side of the street . . . We simply do not have the feeling of coercion except in connection with one of ethical disapprobation . . . Freedom cannot afford an objective standard of policy, a way of escape from the subjectivity of moral judgments, when the feeling of freedom itself is derived from, or at best is another aspect of, moral approval [1947*e:* 10–11].

Disapprobation, condemnation, adverse reaction – it is this that is the central fact of a situation in which human beings are deliberating upon and in the act of jointly choosing modifications of their law. And it is not countable things in the law itself that are being reacted to, but rather things that are apart from the law, yet believed to be dependent upon it.

The fallacy comes in seeking an objective standard, or one which does not finally rest on a judgment of ethical approval and disapproval . . . In no other sense is it possible to speak of coercion . . . Freedom cannot furnish an objective criterion for . . . legislative policy . . . No discussion of policy is possible apart from a moral judgment . . . An appeal to maximum freedom as a "standard" involves a . . . dogmatic acceptance of an existing distribution of power . . . Freedom and coercion are ethical categories, and the only question in regard to which *discussion* can be carried on is the question of what power *ought* to be exercised, or how and under what circumstances [1947*e:* 12–15].

A player of a game, as we noted, may experience a sense of being coerced by rules deemed unfair – but also by rules that appear to him to be stupid, which is a word Knight used to characterize wastefulness, that is, "inefficiency." But again, *efficiency* affords no more objective a standard of legislative policy than does *freedom* (1947*e:* 13; 1956*d:* 26–27). And the same must be said for any other "objectification" of the choice of the law; nothing at all is being maximized or minimized or optimized by persons genuinely participating in a joint choice of a modification of the law. It is a wrong nuance, a falsifying of the circumstances of the choice that is being exercised, for one to conceive of such a chooser as being in an optimizing frame of mind. Of course, one does find laws being chosen by persons who look very much like strategists acting on behalf of coalitions with objective ends in view. It is in this, however, that Knight locates the source of the "sickness" of liberal societies: "the sinister fact of the rarity and difficulty of genuine discussion or of the discussion attitude" (1947*b:* 219) – "the vitally important fact that capacity to play intelligently is much more highly and commonly developed among human beings than is the capacity to improve the rules" (1947*a:* 392).

In dialogues among legislators and their economist advisors, in the act of deliberating upon how well or ill a presently operating system of statutory law is working, there is frequent use of medical terms like *pathological, sickness, remedy, ailing, blighted, depression, unhealthy, underdeveloped, malfunctioning;* and the participating specialists assume almost naturally the postures of the medical diagnostician and clinical practitioner. Knight commented upon this medical analogy on a number of occasions (e.g., 1936: 278–80, 284), always with a caution upon where it fails to fit. The concept of *sickness* involves a relation: an ordering of conceivably observable states of some entity with reference to a standard or normal state. In the medical context it is clear enough from a commonsense point of view what the entity is and with what norm its observed state is being compared. But in the context of the economist's practice, these are matters about which there is presently no commonsense mutual understanding.

Individual medicine itelf is "scientific" only to the extent that men agree on the meaning of health and disease . . . In this field, the degree of agreement which is practically requisite may be taken for granted. In "social medicine," the case is distinctly to the contrary; the main problem of realizing social health is that of defining it, of agreeing as to what is to be striven for . . . The practical problem of achieving . . . a "healthy" society is not a scientific or technical one in the proper, instrumentalist sense. To begin with, it is the very different kind of problem involved in formulating, which means rationally agreeing upon, "rules of the game," which is not a matter of means and end [1947*d:* 182–3].

Nonetheless, in any case of the practice of the economist as legislative advisor, there is this fact – I have come to think of it as the most basic fact of the subject field of political economy, the very starting place of our studies – namely, the fact of earnest, intelligent, responsible human beings in the act of making measurements upon a real entity π_t and being induced by the results of these observations to declare its present state to be indicative of something being wrong with the way an existent economic system $\{\theta, S\}$ is working. We may avoid at will the use of medical terms and analogies and proceed directly with our identification and naming of the fundamental elements of which this situation consists. Among these elements there is evidently a relation remindful of the one in medicine: between an observed state of some aspect of the real entity that we are denoting by π_t and some imagined state momentarily conceived of as a norm – an observed state in which the variation that is manifested (say, among family incomes, or individual employment statuses, or sizes of firms, or commodity relative price changes, or the like) is said to be excessive or in some sense aberrant, and an imagined idealized state of this entity an observation of which would not induce this adverse reaction. And the actuality of this comparison sets the empirical tasks that we try to make a start at doing in Part II of this book: (1) to be specific and concrete with respect to what the entity is whose present state is suspected of being aberrant; (2) to experiment with methods for depicting and describing it and of discovering and provisionally specifying the norms implied in particular instances of such actually experienced adverse reactions.

2.2 A preliminary exhibit of the circumstances in which the descriptive tasks are posed

Such conceptualizing as this by Knight, as we have earlier stressed, is itself an empirical undertaking. It is a matter of identifying and delineating and setting forth the essential features of a class of observable behavioral situations. There are particular human beings who are in fact held responsible for how well or ill the economic system works. Scarcely a day passes that there is not a news account of such persons reacting adversely to what they purport to observe as "the performance of the economic system," and I shall use a recent one of these to illustrate what it seems to me that Knight is expressing, in the last-quoted paragraph, about the unique descriptive and analytical problems that are involved in a specialist's efforts to elucidate this reaction.

I have before me a front-page photograph of two leading legislators seated at a conference table and accompanied by a distinguished economist practitioner who is advising them.[3] They are in the act of explaining a proposal for improving the performance of the currently operating economic system – that is, for modifying it so as to make more nearly right the outcome of its working. The news account of the occasion is this:

A fact sheet said that long-term objectives would be set out for *full employment, price stability, balanced regional development,* and an *equitable distribution of income,* among other things . . . Asked if these goals would be set out in specific numbers, [Senator Hubert] Humphrey [first] said they would not . . . But later the Senator said that numbers may be necessary.

Humphrey observed that the need for setting out national goals "arises from the poor performance of the economy." Inflation, recession, and the energy crisis have demonstrated, he added, that "our economic problems are interrelated and cannot be dealt with in an isolated way [*Washington Post,* May 13, 1975: D8, D11; emphasis added].

Wassily Leontief, the economist and Nobel laureate, . . . said that keeping the American economy in good working order required more than just watching a few major statistics and making changes in the budget and the money supply. He explained: "It requires lifting the hood, observing and if necessary adjusting the operation of all moving parts of the engine, and occasionally replacing those that turn out to be defective. What the Government and the public need is a service manual describing gears, nuts, and bolts" [*New York Times,* May 13, 1975: 58].

In Chapter 3 we shall submit more extended exhibits of legislators and their specialist advisors in the act of critically reviewing the performance of the economic system for which they are responsible. But this brief news account will do for our immediate purpose; and having it in view, let us consider further the just-quoted remarks of Knight, which I take to be allusions to the truly fundamental descriptive and analytic problems of the subject field of our science: (1) "In 'social medicine' . . . the main problem of realizing social health is that of defining it." (2) "The practical problem of achieving . . . a 'healthy' society is [the] kind of problem involved in formulating, . . . and rationally agreeing upon, 'rules of the game,' which is not a matter of means and end."

[3] The legislators are Senator Hubert Humphrey (D., Minn.) and Senator Jacob Javits (R., N.Y.), and the specialist advising upon technical and scientific matters is the eminent economist Wassily Leontief.

We may easily dispense with the medical analogies and thus understand Knight's problem of "defining 'social health' " as that of discovering and specifying and depicting what the salient aspects of the economy π_t look like – what their stable properties are – during a time when persons responsible for the state of the thing tentatively join in finding little or no rational grounds for one's experiencing a sense of disapprobation toward them – that is, little or nothing about these aspects that can be made more nearly right.[4] The two legislators, as reported in the news account, did not speak of sickness and health; but they nevertheless expressed an adverse reaction to what they observed as properties of developing populations of things and of processes of events that were taking place. And just as in Knight's comments, the concept of sickness entails the complementary concept of health; so this provisional judgment to the effect that the observed properties are indicative of an aberrancy entails the complementary concept of a mutually comprehensible standard of comparison, a conceivably existent state of the economy that would not induce in its observers this adverse judgment. The legislators refer to various facets of this idealized state by the familiar names: The economy, while in this idealized state, would manifest, "among other things," *full employment, price stability, balanced regional development,* and an *equitable distribution of income.* Each of these terms is a name

[4] I think I should perhaps interpose here the caution that we are reading into his remarks a meaning about which Knight himself might well have entertained reservations. When he was nearing the age of 85, in 1970, I corresponded with him about his use in this essay of such terms as *sickness* and *health* and how this usage conforms with the posture often assumed by the practicing economist that so reminds me of the clinical diagnostician. The notion thus baldly put was disagreeable to him. "[It] rebuffs me a bit," he said. "You quote me on social 'sickness,' but that was twenty-odd years ago, and I wouldn't do it now. Apart from [its] suggesting the 'social organism,' I wouldn't call a society 'sick' unless I felt I knew the meaning of a 'well' one – and I do not . . . I do not disapprove of anything, that is, except in comparison with a realistic alternative – at least an intelligible [one]. And again, I'm 'stumped' – except for 'details' which it seems reasonable to think could be improved by available means."

In the course of his writing the essay "The Sickness of Liberal Society," Knight assumed two distinctly different roles: the first as a quasi-legislator discussing the performance of a currently operating economic system and how it might be altered for improving the outcome of its working; and the second as an observer and student of this characteristically modern behavioral situation in which officially responsible persons are engaged in such a discussion and in the process of choosing a modification of the economic system. The statement quoted from the letter is a despairing comment of one who will have assumed the first role.

But for one who assumes the second role, the statement serves to point up the fundamental descriptive problem to which I think Knight alluded in his essay – a problem that would seem inherent in the very notions of public policy, of government by discussion, of a people's rationality in its choosing of changes in its law.

for a state of an aspect or component of what we are denoting by π_t – in plain fact, a state of some population of real, conceptually identifiable elements or else of some process of events that really do occur. The said state is spoken of as a goal or objective of the choices that the discussants participate in exercising; but Knight made something of a point of its being more in keeping with the circumstances of the choice that these idealized states be thought of as norms or standards rather than as goals (1956*d:* 28). There is a difference in the frames of mind these words engender. A goal is subject to being well defined and exhaustively specified, an end the finding of a best means for the attainment of which is a technical problem – and Knight stressed as a fact that a people's choice of changes in its law is not "a matter of means and end." A standard or norm, against which an observed state of something is adversely compared, cannot be exhaustively specified. It is directly perceived, and its particularities and their relations can be depicted and described with varying degrees of comprehensiveness, but, as with a face or topography or skill, never exhaustively.[5] One learns by practice and experience and emulation to recognize and communicate variously selected particulars of what it is with which an observed state is being compared.

The legislators speak of the need for setting out these standards "in specific numbers" as arising from "the poor performance of the economy." We shall phrase this differently in two respects. In conformance with the terminology proposed in the preceding chapter, we shall first urge the distinction between that congeries of real developing populations in whose statistical properties performance is manifested and the no less real directly modifiable system of constraining and prescriptive rules upon which these statistical properties are presumed to depend. The former is the economy π_t; and responsible persons, of whom those reported upon in the news account are instances, make observations upon it in guaging how well or poorly the economic system $\{\theta, S\}$ is working. The latter is the thing that performs; and hence it is the economic system, rather than the economy, whose performance is declared by the legislators to be poor.

But then the need for setting out the standards in specific numbers cannot reasonably be said to arise from the poorness of the performance of this system. Standards will have been applied in, and thus in some sense will have existed prior to, the recognition of the poorness. The need for explicit specification of what these standards

[5] Michael Polanyi (1961) discussed and gave many instances of such recognizable but not exhaustively specifiable phenomena.

are, partial though any such specification must be, arises from the circumstances that the judgment is ultimately a joint one. This depicting and specifying what the thing looks like in fact as it develops over time, in contrast with what it would look like were nothing much found to be wrong with it, is an integral part of the discussion in Knight's "government by discussion."

This is the descriptive problem to which I think Knight alluded in his remarks; and it is to this problem that the chapters of Part II of this book are addressed. It is my impression that Knight in his day would have felt doubtful about, even a little hostile to, the emphasis that I shall place upon visualizing, as a physical entity in a literal sense, the economy π_t in whose stable statistical properties performance is manifested. He would perhaps have associated this that I denote by π_t with the notion of the *social organism,* an eighteenth- and nineteenth-century concept that he looked upon as mischievously false to the facts at crucial places for intelligent discourse upon social problems. But the concept that I am delineating has nothing at all to do with this. It is to be found among the strictly factual features of a real, observable situation in which actual human beings are jointly choosing modifications of a system of statutory and administrative law. What such persons initially make observations upon, in forming judgments upon how well or ill the currently operating system is performing, is evidently physical phenomena – it is literally, as anyone may see, one or another population, whose identifiable elements are distributed over geographic space and the whole of which is developing over time. It will have been selected out from the mass of others for the sense of performance its statistical properties commonly convey. Any of the familiar names mentioned by the legislator in the quoted news account – full employment, equitable distribution of income, price stability, balanced regional development – is a name of an idealized state of some real population in terms of which an observed state of that population is judged to be aberrant. I do not at all presume that a discussant who experiences or expresses this judgment has much if anything concretely in mind regarding what this idealized state is – nor that he typically knows much if anything accurate about the properties of the population as it is actually developing over time. But the intelligibility of a discussion of an expressed judgment of this kind – a judgment endemic to the idea of public policy, of a people's rationality in the choice of modifications of the law – implies at least the possibility of discussants becoming reasonably clear about the facts of these contrasting population developments.

The organization of a description of what one of these populations looks like in fact, over some particular span of time, has been for me an exceedingly difficult undertaking. But if its elements can be concretely identified and visualized, it at least lies there in fact at any point in time to be described; and it is a straightforward matter of devising ways of effecting a sufficiently comprehensive description. For example, when a discussant expresses doubt about the rightness of what he observes the income distribution to be, it is clear enough what population it is to which he is referring. In Section 1.4 of the preceding chapter we briefly outlined which population development over time that a measurement of the degree of inequality of income distribution is in fact a measurement upon. Similarly, when a discussant reacts to what he observes as employment phenomena, the identity of the population to whose properties he is referring is evident. At any moment, each person within the nation is located in geographic space and is subject to being classified by employment status as well as by other characteristics – so that one may sensibly visualize the construction of a scaled-down physical model to represent the employment state of this really existent population at each of a sequence of points in time: each individual member being represented by a small object placed at its momentary location, and each being differentiated, say by color, to correspond to that member's momentary employment status. The familiar unemployment rate computed for the nation at large is a measure of what one would observe in this model as the density of unemployed members among all who are classed as qualified for and seeking employment. There is, of course, spatial variation among local densities at any moment in time; and with individual members moving about with the passage of time and also making transitions from one employment state to another, a sequence of such physical models would show an evolution of these local densities, and a continuous process of change in the membership of the unemployed, however stable over time the "global" density might be.

Apart from what may be thought of its quality, there is a considerable amount of easily available data suited to one's experimentation with methods for depicting this process of development of the employment state of an actual population over specific spans of time. And in Chapters 4 and 5 in Part II, we try our hand at this descriptive task: describing certain features of what the thing looks like in fact.

Describing what it would look like while in the idealized state is something else. The description would consist, we shall presently presume, of a representation of a population in a stationary state – its individual elements moving about and making transitions from one employment state to another as time progresses. To specify the relevant properties of this development over time, those that convey meaning to observers as features of the system's performance, one must find some way of assigning forms to distributions and values to parameters. Following Knight, we shall hold that these properties are not "scientifically" deducible from an application of any conceivable technique, nor determinable from empirical studies that are restricted to the thing itself. A specialist's thinking otherwise would be a case of what Knight disparagingly called "scientism." I shall treat the problem of discovering what the statistical characteristics of this idealized state are as a proper subject of a delicate kind of empirical inquiry, directed to but also extending beyond the thing itself, and shall make this a point of discussion in the subsequent descriptive chapters (see Section 6.2).

2.3 A fundamental distinction illustrated: what the physical reality is of which *price stability* is a statistical property

In these two cases – of the *equitableness* of the distribution of income and of the *fullness* of the employment – it is patent on the face of things what the real elements are of which the populations consist.[6] In another case that we shall comment upon in a subsequent chapter – that of a specialist advisor's reference to a "stable monetary background," the growth of the *stock of money* being "allometrically" suited to the growths of other components of the economy – the momentary placements and state transitions of the real elements of the population to which this discussant is referring can be visualized with almost as much concreteness (see the Appendix to Section 4.5). But the latter two references of the legislator in the news account – to price stability and to balanced regional development – are illustrative of cases in which the identity of the elements of the populations in question is not immediately evident. We shall postpone to another time our consideration of what specifically it is that one is looking at and reacting to when one experiences doubt about the balance of the regional development that he observes – only remarking here that it is assuredly not the "region" that is "develop-

[6] I mean to say here only that it is evident that the elements in question are actual people; and I think I am aware of the exceedingly difficult matter confronting discussants in trying to reach agreement upon how these elements should be classified to suit the sense of their deliberations.

ing" or that is or is not "in balance." A *region* is a geographic area arbitrarily delineated; and the developing thing that manifests balance, or imbalance or some degree of balance among its parts, is something contained within or partitioned by the lines demarking the regions. At some other place and time we shall try to identify what this something is and what among its observable properties conveys the sense of "degree of balance." But I shall include here a commentary upon this other case of ambiguity – that pertaining to what the real thing is that a measurement of the degree of *price stability* is a measurement upon – for it affords a better than ordinary illustration of the distinction to which I am attaching much importance: between the physical reality whose statistical properties convey to an observer a sense of the performance of the system, and the measurements that are made upon this reality for numerically specifying these performance properties.

Were I to undertake the task of describing what this thing looks like in fact as it develops over some specific interval of time, I should begin by drawing upon F. C. Mills's effort many years ago to do substantially this (Mills 1927). That author devoted some considerable attention to what he called "the population of prices," and he speculated with his reader upon just what measurements he would have had made and recorded had he been able to have for the asking anything for which he felt a need. As one may see, he was able to do much with the haphazard data that he was obliged to adapt to his purpose – much more upon what I see to be the problem than anyone since has done. But he missed the mark, I think, in his preliminary conceptualizing of what it was in fact whose properties he was describing.[7]

[7] Jacob Viner (1929) reviewed Mills's book at some length. He also participated, as did Mitchell and Mills and other leading figures of the day, in a conference upon the methods and results reported in it (Viner et al. 1940). Viner was heavily critical of Mills's study, holding it to be not really an "economic" study: "I find lots of theorizing in your book, Mr. Mills, but it is probability theory; it is not economic theory" (p. 209).

The record of that conference affords a dialogue among prominent representatives of two schools of economic studies: the conventional neoclassical on the one hand, and the institutional, as interpreted by Mitchell, on the other. One may see in it how utterly different these two subject fields really are. *Value* is as factual a property of an object as its mass or intensity or temperature or density; and to Viner this value of a thing and the theory of what determines its amount are what economics is about.

But to Mitchell, the orienting fact is not the value of a thing but rather the working or performing of an economic system. The two subject fields are very nearly independent of one another. In Viner's there is no essential place for a formally defined concept of a generating mechanism called by the name *economic*

The thing whose properties are being described is a random process of events in geographic space and time. The thing upon which measurements are actually made for an estimation of these properties is a kind of population – but not a population of prices. A price, being a number, is a measured characteristic of an element of the quasi-population in question and is not itself an element. Nor is the element, of which a recorded price is a measured characteristic, a *commodity*. Mills's data covered a period of some 36 years. During this period, billions upon billions of transactions occurred as events, each having a momentary existence at some time and place[8] and each involving an exchange of goods for money. That which bears the name *price* is a variable defined upon this event and whose value is given by the ratio of the number of units of money to the number of units of goods exchanged in that transaction. A *commodity* is a defined class of goods, so that each transaction is subject to classification by the commodity class to which the goods exchanged belong and by the price registered in that transaction. But the primary reality is the transactions in themselves, occurring as events in time and geographic space. It is this process of events that manifests the properties that Mills adapted his data to describe.

The organization of a description of the properties of this process, based upon its actual realization during some specific span of time, is an undertaking that I have found difficult to even think about. But corresponding to any period of time that will have passed, the thing whose properties are to be numerically specified assumes the form of a kind of population. And, as expressed earlier, with its elements

system. In Mitchell's, while not formally defined, it is by implication the central concept: the modifiable operating mechanism whose performance characteristics are manifested in the statistical properties of the populations and processes of events that he studied.

There is confusion, however, in Mitchell's and Mills's usage of terms that bear reference to this basic concept. Mills spoke of "the working of the price system," and he used "system of prices" and "price system" interchangeably to refer to what he called "the population of prices." Viner made sport of this: "I think you speak of the 'price system' . . . The word 'system' is nowhere defined [p. 213]. I would like a discussion of the concept of 'system' . . . That is one of my stumbling blocks" (p. 209). And in a light mood he imagined a biologist proceeding as Mills in a study of a "height system" or a "system of heights" (pp. 169–70).

It is at least our intent to dispel this confusion and to clarify the distinction: between the statistical properties of populations and processes, such as Mills undertook to specify and describe, and the modifiable mechanism, the economic system $\{\theta, S\}$, upon which these properties are presumed to depend.

[8] It may occur to the reader, as it occurs to us, that for many or most transactions some convention is required for assigning the respective places of occurrences. But there is sense in the notion of a "transaction point," and a defining rule for capturing this sense is surely within one's reach.

concretely identified and visualized, one may view it in his mind's eye lying there in fact to be described. With two dimensions to locate the place at which it occurred, and a third dimension to locate that occurrence in time, each exchange of goods for money that in fact happens within the area of the nation is precisely representable by a point within an imaginable three-dimensioned figure. The point locates the transaction in geographic space and time; it is classifiable – ways could be devised for visually differentiating it: by commodity and by the price registered in that transaction and by other characteristics that observers may deem pertinent – size of transaction, conditions pertaining to the financing and services involved, the respective financial statuses of the parties to the exchange, and so forth. For any specific period of time, there would be a finite population of differentiated points thus represented.

However difficult the undertaking might be, it would thus be seen as a straightforward matter of devising a way of effecting a description of this population whose elements are distributed over time as well as space. This would be a description of what the thing looks like in fact – the particularities of it that convey sense as performance. Describing what it would look like were it such as not to induce adverse reactions in a responsible and rational observer is, again, a different matter – involving, as noted earlier, a somewhat different kind of empirical inquiry which we shall consider in later chapters.

Any reader may immediately bring to mind the universe of discourse of the traditional textbooks and teaching of our subject, in which it is sensible for one to abstract from the reality of the transaction – the real event that occurs in fact at some determinable place and time and that assigns a recordable value to the defined variable *price* – and to interpret the concept of *price* as a measured characteristic of an abstraction called a *commodity*. But in his practitioner role as expert advisor to legislators and their agents, discussing with them how well or ill some component of an economic system is currently working, the economist is placed in a different universe of discourse. And it is in this one, rather than in that of the textbooks, that the descriptive problem to which Knight alludes is posed.

2.4 What that working mechanism is for which *economic system* is the name

We come now to the analytical problem – to the peculiar character of that part of the basically descriptive problem to which I think Knight points in the second part of his quoted statement. And an elucidation of it here involves our returning to the matter of Section 1.6 in the preceding chapter. In the two sections immediately preceding, we have been somewhat more explicit than we were in the earlier section regarding what it is that responsible discussants and their advisors make observations upon and describe to one another; so that the point for us of the remark of the physicist quoted there would seem evident enough: that it is "the working of the *statistical mechanism* itself" that such persons "are really interested in." Their intent is that certain statistical characteristics of stochastically developing populations of things be altered in some predetermined respect. These are seen as properties of variables defined upon the populations in question and whose variations are "generated" by the "working" of some presently undisclosed "statistical mechanism." To effect the intended alterations of the properties of this population process, they must efficaciously modify this "generating mechanism." And thus the essential questions are posed as to what it is and how it "works."

The concept of this generating mechanism, this constituent of the S of the operating system $\{\theta, S\}$, is missing from the only "economic" theory admitted as such in textbooks on the subject.[9] But throughout

[9] A reader whom I take to be not entirely unsympathetic with the argument herein presented nonetheless maintains that this statement is flatly not true – that the concept of an economic system, as a generating mechanism, is not missing but on the contrary is "central to contemporary micro-theory." He goes on to express the view that "the possibility of public policy depends on [the existence] of regularities but not necessarily statistical regularities" and comments dubiously to the effect that "if the 'generating mechanism' [does in fact] produce a *random* variable it is not clear that any policy choice is available" (emphasis added).

I am sure that such thoughts as will have prompted these remarks will cross the mind of almost any reader that I am likely to get; and I believe them to be mistaken. There is nothing remotely similar in the literature of economic theory to what we are denoting by $\{\theta, S\}$. There is, of course, the term *economic system;* but whatever it is for which this is supposed to be the name, it is not a generating mechanism in a sense suited to the factual circumstances of the practice of the economist as legislative advisor. As remarked earlier, the components of S are not what economic theory is about; it is the literature of the theory of stochastic processes that treats of such as these – but not yet in this specific context. The supposed regularities to which actual persons are reacting, in their deliberations upon how well or poorly a currently operating economic system is working, are statistical regularities. This I state to be a factual feature of any instance of such deliberations. A numerical record of the outcome of the working of an economic system, the essential substance of what is being talked about, is formed from observations upon variables defined upon developing populations of really existent elements and processes of really occurring events – that is to say, from observations upon random variables. A *description* of a random variable, as probabilists use this term, is given by a specification of its distribution function – which tells one the relative frequency with which the value of the variable falls within any interval of the range of its variation. (*cont.*)

the history of the practice of the profession, practitioners have alluded in their speech to something that would seem to be on the order of that thing. For example, Keynes, 50 years ago, spoke ruefully of our having "involved ourselves in a colossal muddle, having blundered in the control of a delicate *machine*, the working of which we do not understand" (Keynes 1931: 136; emphasis added). And in our news account we have Leontief presently speaking of what is required for "keeping [this machine] in good working order": "lifting the hood, observing and if necessary adjusting the operation of all moving parts of the engine, and occasionally replacing those that turn out to be defective."

This mode of speech – this usage of some name for a something that is working – is essential and to the very point of the practice of this advisory science. But an identification of just what this something really is has not yet been accurately settled upon among the students of this science. Had Keynes set forth what he had in mind as the machine of which he was speaking, it would perhaps have been something like one or another of the econometric models that were later founded upon his thought[10] – maybe something similar to the one described by T. C. Koopmans and J. M. Montias (Koopmans and Montias 1971). And had Leontief gone into some detail about the engine of which he spoke, I presume that he would have set forth some version of his own input–output model. Each such model consists of a system of equations – so that from an operational point of view, the thing that is working will have been reduced in either case to a system of equations relating some collection of conventionally defined variables. In the higher reaches and purer forms of economic theorizing there is this same kind of reduction and closely similar linguistic usage – as in the Hicksian "Laws of the Working of the System": *system* being the name of the something that is working; this system being in fact a Walrasianlike system of equations; the *laws,* in the scientific sense of law, having been deduced as implications of certain postulated conditions specified in these equations.

But this conception of a working system – this that corresponds to

(*Footnote 9, cont.*)
The "policy choice" is intended not to determine the value of the variable itself but to have some effect upon the shape and form of what this description shows.

The views expressed by this reader are shared by others with whom I have discussed these matters; and certain of the footnotes in this and the preceding chapter are intended as responses to them (see footnotes 3, 6, 8, 10, and 12 in Chapter 1 and footnote 7 in this chapter; see also Section 1.8).

[10] But then again, perhaps not. See the exchange between Keynes (1939; 1940) and Tinbergen (1940).

the names that one may note in the textbooks and treatises of economic theory – is not the right one. It will have evolved out of studies not specifically focused upon the legislators' identification and descriptive problems. It is factually not descriptive of the mechanism the outcome of the working of which the legislators are deliberating upon. Identifying the kind of thing this pertinent mechanism is, and describing instances of it, is first and foremost a matter for empirical inquiry. Legislators in the very act of deliberating upon how well or poorly a presently operating system is working – that is where one must go to find out what specifically it is that is working. And the "it" in Hicks's "laws of its working" (Hicks 1946: 273) is not that "it."

The first step in one's identifying what it is that is working – in this observable set of circumstantial facts – is that of determining and describing what the manifestations of this working consist of – what the particularities are that are conveying to the deliberators a sense of the system's performance. The mechanism of the system would then be identified as that special kind of thing that generates in its working such particularities as are being reacted to. I have already set forth in general terms what I think one will find to be the case in this regard (see Sections 1.4, 1.5, 2.2, and 2.3). In any instance of these deliberations, the particularities to which the law choosers are reacting can be seen to be certain statistical properties of some population process or some process of events. This is not to say that the advisees themselves use or think in such terms. But a practitioner of a special science so formed as to be specifically applicable in this actual practice – that is, in expertly describing what in fact is being reacted to and what then in fact the properties of this that is being reacted to depend upon – should be prepared to recognize this that the advisees point to and talk about for what it really is. And what it is, is a congeries of population processes.

The manifestations of the working thus being in the form of statistical properties of variables defined upon certain population processes, and *economic system* being a name by which legislators designate the something that is doing this working (i.e., that is generating the variations of which these observed properties are characteristic), it then would seem to follow that the working part of this system consists of a collection of statistical mechanisms, in precisely the sense in which natural scientists use this term (see Sections 1.6 and 4.5 and the Appendix to Section 2.5). This is the S of our notation $\{\theta, S\}$, the θ being the directly modifiable system of statutory law and administrative rule (i.e., the rules of the game) upon which the constituent mechanisms of the S are presumed to depend.

As for certain other matters that we have mentioned (see Sections 1.4 and 1.5), the best way that has occurred to me for one's acquiring a firmer feel for what this means is to painstakingly try to describe, with as much comprehensiveness as can be mustered, some population process the properties of which do in fact convey to responsible observers this sense of the working of the system. In Chapter 5 I report the results of my trying to do this – describing, as a population process, the employment state of the nation's population of people, dispersed as it really is over the national area and developing as it really does do over an extended period of time. And this illustrative exercise serves to demonstrate, I think, the kind of problem with which specialists will come to be involved in trying to find out what the generating mechanism is whose alteration would be required in order that the properties of this process be changed (see Section 5.5). There is also the cardinal fact made evident that this *S* that constitutes the mechanism is no more subject to direct and immediate modification than are the properties of the variation that it generates – that what is subject to direct and immediate choice, by these agents on behalf of a people, is strictly confined to statutory law (i.e., the rules of the game).

I shall put at this place what seems to me to be the bearing of the quoted remark by Knight: that one's figuratively applying such terms as *health* or *disease* to observable states of the economy lends a false and misleading cast to the nature of the problem confronting agents of a people in the process of choosing modifications of a currently operating economic system; that there is never in this context a prior principle of purposeful structure and functioning that would give meaning to *health* or *disease* or *defectiveness* as objectively recognizable states of an economy; that the primary problem of participants in such deliberations is not scientific or technical in the instrumentalist sense of the medical or engineering sciences, but rather is identically the same kind of problem with which a group of persons involve themselves who undertake to formulate and rationally agree upon " 'rules of the game,' which is not a matter of means and end" (Knight 1947*d:* 182–3). (Also see footnote 12 in Chapter 1 and Sections 3.4, 3.5, and 3.6.)

In an application of medical or engineering science there is the external reality of health or disease or defectiveness – a state of things "out there," as Knight called it, by virtue of a prior understanding of a principle of purposeful structure and functioning of the object that is subject to being in this state. In an application of our science, this is missing; and in place of the external fact of disease or defectiveness there is the internal fact of adverse reaction or disapprobation – Knight's "mental fact" of the comparison that free human beings make between the "is" and the "ought-to-be" (1949: 282). This "is" is a normal (in the probabilistic sense of *expected*) outcome of the working of a currently operating mechanism. There is not in it on its face a manifestation of disease or defectiveness – for there is no prior mutually understood principle governing structure and functioning which would give objective meaning to *defectiveness*. The "ought-to-be" is a contrasting normal (in the same probabilistic sense of *expected*) outcome of the working of an efficaciously modified version of this mechanism. Far from there being a prior agreed-upon principle which would give objective meaning as "health" to this "ought-to-be," it is this very agreement that is primarily being sought for in the discussions. The utter absence of a prior principle of purposeful structure and functioning is the basis for Knight's strong aversion to the concept of the social organism.

This difference – the *internalness* of the fact of the adverse reactions experienced by responsible observers, in contrast to the *externalness* of the fact of disease or defectiveness in the applied natural sciences – gives to our social science its special form – rendering it strictly descriptive: of population processes, those in particular whose properties convey sense and meaning as performance – and with observational problems that are unique to it (see Section 6.2).

2.5 The meaning of *statistical*, as in *statistical economics*: illustrations from a peripheral literature

In the passage quoted in Section 1.6, Schrödinger spoke of the gradual emergence of the statistical point of view among natural scientists – *statistical* being understood in its probabilistic sense, as in statistical mechanics. We added that among economists this had not yet occurred – that there was not yet a *statistical economics*, in this same probabilistic sense of *statistical*, that economists generally recognize as such (see footnote 10 in Chapter 1). However, one may pick and choose within the literature of economics and set apart a growing segment of it that would seem to be in fair conformance with what we are here presenting.

The works of Wesley Mitchell and his early (1925–35) NBER associates are illustrative of the beginnings of what I have in mind – in particular, three research reports: Mitchell's *Business Cycles: The Problem and Its Setting;* F. C. Mills's *The Behavior of Prices;* and A. F. Burns's *Production Trends in the United States Since 1870*. One must rearrange things somewhat, for these studies are not laid out precisely along the lines that I think the nature of their subject requires. As with Knight, the formative years of Mitchell and his associates came just before the development and clarification of the basic theory of the probabilistic phenomena with which their studies dealt.[11] But in the light of this development, one may see these three studies as being aptly addressed to the descriptive problem outlined in Sections 2.2 and 2.3: that of describing what certain population processes look like in fact as they develop over extended periods of time. They conceived of the economy, or so it would seem, as we are conceiving of it here – as that immense real object upon which the Census Bureau makes periodic observations, a congeries of stochastically developing populations of things. The population processes that were the subjects of their studies had been selected out as prominent ones among those whose properties do in fact convey to responsible observers a sense of how well or ill an economic system is performing. And their descriptions essentially consisted of specifications of distribution functions and of statements of how the forms and parameter values of these functions evolved over time. Their thought seems to have been primarily directed to describing in this way aspects of the outcome of the working of a presently existent system; but if one looks for it, the other side of the descriptive problem also comes through to some extent, at least the authors' awareness of it: that of finding out and specifying what the idealized states of these population processes may be taken to be – the standards or norms against which the actuality is being contrasted when adverse reactions are experienced by responsible observers.

When Mills undertook to identify the specific analytic form of the distribution of relative price changes, his objective was that of concise description – of "reducing the data," as it was called. He did not see it – at least he did not stress it, as he would undoubtedly see and stress it now – as an essential step toward discovering just what statistical mechanism was presently at work. Had he done so and proceeded toward this discovery, he would have become engaged upon the first of two stages of what we have set forth as the analytical part

[11] I am inclined to think that the history of our subject would have been very different had Mitchell come after, rather than just before, the spectacular development of probability theory that has occurred over the past 50 years. William Feller's *Introduction to Probability and Its Applications*, first published in 1950, two years after Mitchell's death, marks the beginning of the accessibility to nonspecialists who would apply it, of this technical knowledge that is essential for the line of thought that Mitchell was pursuing.

of this descriptive problem. By now, there are any number of studies that may be cited as having been directed to this first stage – in which some one or another probabilistic model or conceptual experiment is devised, which when set in operation will generate random variation similar in its properties to the variation actually observed, among, say, family incomes or relative changes of family incomes, or firm sizes or firm growth rates, or city sizes or city growth rates or unemployment rates, or some other such variation that commonly conveys meaning as *performance*. Work of this kind is still, as it seems to me, on the far periphery of economic inquiry, in the sense that not many of the general run of economists are so trained and directed in their thought as to find much if any interest in the details of what these inquiries purport to show; but a considerable literature could nonetheless be formed of just such probabilistic studies as one might imagine a present-day Mills pursuing in a continuation of his inquiry into the variations among price relatives at any moment. Yet, of this growing but still peripheral literature, I can bring to mind only one series of studies whose authors show an indication of realizing that this is but the first stage – that of finding out and specifying what mechanism, in the narrower natural science sense, is at work in the generation of the variation whose properties are being responsibly reacted to – and that there is a second stage which is the crucial one in the practice of our advisory science: that of finding out the dependence, if such there be, of this mechanism upon what specifically it is to which legislators are restricted in the choosing that they actually do, that is, the system of statutory law and administrative rule, the rules of the game that individuals, including administrators, play. These are the several articles by H. A. Simon and his associates reporting their descriptive and analytical work and reflections upon what is familiarly called the *concentration of power* in industry (Simon and Bonini 1958; Ijiri and Simon 1977). I see these studies as companions, in a way, of the works of Mitchell and his early associates – they being illustrative of inquiries directed primarily to the analytical problem, as Mitchell's had been primarily directed to the descriptive.

Just as I may be reading more into the disparate writings of Knight and Mitchell than these authors would have wished to have attributed to them, so too may I be reading more into Simon's expressions than he would want to own. But whereas there are technical as well as conceptual details in this work that I presently find difficult to understand as entirely cogent, taken as a whole and with stress upon point of view and method rather than specific results or findings, these articles seem to me to fall within our general conceptual scheme of things. Simon's studies are also aptly addressed, although not so meticulously as were those of Mitchell, to what we have set forth as the initial descriptive problem: that of depicting and specifying selected particularities of the economy π_t as this immense object develops over time. He, too, would seem to be perceiving the reality of what is called by that name as we are viewing it here – as a vast congeries of populations and processes of events. The population that is the subject of his studies is a prominent one among those whose properties commonly convey sense and meaning as *performance.* Legislators and those for whom they act do in fact upon occasion experience and express adverse reactions to what they see in this population process as a tendency toward an excessive degree of concentration of power. And his description of what he seems to think such responsible persons are in fact reacting to – what they are looking at that so induces in them this feeling that something is not as right as it might be with the way the economic system is working – is a description of certain statistical properties of a developing population of identifiable elements.

It consists of a specification of the distribution function of a variable defined upon this population; and the analytic form that his empirical studies led him to tentatively assign to this distribution has a fundamental bearing upon the choice of a measure of the degree of concentration that this population manifests. It is in this consideration – in the intricacy of the part that the form of this distribution plays in his defining of a measure – that I think I notice the author's recognition of the second stage of which we are speaking; and this marks, as I propose to view the method in it, a distinct advance over the thought and practice of the earlier Mitchell and his associates. Simon would, of course, require that the measure selected have the requisite intuitive appeal to responsible discussants of the problem: It must be such that they can confirm for themselves that variations in its value correspond to variations in the degree of what they directly perceive as concentration. But it must serve for something more than that; it must also be such as to provide hints as to how the mechanism that is generating the variation will respond to some proposed change of statutory law – that is, as to what will "tend to emerge" respecting this mechanism as a result of some specific change in the "rules of the game" (see footnote 8 in Chapter 1). And Simon accordingly adds this other desideratum: The defined measure must be intimately related to, some hopefully determinable function of, one or more of the parameters of the distribution function that describes the variation that is conveying to observers the sense of concentration. His tentative identification of the analytic form of the distribution tentatively indicates to him what kind of statistical mechanism it is that currently is at work. And thus this method proceeds to a devising of a "conceptual experiment" a laboratory model of this particular kind or class of mechanism – constructed on the numerical basis of certain measurements made upon an observed *realization* of the actual population process, and such as can be set in operation so as to experimentally generate variation that is similar in form and shape to that which the discussants are observing and reacting to. With this device – by tinkering with it, to some extent mathematically, but primarily by Monte Carlo procedures – he would then undertake to throw some modicum of light upon what changes are required in those numerically specifiable properties of π_t that constitute the mechanism in order to effect the intended alterations in the values of the parameters in terms of which the degree of concentration is measured. I shall add, too, that in this case of what is reported in these articles, the author's experimenting with the laboratory mechanism – experimentally generating such variation as that which is actually being reacted to – led him to reflect most pertinently upon just what it "really" is that induces in responsible observers the reactions that they experience – and to tentatively identify this that conveys a sense of concentration or inequality with properties that lie "deeper" than those reflected on the face of the shape and form of the distribution in question (Simon and Bonini 1958: 616).

I cannot vouch for this being the way that Simon himself would have his reported thought interpreted. It is what I see in these writings that fits into the conceptual scheme of things that is herein being presented. And I wish to make it plain that although a nonspecialist reader might be surprised at how much is already known that could go into the devising of techniques applicable to what we have called the first stage of this analytical problem – finding out what mechanism it is that is generating the observed variation whose properties are being responsibly reacted to – there is virtually nothing of which I am aware in the literature of our subject that is applicable to this second stage – determining the dependence of this mechanism upon what it is that is immediately and directly subject to legislative choice – that is, nothing beyond intelligent and experienced common sense, which is notoriously unreliable upon probabilistic matters. So that the reader need not expect to find much along this line were he to look for it in Simon's articles. What he might find, I think, is an underlying recognition of the necessity of the problem – the necessity, if the reality that is being reacted to is to be altered in some reliably predetermined way, of finding out how the generating mechanism will be changed by a changing of the law. It is a grossly simple matter for some group to devise something in the form of legislation that effectively betters the momentary circumstances of a specified set of presently existent individuals. But whether instituted by peaceful choice or by violent force, the newly legislated law remains as new "rules of the game." In "what tends to emerge," after as before, there are yet the variations, among the circumstances of individuals, of all those things that convey sense regarding how well the system works. And recognizing the problem of anticipating what the character of these will be is, of course, a necessary step toward devising methods applicable to it.

An Appendix to Section 2.5 containing notes upon the nature of the statistical problem and upon a training program for students who would concentrate upon it

A present-day student having a modest grasp of probability theory would know how to construct a probabilistic model that, when set in operation, would generate a random series of values of X_t with statistical properties that he could specify and predict in advance of its being observed. These properties would be described in terms of the frequency function of X_t, which the student would know how to deduce from the specifications of his model. Were this designed mechanism repeatedly operated n times, each over an extended interval of time and with the value of X_t recorded for each of a succession of values of t, there would be provided n observations upon X_t for each of these values of t. And the student could make known beforehand the properties of the variation of X_t for any t, and would be able to furnish a description of this expected variation in the form of a graph and table that would anticipate the shape and form of a frequency distribution constructed from the n values of X_t yet to be observed. The X_t itself is called a *stochastic process*. The record of the values of it that result from a single "run" of the model is called a sample function or *realization* of the process. And if the deduced frequency function of X_t tends to a stable analytic form with stable parameter values as t is made large, this stable distribution is said to be the *steady-state distribution* of X_t.

This is one type of problem or task for the student to undertake: to design the details of a statistical mechanism the operation of which generates a random series of values of X_t, and from the details of the design to deduce the operating characteristics of the mechanism, these characteristics being described by the specification of the frequency function of X_t for any t.

Consider now the obverse of this problem. Suppose the student were given a large sample of n series of values x_t, not being told what statistical mechanism it is whose operation generated these series, but being nevertheless assured that the model in question is among the types usually discussed and analyzed in textbooks on stochastic processes. His task is that of inferring from what he can learn from these n observed series the nature of the model that generated them, and of then constructing a mechanism of his own that will generate a random series X_t the statistical properties of which are substantially the same as those found to be characteristic of the observed values x_t.

A student who knows how to proceed with the first problem would naturally enough begin with the second by experimenting with various arrangements of the data in an effort to discover what statistical regularities and uniformities characterize the observed variation. A finding of these would lead him to the type of probabilistic model associated with the form of variation shown by his data. If he were assured that the X_t upon which he had n observations was of a kind that had a steady-state distribution, it would be the form and parameter values of this that he would first try to estimate. But there might be many relevantly different designs of models that would generate random series of values having the same steady-state distribution. His data consist of n random series. Let x_{it} be the value of the ith of these at time t. At that time it will lie in some one or another of the size classes that the student will have used in constructing his observed frequency distributions. At $t + 1$ this ith value may have made a transition into some other size class. The rates at which such transitions respectively take place from one size class to another are a relevant property of the variation; and it would be required of the student that the mechanism that he designs be such as will generate a process X_t that not only will have the same steady-state distribution as the one observed but also will show transition rates that are approximately the same.

To indicate the sense of our use of the term *relevantly different,* we may note that elementary models of this sort may be constructed which, when set in operation, generate samples of time series x_{it} that would be said by reputable persons to resemble in certain respects some one or another collection of time series formed from measurements made upon an actual outcome of the working of a real economic system.[12] For example, the x_{it} may be imagined as representing the size of the income of the ith family at time t, or the mean size of family income of the ith city, or the size of the ith firm of an industry, or the price relative of the ith commodity, or the size or rate of growth of size of the stock of money concentrated in the ith city, or the unemployment rate of the ith city. The n series generated by the mechanism would look like the real series in the sense of being characterized by similar statistical properties – the frequency distributions of the x_{it} values for each t would be similar. With the passage of time, an x_{it} makes transitions from size class to size class along the range of variation of this variable. And the relevance to which we alluded earlier has reference to this: that when an observer reacts to what he takes to be some degree of inequality of income and opportunity, or of concentration of power in an industry, or of price and monetary instability, or of depression and blight, the rates at which individual elements of the population in question are making transitions from size class to size class are as prominent a feature of what he is reacting to as that represented by the form and shape of the steady-state distribution of the variable.[13]

We have been contemplating a kind of game that an instructor might play with his students: he devising a statistical mechanism and generating with it n time series x_{it}; they inferring from the statistical properties of these observed series the details of the mechanism that generated them. There are evident ways for the instructor to make his model progressively more complicated and elusive of detection. In the case that we have envisaged as an initial exercise, the n series of x_{it} are independent; what we have spoken of as a "run" of a model is in truth n independent runs of a model, each such run generating a series x_{it} so that for each t there are n observations upon x_i. The instructor might advance from this rudimentary design to a model for which X_t is a vector having n mutually dependent components x_{it} – so that a single run would generate a sample of n mutually dependent series x_{it}. Also, in the initial exercise the conditions would be such that parameters of the distributions that describe the random variation are constant. In advanced versions of his exercise, the designer of the model might have these parameters subject to varia-

[12] See, for example, the series of articles by H. A. Simon and his associates that were cited in Section 2.5. I also have in mind several articles in a volume of reprints edited by P. H. Cootner (1964), particularly those by M. G. Kendall, Holbrook Working, M. F. M. Osborne, and Benoit Mandlebrot.

[13] This is the point to which we referred in Section 2.5 as having been made by H. A. Simon (1958: 616).

tion, random and perhaps in some way dependent upon things that change with the passage of time.

Complexities of one sort or another might readily be contrived so that even though the generated series were validly called random and had statistical properties subject to being specified and predicted by the designer, the problem of discovering and making known these regularities from a study of the data, and thence to an identifying of the germane features of the mechanism that generated the observed series, might well be put out of one's reach, whatever the state of one's skill and learning. But were the really clever and inventive specialists in the theory of the subject somehow induced to take a serious interest in the playing of this game, would anyone doubt that there would accumulate a body of progressively more powerful techniques and methods for analyzing a sample of n randomly generated series x_{it} and inferring the design of the statistical mechanism that generated them?

Notice that the problem situation that we are now formulating is different from the one that gives rise to the familiar sampling problem of statistical inference. In this conventional sampling case the state of the population is not conceived of as a probabilistic phenomenon – the measured characteristic X_{it} corresponding to the ith element of the population is interpreted as a fixed value, not a random variable. The randomness is introduced into the situation as a feature of the sample survey design. This latter is an instance of a statistical mechanism, but not of just the kind with which we are presently concerned. A sampling specialist has the problem of constructing an *efficient* such mechanism for use in obtaining stipulated information about how these fixed values vary among the elements of a "dead" population. The problem situation that we are now contemplating is distinctly different. The measured characteristic X_{it} of an element of the population is itself a random variable. The primary problem of our specialist is not that of designing an efficient mechanism but rather of inferring from what regularities and uniformities he can discover in the data the pertinent details of an existent mechanism that is generating the variation thus described. In the course of his proceeding with this primary problem, he encounters estimation and testing problems of the conventional kind; but the efficiency with which he deals with these subsidiary problems is an utterly minor matter.

It is a statistical inference problem, different from the familiar textbook problems of sampling and statistical inference, but similar in its analytical respects to the inference problem that is posed in the situation in which the earlier Mitchell, Mills, and Burns played specialist roles. And to indicate the outlines of an analytical theory that would seem to be implicit in Mitchell's thought and method, we shall try to identify what there is in the real situation in which Mitchell assumes his role that is missing from the artificial situation that would be simulated in the laboratory.

In the laboratory situation, the person who is to undertake the task is furnished with n observations upon some initially unknown stochastic process X_t for each of a succession of values of t; and he is to take for granted that telling statistical regularities may be found that characterize the variation thus represented, if only he can hit upon arrangements of the data that will reveal them. If and when he finds them, they will take the form of transition rates, analytically specified distribution functions, and parameter values, all stable in some one or another sense – absolutely or functionally or stochastically, depending upon how advanced the problem will have been made. Some of these would be illustrative of components of what we have denoted by β_t, descriptive of the *operating characteristics* of the mechanism that generated the variation upon which the observations had been made; and some would be components of the mechanism itself, illustrative of a constituent of what we are denoting by S. From what this person estimates these components to be, he is to be led by some inductive process to a specification of this initially unknown design of the mechanism; and having detected what mechanism it is that generates such variation as this that he has observations upon, he might then devise modifications of it so that its operating characteristics β_t will be altered in some reliably predicted respect.

When the person in the laboratory takes note of and reflects upon the regularities and uniformities descriptive of the variation shown in the observed series, his reaction is not of the kind that can be sensibly referred to as adverse or favorable. He sees operating characteristics in which he tries to find hints regarding what the generating mechanism is; but they do not convey to him a sense of how well or ill this thing is performing. In what is observed in this laboratory situation there is no sense of well or ill. In Mitchell's problem situation, however, there are observers who do react adversely or favorably or acquiescingly to what they observe; and what they observe and react to initially are not in numerical form but rather are physical states and changes of states of populations of people and other things and of events occurring in space and time. This congeries of populations and processes is the reality for which π_t is our notation; and a variable X_{it} as it would appear in the real situation is defined as some count or measure upon this physical reality. A person in Mitchell's role is not furnished with n observations upon some defined X_{it}, nor even with a definition of X_{it} in accordance with which he might himself collect these numerical data. He has the added task of defining the variable for measuring the *instability* or *inequality* or *concentration* or *depression* or *inflation* or *underdevelopment* or the like that is conveying a sense of performance to observers who are responsible for how well the system works.

But having reached the stage at which numerical data are in hand, Mitchell and his associates of that day proceeded much as we have imagined the person proceeding in the laboratory situation. It was the hallmark of their method that they concentrated upon a search for statistical regularities and uniformities descriptive of the variation manifested in the data – which was the first step we thought the student would be "naturally" led to take in dealing with his special inference problem. And upon the occasions when such were thought to have been found, they took the form of what now would be called transition rates, distribution functions, and parameter values. As in the laboratory situation, these statistical regularities, discoverable in observations made upon the n time series X_{it}, are attributed as operating characteristics to an economic system $\{\theta, S\}$. The inference problem, however vaguely they may have sensed it at that time, is essentially the same as the one confronting our imagined person in the laboratory exercise: Having discovered in the data what appear to be stable rates and functional forms and parameter values that characterize the variation that is observed, a person in this role, as in the simulated case, is to be led by some inductive process to a tentative specification of what the mechanism is that will have generated the observed series.

The problem situation confronting a Mitchell or Mills or Burns, in his undertaking to measure and analyze the instabilities or divergencies or inequalities that characterize the outcome of the working of an economic system, is closely similar to the problem situation confronting one who undertakes to measure and analyze the congestion that characterizes the outcome of the working of a traffic system. The last three sections of the first chapter of an introductory monograph on queueing theory (Cox and Smith 1961: 26–32) appear almost as if intended for an illustration of this similarity: "The Measurement of Congestion," "The Investigation of Queueing Systems," "The Modification of Queueing Systems." The nature of the operating thing called system and the sense of the notion of its working are the same in the two situations. The measurement problems posed and the natures of the phenomena respectively measured are the same or of the same kind. The analysis of the functional dependence of the quantitative properties of what is measured upon the modifiable components of what is working involves an application of the same basic theory in the two situations. And the motivating settings for the respective investigations are essentially the same: in the one instance, a people trying to be rational in its choice of a modification of a traffic system with the intent of mitigating the degree of congestion that has been a feature of its working; in the other, a people similarly trying to be rational in its seeking for a modification of, say, a monetary and pricing system with the hope of lessening the amount of price instability that has been a feature of its working.

In Section 1.2 we commented upon this similarity; and in this extension of our remarks in the present chapter regarding Mitchell's thought and methods and the theory that goes with them, that discussion of this contrast would seem to be again in point.

CHAPTER 3

On norms that are implied in observers' adverse reactions to an economic system's performance

3.1 The sense in which a norm is said to exist

In continuing with our effort to identify the things to be described, and the suppositions required for the intelligibility of the talk about those things, we shall keep before us the quotation cited earlier as Knight's allusion to the fundamental peculiarities of economics as a descriptive science (1947*d*: 182–3). He there stated the problem – which I shall take to be that of specifying those idealized states of things to which such names as *full employment, price stability, equitable income distribution,* and the like are given – to be an intellectual but not scientific one. I think these two terms do not express clearly the contrast that he intended to place emphasis upon. He indicated his usage of *scientific* by observing that "medicine itself is 'scientific' only to the extent that men agree on the meaning of health and disease," that "in this field, the degree of agreement which is practically requisite may be taken for granted," but that "in 'social medicine,' the case is distinctly to the contrary," that "the main problem" facing persons jointly responsible for "realizing social health is that of defining it" – that is, of agreeing upon a description of it – but that it is to misconstrue the facts of the situation for one to regard a legislative discussion of what a "healthy state of things" looks like as a stage in the defining of an end for which an optimal means may then be technically sought, that in fact it is of the same order of *discussion* as one may see in simpler form when players of a game forgo for a while their play in order to deliberate upon how well the present rules of the game are working out and upon what changes might be effected in them to render the outcome of its play more nearly fair or otherwise felicitous – "which is not a matter of means and end." And the difference to which I believe he was drawing attention, which his contrast of the intellectual with the scientific does not quite convey, is the difference between what would be represented by a figure so constructed as to depict a norm of some population process under review in a discussion of how well or poorly an economic system is working (see Sections 1.4, 1.5, 2.2, and 2.3) and what would be represented by a figure descriptive of the normal structure and functioning of some biological organism. The subject matters respectively depicted by the two figures exist as real phenomena in basically different senses. The requisite data for the respective constructions must be sought in fundamentally different ways.

In subsequent chapters we shall make an illustrative try at constructing such a figure – that is, at describing one such norm for which there is a familiar name: in particular, this nation's population of people, distributed as it characteristically is over the national area and developing over a time when it would be said to be in a state of full employment. It is the reality of such a thing as this – a population in space and time while in a state of *full employment,* or this same spatially distributed and developing population while in a state of *equitably distributed income,* or a population of firms or else of families developing over time while in a state of *benign concentration of power,* or a congeries of populations of things in space and time while in a state of *balanced regional development,* or a process of commodity-money exchange transactions occurring in space and time while in a state of *price stability* (see Section 2.3) – that Knight places in that radically different category of existence from that which is the subject of study in the natural sciences. At least this is how his expression of this essential distinction comes across to me – so that in my experimental attempts to observe and describe a specific instance of it, I must somehow find ways of proceeding that are appropriate to the task. And I shall comment here upon certain other references that have been particularly provocative in my thinking about what one might properly do in the forming of a description of this different kind of thing.

I realize that in this dwelling upon these abstract distinctions I do indeed risk losing the attention of any reader I may have gotten – but what could be more important to students of our subject field than coming to some understanding about the bearing of whatever this difference is?

3.2 Two categories of norm as reality

The nine statements listed at the end of Section 1.8 were drawn from Knight's highly critical review of a series of lectures by the distinguished scientist Michael Polanyi (Polanyi 1946). These lectures had apparently been bothering Knight for some time, for in an article written two or so years earlier about another author's work he had included two long disapproving footnotes referring to the views that had been set forth by Polanyi. The theme of the lectures, as Knight expressed it in these earlier footnotes, was "the moral and social character of scientific activity" and the identification of the "reality studied by science" with that which is the subject of any seeking for answers to questions. Polanyi spoke, at another place (Polanyi 1961), of *knowledge* as consisting essentially of "knowledge of a problem," the perceived truth about the subject of a question being "developmental," what competently thoughtful persons momentarily agree upon in a continuing process of discussion (Buchanan 1967: 304–5). Hence, when the question comes to the matter of what constitutes a good system of economic legislation – that is, what the truth is in this regard: tax law, property law, monetary law, labor law, welfare law, regulatory law, or any of such kind – the reality of the subject of this question, a *true* system of law, is to be looked upon as a reality "out there" like any other, subject to being found out and made known through systematic inquiry by competently thoughtful students of the law and jurisprudence.

It is precisely this that Knight would not have, vehemently holding this view of things to be contrary to the "fact" of the fundamentally different categories of reality that are involved; and in the two earlier footnotes he stated and then nearly identically repeated a curiously cryptic remark:

> He ignores the fact that agreement is reached without formal coercion in natural science and certain aspects of social science but not in the field of law and morals, which is the factual root of the whole social problem.
> Polanyi makes natural science itself a process like that of discovering a transcendental reality. This has a certain . . . appeal, but one must note that it ignores the basic facts. Scientists agree and masses accept their authority without any coercion, while the opposite is true in the fields of jurisprudence and morals [1956*c*: notes 3 and 7 on pp. 228–33].

Whether or not this is an accurate representation of Polanyi's views,[1] I think I see a useful hint in what he alludes to here as "the factual root of the whole social problem" – useful, that is, to one seeking a proper way of finding out and provisionally describing certain things for which descriptions are required in any instance of responsible human beings in the act of choosing changes in the law. I have placed at the end of this chapter two exhibits of actual cases of legislators and their economist advisors in this very act. And in Sections 3.6 and 3.7 I shall comment upon several passages drawn from these exhibits – in one of which the advisor, in his explanation of

[1] Later on, Polanyi reissued his lectures with a new introduction but with no reference to Knight's criticism. See J. M. Buchanan (1967: 303).

how it is that a legislator's expressed diagnosis is not a correct one, requests that the other discussants raise to mind an economy developing over time while in a state of full employment and also of price stability. One's visualizing such a thing – that is, laying out in his mind's eye a real something ready to be described while in these named idealized states – cannot be other than a visualizing of certain isolated aspects of "what tends to emerge" as a result of a nation's people working out their respective lives within the constraints of a "true," in the sense of "good," system of statutory law. This poses the concrete descriptive tasks in the trying of which I hope to elucidate certain of the abstractions in terms of which Knight's critique is expessed; and I shall return to this "factual root of the whole social problem" in the later sections in which these passages are discussed.

3.3 Avoiding the fallacy of "scientism"

I shall include this one other reference – drawn from another of Knight's articles of about the same vintage (1956*a*). In it he is castigating another author whose form of "scientism" apparently upset him even more.[2]

The illustration is that of two imaginary economists in an argument as to whether the check system did or did not exist in present-day Paraguay. If they are scientific, they might themselves go to Paraguay and investigate. In that case the argument might be settled by their actually having a check before them. "Then, having settled the scientific dispute, they might begin a philosophic dispute" . . . as to whether they had "the real check-an-sich" or only "the idea or appearance of a check." Now it is surely obvious, without any reference to transcendental reality, that it would be impossible to assert on the basis of any printed slip of paper or other object "before them" whether "the check system" existed or not. One would certainly have to know the history of the "object" and the laws and business usages connected with it. In fact, it is inadmissible to speak at all of "the" check system, if one is making any serious pretense to accuracy; and if one is talking about a check system at all, one is certainly concerned with purposes aimed at and results achieved as well as with the existence and paths of motion of printed pieces of paper or any physical events . . .

Hutchison continues: "The scientist proceeds by means of the two inextricably interconnected activities of empirical investigation and logical analysis, the one, briefly, being concerned with the behavior of facts, and the other with the language in which this is to be discussed" . . . His philosophical position . . . would seem to be that of "logical positivism;" that is – if one can hope to state a position which one does not believe to be tenable in a way that would be acceptable to someone who does believe it – knowledge is (or

[2] Knight's article is a review of Hutchison (1938).

true propositions are) relative to objects of two sorts: (a) "things," such as printed pieces of paper, which can be identified by pointing and naming, and (b) verbal definitions, which are a pure matter of the use of language in accord with conventional or arbitrary rules . . .

Now, in the present writer's opinion, all this is fundamentally misleading and wrong . . . The . . . propositions and definitions of economics are neither observed nor inferred from observation in anything like the sense of the generalizations of the positive natural sciences . . . and yet they are in no real sense arbitrary. They state "facts," truths about "reality" – analytical and hence partial truths about "mental" reality, of course – or else they are really "false." Economics and other social sciences deal with knowledge and truth of a different category from that of the natural sciences, truth which is related to sense observation – and ultimately even to logic – in a very different way from that arrived at by the methodology of natural science. But it is still knowledge about reality [Knight 1956*a*: 152–5].

Once again I shall interpose a reminder that Knight himself might well have disowned the interpretations that I am reading into his remarks. As I have mentioned earlier more than once, I harbor a strong suspicion that at least on first encounter Knight would not have taken well my efforts at specifying and depicting such actual population processes as those of which we have been speaking – that he perhaps would have looked upon one's involvement with the descriptive exercises of the following chapters somewhat as he viewed the preoccupation of Hutchison's two economists: examining specimens drawn from a population of "pieces of paper," studying their "paths of motion," scientifically intent upon establishing whether or not "the slips of paper" they had "before them" were checks, and thus whether it may be truthfully said that a check system was now "at work" in the locality of their observations. Knight's regard for "the two economists," and what he apparently took to be their identification of a check system with a tangibly real "population of checks," is remindful of Viner's attitude toward Mills and his apparent identification of a price system with what he called a "population of prices" (see footnote 7 in Chapter 2). Neither seemed to take the matter seriously – Viner jocularly imagining a biologist proceeding as Mills in the study of a "height system" and complaining of what that author was leaving out: "The word 'system' is nowhere defined . . . I would like a discussion of the concept of 'system'. . . That is one of my stumbling blocks." But one may doubt that either Viner or Knight would have "really" liked to sit through such a discussion, although Knight did make an offhand start at one – asserting that the thing for which *check system* is a name is not a "population of checks," and going on with a certain cogency that we shall later remark upon. But these statements about what such things really are were not among "the propositions of economics" to which he was referring in the quotation. The propositions of economics of which Knight spoke – the context in which the quoted passage is found shows this – are the familiar ones of conventional textbooks: about consumer preference, firm costs, demand and supply, capital and interest, and the like. So far as I can tell, there was in Knight's conscious mind nothing close to what we have been discussing as proper subjects of propositions suitably called "economic": what specifically that modifiable thing is that is said to be working and to which the name *economic system* is given; what its working parts are and what these depend upon that are subject to being altered by persons responsible for the outcome of this working; what it is that these responsible persons look at and react to as showing how well or poorly the thing is presently performing; what this that is being reacted to is being contrasted with on the occasions when adverse judgments are experienced.

Yet, it is from Knight's writings, I do earnestly believe, that I have been led to these latter subjects, not to those that I am sure he had consciously in mind, as being the central ones in an applied science by whatever name but not inappropriately called *economics* – appropriately in the sense of being specifically and directly applicable to the tasks that economists are called upon to do as specialists in the actual practice of their profession. And from the point of view that I am thus led to adopt, what would be found "fundamentally wrong" with "all this" that Knight attributed to Hutchison and his "two economists" is its being artificial and basically out of touch with the factual circumstances of this ongoing professional practice. Later in this same essay is the passage quoted at the beginning of the Preface. The methodology of a scientific discipline, he remarks there, must of course be worked out with reference to the peculiarities of the problems which have given rise to it and which sustain an interest in it. And for our special field, he goes on to say that "the first fact for emphasis" is the fact of what these problems are: They are ones that are unavoidably encountered by citizens and their legislative agents in their deliberations upon the choice of what is called "social policy." A special science comes into being as a matter of course as persons in this role of citizen and lawmaker strive to refine their capacities for "talking sense" about this choice problem. "And the first requisite for 'talking sense' about social policy," he asserts as a presumably demonstrable matter of fact, "is to avoid the nearly universal error of regarding the problem as in any sense closely parallel in form to the scientific-technological problem of using means to realize ends."[3] Rather, the central problem for which he exclusively reserves the adjective *social* is "that of establishing a social consensus" on the choice of a "social action." And he then states what this is – presumably identifying what a social action is by observing in some sense the very fact of it in any such situation of which the illustrative exhibits at the end of this chapter are instances: "The social action which the study of economics has as its function to guide, or at least to illuminate, is essentially that of making 'rules of the game,' in the shape of law, for economic relationships."

It is with specific reference to this factual situation – citizens and statesmen striving to be reasonable in the reaching of a consensus upon the choice of changes of the law – that Knight asserts that the object for which *check system* is the name is not a population of checks. It is in the thought of such discussants, as indicated in their utterances as they jointly review how well or ill those things that are subject to their choice are presently working out, that he would apparently have one begin his identification of that thing; and in this context a check system is an item in a more extensive object called a *monetary system,* this in turn a component of a much more comprehensive thing called an *economic system.* And as a sensible beginning for a settling of the matter of just what this thing is, one may point to instances of proposed modifications of it, or of what experienced and responsible observers discern as gradual changes in it; and these assume the form of statutory law and business usages worked out within the constraints of law.[4]

The essential context of empirical inquiry in this special subject field is thus that of a review by "citizens and statesmen" of how well or poorly a currently existent economic system is working. It is a *fact* that such responsible reviewers of the working of this thing, together with their specialist advisors who will have been authenticated as economists, "see" this performance in the structural and developmental properties of real populations of things and of random processes of really occurring events – this is what they talk about when they talk about the performance of a currently operating economic system for whose working they are responsible (see Sections 2.2 and 2.3). "If one is making any serious pretense to accuracy" – that is, if one is diligently bent upon describing faithfully just what is the case in any such situation of which the exhibits at the end of this present

[3] See Section 1.8, and note the radical difference of Knight's characterization of what economics is about from that of Tjalling Koopmans in his Nobel lecture (Koopmans 1977: 261).

[4] But see Sections 2.4 and 6.1.

chapter are instances – "it is inadmissible to speak at all of 'the' check system" – just, we may add, as it is inadmissible for one to speak of "the" price system or "the" monetary system or "the" economic system. It is a class of objects the form and detail of whose members undergo continuous change and are presumed to be subject to deliberate modification by statesmen acting on behalf of a people. "And if one is talking about a check system at all," Knight continues, "one is certainly concerned with purposes aimed at and results achieved as well as with the existence and paths of motion of printed pieces of paper or any physical events." It is certainly the lawful rules – the "rules of the game" – that are deliberately changed when persons authorized to change the system are in the very act of changing it. And the ones "talking about it" in the process of choosing whatever change is chosen will have had their concerns aroused by seeing a discrepancy. But the language he happened to hit upon for conveying what the discrepancy is between – "purposes aimed at and results achieved" – carries, I think, an "inaccurate" nuance of what he had called "the nearly universal error" of confusing this situation in which a "social action" is being decided upon with the distinctly different one in which a means is being sought for the realization of an end. And he seems to be asserting that what in fact is being sensed as a discrepancy is virtually a thing apart from what can be observed in such real phenomena as "paths of motion of printed pieces of paper or any physical events." But it is not a thing apart – that is, if one is to be "accurate" in his description of just what is going on – no more than the physical sounds of a spoken sentence are a thing apart from the sense that a listener reads into this sequence of sounds. This *sense,* of course, cannot be deduced and learned about from a study that is restricted to the physical properties of sound; but it is the sequence of sounds that conveys the sense, and as a practical matter it must be clearly heard and registered as a fact. Nor can this discrepancy be discerned and learned about from a study that is restricted to the physical properties of the populations and processes that are being reacted to; but, again, it is the physical properties that convey to responsible observers the sense of the discrepancy that they experience – and there is the similar practical matter of finding out and being clear about the form of it that is jointly seen for the sense that there is in it. The population of "the printed pieces of paper" – or the quasi-population of the events that would occur in the working of any electronic system that might supersede the usage of checks – is a member of that vast congeries of populations and processes of events that we are denoting by π_t and calling the *economy;* and although it may not be one in whose statistical properties discussants may be brought to see meaningful features of performance of a presently operating economic system,[5] it is in the properties of some one or more of those of which π_t consists that performance is in fact observed and reacted to. It is only in the real world that discussants will have observed "results achieved," that is, what the things that convey sense as performance look like in fact; and it is only in imaginably attainable states of the real world that he conceives of the discrepancy between this "is" and the "ought-to-be," that is, what these things would look like were they such as not to induce in rational choosers of the law the adverse reactions that they are in fact experiencing.

3.4 The reality of *health* contrasted with that of *fairness* – or of *fullness* of employment

Return now to the quoted remarks with which we began this chapter. A medical practitioner "sees" disease in an organism as a discrepancy between the state of the thing as it exists in fact and the state of it were it normal (i.e., healthy) in its structure and functioning. The reality of this discrepancy is of the "scientific" category in Knight's usage – being "out there," subject to investigation by "the methodology of natural science," the "truth" about it being "related to sense observation" in the ordinary way – by virtue of a prior taken-for-granted agreement upon "the meaning of health and disease." But the reality of the discrepancy that is the subject of our special science, this that responsible persons have the sensation of "seeing" in the properties of the population processes that they make observations upon, exists in a distinctly different sense – and *truth* about it "is related to sense observation . . . in a very different way." The medical practitioner will have come to *know* by way of scientific studies of the thing itself, and independent of the person whom he is treating or advising, what the ought-to-be state is against which the observed state is being contrasted. The practitioner of our special science can know nothing of the kind from studies that are restricted to the thing itself. In the practice of his profession, this ought-to-be *norm* of the thing, this that validates the reality of the

[5] On the contrary, I believe that persons responsible for monitoring the working of a monetary system will come to recognize the statistical properties of this and related populations as an essential feature of this working – e.g., as a detail in the process of growth and development of a nation's stock of money. See the Appendix to Section 4.5.

existence of the discrepancy in question, is in the process of being found out and agreed upon by rational discourse among persons whom he is advising in their choosing of the law.

In his critique of Polanyi's lectures, Knight seemed to be making a linguistic play upon the two uses of the word *law:* the laws of natural science on the one hand and the juridical laws of a society on the other (Knight 1949: 282). And he ends with a rhetorical question a rephrasing of which I think affords the best hint ever as to how a practitioner in our special field might appropriately proceed in tentatively describing a current instance of such a norm. Polanyi spoke, at still another place, of scientific discoveries being made "in search . . . of a reality that is there whether we know it or not; . . . the search is of our own making but reality is not."[6] The laws of natural science describe, in a manner of speaking, "what tends to emerge" (see footnote 8 in Chapter 1), in a universe the constituents of which are governed by these laws. They are *true* if the "what tends to emerge" that the laws describe is *truth – truth* being the name of the reality that exists in fact independent of any observer of it. But the juridical laws of a society, in the contrast as Knight seemed to be expressing it, are descriptive of a distinctly different category of thing. There is in them an implication of what Knight calls a "social order" – which, in our interpretation, has its concrete manifestation in the properties of developing populations of real things and of processes of really occurring events – and thus in this manner of speaking they describe a "what tends to emerge" in a society whose members are governed by these laws. The juridical laws are *just,* this term corresponding to *true* laws of the other kind, if the "what tends to emerge" is *justice* – as Knight expressed it, " 'justice' in the widest meaning . . . describing the social order which embodies the ideal" (Knight 1949: 282). *Justice,* then, is the name of this other kind of truth or reality, the one that is being sought in the search for true juridical law – a state of things that would be said to exist when, among other details, employment is *full,* income *equitably* distributed, prices *stable,* personal and industrial power concentrations *benign,* regional development *in balance.* Knight apparently understood Polanyi in his lectures to be holding that the way of proceeding in the search for juridical law that is true, in this sense of *just,* is the same as that which has been an "undoubted success" in the search for true laws of natural science: "an explorative investigation of 'reality'." And Knight asked rhetorically of him: "Is 'justice' a real-

[6] This is from a mimeographed lecture by Polanyi, quoted by J. M. Buchanan (1967: 310, note 7).

ity, essentially like that of the everyday world . . . especially in the sense that we get 'knowledge' of both in the same way?" (1949: 282).

Now put the question equivalently: Is the *fairness* of a simple game a reality? Knight refers to what he calls the *plain man* and what his views are upon such matters; and surely to this plain man *fairness* is as real an attribute of a game as mass or temperature or color is of a physical object – or *sense,* as opposed to nonsense, is of a linguistic sequence of sounds. He sees it or in some way tells whether or not it is there in some degree. But by what operations does he do this? What does he look at – and what does he do to convince himself or some other person of what the truth is in this respect – and if the game is found to be not so endowed with a tolerable degree of this quality, how does he go about finding what to propose be done with it to make it so? And with these questions in mind, recall the tentative answers that were submitted for ones much like them in the ancient theory of a fair game (e.g., Feller 1950: 196–201) – and particularly how these answers were successively revised as the investigations of these fair game theorists continued. In the answers there was putative knowledge, and of the very special kind of which Knight was speaking – and recall especially what was done by these investigators for a "getting" of this knowledge.

First note certain of the suppositions about the circumstantial facts of such games as this theory is about. Corresponding to any such game, fair or not, there is supposed to be a specifiable *outcome* of the game's being played – not the chance occurrence resulting from a single play of it, but an outcome in the abstract as an attribute of the particular game in question. The game itself is an instance of a *conceptual* or *random experiment* – this and related notions being the ones that we discussed in Section 1.7. Its corresponding outcome is described in terms of properties of variables defined upon the *sample space* of this experiment – these properties being numerically specified by expected values, frequency functions, transition matrices, and so forth, of the defined variables. And in the formulation and development of this theory, the games were of so simple and elementary a kind that a definitive description of the outcome in these terms was deducible mathematically, or could reasonably be hoped to be so, as an implication of the rules and assumed conditions of the game in question – that is, one so endowed with requisite mathematical skills would be capable of "seeing" in the rules themselves the *expectation,* in the strict probabilistic sense, of the "what tends to emerge" consequent upon the game's being played. *Fairness* is an attribute of the rules of the game; but this quality is "seen" in this expectation of the physical outcome.

Now, in the initial stages of their thought, the formulators and developers of this theory were obliged to find out about and come to some understanding upon these two factual matters: first, what it is in an *outcome* that conveys meaning to the plain man as *fairness* – that is, what he is looking at, generally speaking, on those occasions when he experiences the sensation of seeing fairness in some degree; and second, what the criteria are that he is applying when the sensation experienced is that of seeing a discrepancy: between what this aspect of the outcome is in fact and what it would be were the game a tolerably fair one. It was, of course, the mathematical problems posed in the seeing of the expectations and the applying of the criteria that attracted to this subject the attentions of those formidable mathematicians of long ago; and these essentially empirical problems were dealt with on short order. But however cursory the order of their dealing with these matters that were perhaps for them of only preliminary and incidental interest, this problem that is of main interest to us was nevertheless there; and their getting of this knowledge – of what is to be looked at, that is, what it is that carries this meaning, and what criteria are to be applied, that is, what this that is to be looked at looks like when it is right – affords for us an illustration, in a very rudimentary setting, of a getting of identically the same kind of knowledge as is required, in a stupendously complicated setting, for rational deliberations by a people's agents in their choosing of its law.

3.5 Fair game theory as simple prototype of a theory of political economy

The nine statements listed at the end of Chapter 1 pertain to certain factual circumstances of a people's choosing changes in its law – which centers, as was said, "in a relation between reality as it is and reality as it ought to be." It is this latter that is presently our main concern: "the notion of a kind of reality or objectivity in what ought to be." In the rudimentary circumstances of a group of players of a game who will have stopped their play to deliberate upon a changing of its rules, this special kind of "reality or objectivity," at least one essential aspect of it, is called *fairness;* and a description of its principal attributes assumes the form of a criterion – for telling in an outcome resulting from their play whether or not there does indeed exist a discrepancy between what it is in fact and what it ought to be. In the exceedingly complicated circumstances of a people's agents in the act of choosing changes of its law, the form assumed is that of the idealized states – for telling exactly the same thing. A description of a nation's population of citizens as it develops over time while in a state of *full employment* – or of any of the other aspects of an economy π_t while in its idealized state – is, or would be were there one that could be agreed upon, a detail in a specification of what is essentially a criterion – the counterpart, in a theory of a people's choosing changes in its law, of the criterion of fairness in a theory of fair games.

"The notion of a kind of reality or objectivity in what ought to be grows out of conflict in what different people want reality to be like . . . together with the necessity of appealing to something beyond these clashing subjective desires if there is to be any discussion looking toward agreement." At several places in his critique, Knight is moved to use the word *necessity* with reference to *agreement* – this last term being a name for an event that really can happen and that really must occur in order for something else to happen, namely, an averting of a society's breaking up. A state of things in which sensations of agreement are scarcely being experienced, nor held in hopeful prospect, is a state of "sickness" of a Liberal Society – that is, a society whose members are themselves the authors of its laws (see Section 2.1). "The root problem is the necessity . . . of agreement, within some limits . . . The general public must reach 'agreement' in some way." And *necessity* is being used here, I think, in its sense of logical entailment: the possibility of agreement among those in the roles of player or citizen, an authentically experienced meeting of minds, and the actuality of a process of rational discourse that leads to and keeps current this virtual state of mind, are entailed in the very idea of a "game" or of a "free society." It is not a "game" or "free society" that is in process when those in these roles hold no prospect of reasoned change and feel coerced by rules or laws they deem unfair. Disagreements, about factually experienced adverse reactions to what can be observed, occur continually over time in any case – but all hopefully to be resolved as subjects of a continuing discussion "looking toward agreement." Incessant repetition of "I want" is not *discussion* "looking toward agreement." There is a necessity – entailed in the idea of a game or a free society as a viable process – that there be "something beyond these clashing subjective desires" to which appeals may be made in the forming of agreeable descriptions of the "what ought to be." And our object now is to identify what this "something" is.

We are to seek guidance in this in seeing first, in the exceedingly simple circumstances assumed, what this "something beyond" was to which the fair game theorists did in fact appeal; and I suspect that the reader will think it anticlimactic when I point to what I see this "something beyond" to have been. As remarked earlier, and to the extent that I can tell, the matter of "objectifying" this property of a set of rules called *fairness* was no more than incidental to the main interests of those investigators of that time. It was a handy point of departure for a posing of crucial mathematical problems in the early forming of a mathematical theory of probability. In turn, these mathematical problems that were posed were entirely technical and incidental to the problem of finding and specifying a "true" criterion of fairness – which is not a mathematical problem at all but strictly a cognitive one.

The two technical problems were these: First, there was the matter of deducing, from the conditions laid down in the rules, whatever their fairness might be, a description of the "what tends to emerge" as a result of the game's being played. This first mathematical operation thus served as an efficient means of observing, a clever way of "seeing," in a set of rules the outcome corresponding to it; and although this certainly is a purpose for which we must also find some way of serving, their way is not for us, at least for the calculable future – for the feasibility of this mathematical mode of observation, the tractability of the mathematical problems posed, strongly depended upon the radically simple and rudimentary circumstances that were assumed to be the case in these investigations. This first operation thus furnished what it was that was to be looked at; but it did not instruct one who would look at it upon how to tell what fairness there was in it. To find this out, that is, to provisionally settle upon a criterion for setting apart the fair from the unfair, something else was done – and we shall comment upon this is in a moment. But a criterion having been tentatively specified, there was next a second kind of technical problem posed – a design problem: Given an incompletely specified set of rules, to complete the details so as to render the "what tends to emerge" resulting from the game's being played a *fair game outcome;* or, alternatively, given a game that is unfair by the criterion agreed upon, to deduce what alterations in its rules are required for making it fair. This, again, is evidently a purpose for which we, too, must find some practical way of serving; but, as before, their way is not for us – for, again, the tractability of the mathematical problem posed in this deductive mode of transforming unfair games into fair most strongly depended upon the radically rudimentary circumstances that were assumed to be the case.

In between these two technical problems there was that nonmathematical cognitive problem that is presently the main one for us: that of provisionally describing the attributes by which fairness is to be identified in an outcome; that is, that of tentatively specifying a criterion – which for us would be that of tentatively describing and specifying one or another of the idealized states. And to the extent that I am able to determine what was done to settle upon a criterion, these distinguished mathematicians found no other way of proceeding than to consult one another's sense of fairness – there was discussion "looking toward agreement."[7] This is the impression that I get from their discussions of such problems as that of the Gambler's Ruin – in which discussants show to one another instances of games that all can directly perceive to be unfair but yet that are classed as fair by previously agreed upon criteria. The criterion in question would thus be shown to have been not the "true" one; and the "error" – a case of Knight's other kind that "is related to sense observation in a very different way" – would have been detected, not by objective test, but by earnest and perceptive people looking at what

[7] I shall point out in passing that, so far as I understand these matters, what is being said here about the technical problems as opposed to the cognitive is also true for the investigations pursued by theorists of strategic behavior and decision – and that in this literature there are perhaps better illustrations of investigators in the act of dealing with the nonmathematical cognitive problem that can be found in the older literature of fair games. These investigators were also obliged to search out a "true" criterion – in their case, a criterion of *best* that a rational person applies in choosing rules of strategic action. Their mathematical problems are, in essential respects, the same two technical ones. And in this literature there are instructive illustrations of such theorists appealing to one another's introspective selves in seeking for the right or "true" criterion of *best* among the many that occur to them as possibilities. (See, e.g., Luce and Raiffa, 1957, *Games and Decisions: Introduction and Critical Survey,* Chapter 13, especially pp. 278–98, in which the authors discuss the choosing, for a theory of choice, of a criterion of choice.) A provisional determination of the meaning of *best* having been agreed upon, there is then the problem of designing best rules of action – for testing hypotheses, controlling quality, allocating resources, assigning tasks, etc. I mentioned earlier (Section 1.8) how useful I thought Jerzy Neyman's small introductory book is for instruction upon the structures of these theories of choice and decision. What he was prompted to call "the fundamental theorem" of his theory had its application in the designing of best rules of action – i.e., in locating, among a restricted set of "admissible" rules of action, the one or several that satisfy the conditions set forth in a previously agreed upon criterion of *best.* The problem of determining what those attributes are by which a *best* is to be recognized in an outcome is in no sense a technical mathematical problem. It is a cognitive problem and was treated as such, a matter of inquiring in some way into the ordinary person's inner self. (Neyman 1950: Chapter V, especially Section 5.3, pp. 304–21.)

is being classified and reflecting upon how players would react to it.[8] This, in some measure, is illustrative, I think, of the sense of Knight's usage of the expression "the factual root of the whole social problem" (see Section 3.2).

Precisely the same cognitive problem is posed in the complicated circumstances of a people's agents in the act of choosing changes in its laws. Whereas in the simple case it is fairness that is being objectified and described, in our complex case it is *fullness* of employment, *equitableness* of income distribution, *balancedness* of development, *stableness* of prices, *benignity* of power concentration. In either case these are names of properties that discussants attribute to sets of rules or law – in that in an intended choosing of whatever these names are supposed to connote it is a modification of a set of rules or laws that is in fact chosen – but properties that are nevertheless manifested and observed in the "what tends to emerge" resulting from actions chosen individually, by players or citizens, within the constraints of jointly chosen rules or laws.

3.6 A case of a distinguished practitioner in the act of practicing Smith's science of the legislator

This is the basic factual situation in which the problems of our subject field are posed: specialists, commonly called economists, supposedly possessed of such special knowledge and technique as to warrant their being called upon for professional advice, in the act of practicing this profession of advising legislators in their deliberations upon how well some component of a presently operating economic system is performing, and upon what changes might be effected in it for making more nearly right the outcome of its working. At the end of this chapter I shall include two observations upon this factual setting – that is, two exhibits of practitioners in the actual process of this professional practice. Each is in the form of a dialogue, which I take to be an instance of Knight's "discussion looking toward agreement." These cases of the actual practice are intended for the reader's study, his task the same as the one we have been trying to do: to identify what things and relations the discussants are talking about – the ones their roles oblige them to talk about – and what suppositions are required for the intelligibility of the talk.

[8] For example, William Feller (1968: 249): "Problem 15 contains an example. [By the criterion] this game is *fair*. [Yet] it is difficult to imagine that a player will find it 'fair'." Also see Feller's Chapter XIV.

Exhibit A, the first case, consists of an excerpt from the *Hearing before the Joint Committee on the January 1955 Economic Report of the President.*[9] I have placed in the margin a number alongside of each of several segments of the quoted dialogue. These mark places at which I think the reader might exercise himself in the doing of this task. Certain of the marked passages pose the descriptive problems to which the chapters of Part II are addressed. And I shall give here a review of the passages marked (1), (2), (5), and (6) to illustrate an identifying of what I think those things really are that the talk is all about – that is, what that special knowledge and technique would specifically be about to warrant a practitioner possessed of them being called upon for advice.

In passages (1) and (2) the legislator is telling of and demonstrating what he sees as questionable about the outcome of the working of the currently operating economic system. A numerical record will have been formed from counts and measurements made upon selected populations of things and upon processes of events occurring in space and time – there is simply nothing whatsoever else upon which variables could have been defined for a forming of such a record. Computations upon and arrangements of these numerical data will have been devised to serve as descriptions of characteristic properties of these developing populations and processes. These appear to me to be not at all well contrived for revealing what it was in fact that this responsible reactor was reacting to; but nevertheless it is to the graphed and tabulated data thus prepared that the legislator points – "Could I get someone over here, please, to move this chart so it can be seen?" – in an effort to demonstrate what he is finding to be wrong with the way the economic system is presently working.

In passages (5) and (6) a distinguished practitioner of this advisory science, by now a Nobel laureate, expresses a directly contrary reaction to what the legislator has shown:

> *Mr. Schultz:* This, therefore, is to say that this is not an abnormal thing that one sees up there.
>
> *Vice-Chairman Patman:* You mean [that this] is not abnormal[?] . . . You [surely] do not want one line to run one way and the other line the other.

This is Professor T. W. Schultz, responding to what he deems to be a misdirected concern of, an erroneous diagnosis by, the legislator, Representative Wright Patman (D., Tex.). There are, to be sure, he

[9] Eighty-fourth Congress, 1st Session, January 24 to February 16, 1955, pp. 624–32.

thinks, questionable things that may be noted in the properties of these and other populations and processes as they are now developing over time; and he will in due course direct attention to them.[10] But this that is being shown in the charts is not among them – with respect to what the legislator has pointed to, he declares that to be "not an abnormal thing that one sees."

In elucidating and elaborating upon this diagnostic judgment, the advisor in effect asks his audience, the legislators and quasi-legislators there gathered, to raise to mind a visualization of what he calls the economy, by which I am virtually certain he means the thing that we are now denoting by π_t – that vast congeries of populations and processes of events upon which a census is an observation – during an extended period of time when it would be said to be in a state of full employment and also in a state of price stability. And he requests that this be done with the apparent intent of proceeding from a visualization of what these aspects of the economy look like when there is nothing much that may be said to be wrong with them to a demonstration of the truth of this: that what the legislator had singled out in them as cause for concern is, on the contrary, a normal feature of the operation of an economic system that is working not poorly but well.

The stance that the specialist thus appears to have assumed seems much like that of the clinical practitioner of medicine – presuming to know from his scientific studies how things look when right and how things look when wrong. But this is not a stance – this that presupposes an objective test of the rightness of what is being reacted to – that fits the factual circumstances of this particular professional practice. Although I am sure that Knight himself would not have regarded this as a case of the "scientificism" of which he disparagingly spoke (e.g., 1956*d*: 28), for me it represents the most prevalent form of that misconstrual of role that Knight's usage of this expression brings to mind. Perhaps I do Professor Schultz a disservice in attributing it to him in his practice of this advisory science; but if I am in error in this, I am also putting him in the very best of company, where I think he undoubtedly deserves to be, among the truly leading figures in the history of this professional practice. One might easily form an exhibit of this practice and have in this role of

[10] This was done in other testimony that we have not included in the exhibit. The views expressed are substantially those submitted in his article (Schultz 1950) and in the two chapters of his book (Schultz 1953*a*; 1953*b*). And to the reader who would undertake the task that I am setting forth for him, I much recommend that he add this article and two chapters to Exhibit A.

specialist advisor any of quite a number of economists with famous names – Ricardo, Marshall, Keynes, Fisher, to mention a few.[11] And the exhibit so formed would show the practitioner in this attitude that I am attributing, perhaps mistakenly, to Professor Schultz: of one possessed of, or who will have at least scientifically striven to acquire, an objective test for telling in an outcome whether or not there does indeed exist a discrepancy between what it is in fact and what it ought to be.

But the factual circumstances of this advisory practice do not admit of any such objective test. These circumstances, to the extent that my observations upon them have been accurate, are nearly identically those of the fair game theorists' studies – the difference being only this: that in the one they are as complicated and complex as can well be imagined, whereas in the other as simple and elementary as required for rendering tractable certain mathematical problems posed. For those simple circumstances, as was noted, there were clever mathematical devices contrived for seeing in a set of rules the outcome of its working, and for transforming rules the properties of the outcome of whose working do not satisfy prescribed conditions to rules the properties of the outcome of whose working do. And in between these two technical operations there was the cognitive problem of finding out tentatively what these prescribed conditions are to be; and there was no objective test of the rightness of this determination. This, I think, and as remarked earlier, is the lesson to be drawn from the fair game theorists' discussions of such problems as that of the Gambler's Ruin – for example, from William Feller's earlier quoted remarks (see footnote 8 in this chapter): to the effect that the game in question is fair by the criterion that had seemed to be a "true" one; but that in a more comprehensive description of this game's outcome it becomes evident to one's own sense of fairness that real players would not regard the game as really fair. The criterion was thus recognized, not as an objective test of the rightness of the outcome, but as a predictor, in this case an allegedly erroneous one, of how players will react to what they themselves will experience this outcome to be.

It is much the same with the two idealized states that the practi-

[11] Sources for a forming of such exhibits of the practice of famous practitioners would be such as these: Ricardo (1952), Marshall (1926), and Keynes (1971), and for Fisher, any of a number of congressional hearings, e.g., Committee on Banking and Currency, House of Representatives, 69th Congress, 1st Session. *Hearings on H.R. 7895, A Bill to Amend Paragraph (d) of Section 14 of the Federal Reserve Act, as amended, to Provide for the Stabilization of the Price Level for Commodities in General, Parts 1 and 2* (1927).

tioner in our exhibit asks his listeners to raise to mind. The one is presumed to be a possible state of a real population process and the other of a real process of events (see Sections 2.2. and 2.3). A specialist's description of either of these states, "correctly interpreted" – that is, "if one is making . . . a serious pretence to accuracy" in laying out what is really going on in any actual case of the practice of our advisory science – is a predictor of what responsible choosers of the law can be brought by discussion to reach agreement upon as a state of things not reasonably reacted adversely to. And so far as I can see, specialists who would undertake this descriptive task, as more or less would seem to be the case with the fair game theorists' seeking for a criterion of fairness, have no other way of proceeding than by discussion "looking toward agreement" – that is, by appealing to persons' senses of rightness in their reactions to what can sensibly be set forth as possibilities.

This setting forth of the possibilities is, of course, an entirely different matter in the enormously complicated circumstances of the advisory practice that our exhibits show, from what it is in the simple circumstances of the problem field of fair game theory. In this latter case, expectations of the outcome of the working of a set of rules are deduced mathematically from the conditions that the rules impose. In the professional practice that we are studying, there can be no such mathematical modes of observing how things will work out – none to be even aspired to for the calculable future. And should this bring to the reader's doubting mind the literature of econometrics and mathematical economics, I bid him study more intensively cases of the actual practice and come to realize that these crucial technical problems, in the forms in which they actually appear in this practice as well as in the theory of fair games, are simply not among the subjects of this literature. For a serving of these essential purposes in the complicated circumstances of this practice, there is virtually a necessity for empirical investigations of actual happenings of outcomes as they really do occur in fact[12] – that is, for improvising, however, primitively at the start, some form of what probabilists call a Monte Carlo procedure. One can organize a progressively more comprehensive description of the "is" – those properties of it that convey to responsible observers a sense of how well the presently operating system of legislation is working. And one can find extended periods of time over the course of which this "is" was at least

[12] It is in the light of this supposed necessity that we have interpreted the method and work of Wesley Mitchell and his associates of the 1920s and early 1930s. See Sections 2.3 and 2.5 and the Appendix to Section 2.5.

said to have been in one or another of certain of the idealized states. In Part II of this book we shall take this as our experimental descriptive task: that of describing the population of this nation, dispersed as it is over the national area, each of its members in some employment state at any moment and from moment to moment subject to transitions from state to state, the whole developing over a time when it was generally said to be in a state of full employment.

3.7 A second case of the practice of this advisory science

Exhibit B shows practitioners of our science in the act of professionally advising upon the monetary system that was in operation at the time – what may or may not be said to be wrong with its working, and what changes legislators would or would not be well advised to make in it. This observation upon the practice of the science has been formed from excerpts drawn from Professor Milton Friedman's testimony submitted long ago upon two occasions: before the Joint Economic Committee of the Congress in 1959, and before the House Committee on Banking and Currency in 1964.[13] I have included from the record of the discussions that took place on that second occasion a brief exchange between a legislator and a member of the board of governors of the Federal Reserve System.

I shall subsequently use this Exhibit B as a point of departure for a commentary of which the Appendix to Chapter 4 consists. Presently, I shall refer to certain episodes in it to illustrate somewhat further what I am led to think the special knowledge and technique must specifically be about to warrant an expert possessor of them being looked to for legislative advice.

In the first of these, a legislator, himself a distinguished economist who had once served as president of the American Economic Association, asks this prominent practitioner of our science, who later was similarly so honored and by now is a Nobel laureate, to express an expert's judgment upon the way the nation's "stock of money" had grown over the course of a recent period of time: Was there something wrong with the pattern of this growth or not? The reply is to the effect that in fact the growth had not been just right during this time; and the advising specialist, as it would seem from the

[13] Joint Economic Committee on the 86th Congress. *Hearings on Employment, Growth, and Price Levels, Part 4, The Influence on Prices of Changes in the Supply of Money,* May 25, 1959, pp. 605–69; Subcommittee on Domestic Finance of the Committee on Banking and Currency, House of Representatives, 88th Congress, 2nd Session. *Hearings on the Federal Reserve System After Fifty Years, Vol. 2,* February 25, 1964, pp. 970 et seq.

record of the discussion, then proceeds to demonstrate upon a chart what a plotting of the aggregate size of this "stock" would have looked like had its growth been more in keeping with the requirements of the economy. For a drawing of such a line, depicting a feature of what would appear to be presented as a norm, a simple arithmetic rule is proposed: Taking due precautions in the selecting of a starting place for the plotting, he would have the line so drawn as to represent a size that increases over time at a stipulated constant rate.

But while his statement lends it that appearance, it is not a norm of an aspect of the reality that we are denoting by π_t that would thus be depicted, that is, a feature of the outcome; rather, it is a detail of a proposed modification of the operating system that we are denoting by $\{\theta, S\}$ that the specialist is illustrating in this passage. The plotted line would convey a sense of what is being proposed for the legislators' choice, a modification of the mechanism – not a sense of what the outcome of its working would look like. The working of it is attended to, at least remarked upon, in other passages; and in one of these we have a distinct reference to such a norm or standard as the kind of which we have been speaking. Were the legislators to adopt this proposed modification, the advisor goes on to say, that is, were they to enact this statutory prescription whereby operators of the system would be instructed to see to it that the rate of growth of the aggregate size of the nation's stock of money – we shall later denote this growth rate by λ_t – be kept nearly constant at a value of about 3 to 4 percent, there would then tend to emerge an approximately stationary state of things – "a stable background" for the accommodation of "the other fluctuations." These references to "the other fluctuations," and the "stable monetary environment" of which they would be a complement, are not to the operating mechanism but to the outcome of its operation – in particular, to the populations of real elements and processes of really occurring events in whose statistical properties legislators do in fact see the performance of the system. And the statements in this context are scarcely intelligible apart from an understanding that "the other fluctuations" of which the advisor is speaking are of that special kind and form: namely, the kind that choosers of the law can be brought by rational discourse to agree upon as being fluctuations and forms of variation not reasonably reacted adversely to.

In another episode, another specialist advisor, this one a person who would have a part in the operating of whatever mechanism the legislators see fit to choose, is asked to express a professional judgment upon the modification that the other specialist had proposed: Would his agency be able to do what the proposal called for its doing? His reply is that the modification is a feasible one, that by doing things that it presently is authorized to do, his agency would be able to see to it that the rate of growth λ_t be kept approximately constant at the prescribed value – but that this modified version of the system would not work the way its proposer had said it would, that it does not have the performance characteristics that had been attributed to it: There would not tend to emerge a state of things for which "stable monetary environment" would be suitable as a name; and "the other fluctuations" would not be of that special kind and form that persons responsible for this working can be brought by rational discourse to look upon as fluctuations not reasonably reacted adversely to.

Now note the response of the first advisor to this same question of the feasibility of the proposed modification (the questioner is Sen. Prescott Bush – R., Conn.):

> *Senator Bush:* The thing that troubles me about your plan is the practicality of it. You have thought about this a lot, of course – and you believe it is perfectly practical for the Federal Reserve to step up that stock of money each year at an even rate?
>
> *Mr. Friedman:* Oh, yes.
>
> *Senator Bush:* Regardless of what the economic conditions may be, or the demand of the Treasury, or what fiscal policy effects may be. That can still be done practically?
>
> *Mr. Friedman:* It is perfectly practical. This doesn't mean, of course, that there won't be consequences. If there are strong inflationary pressures otherwise, upward pressure [from other sources], following this rule would mean that interest rates will rise sharply, and the Government will have to pay a higher price for its [borrowings just as every other borrower will have to pay].
>
> *Senator Bush:* [Your proposal is based upon an expectation] of a gradually rising gross national product?
>
> *Mr. Friedman:* Yes, sir.
>
> *Senator Bush:* You would not advocate it if you looked for a gross national product [that would not show growth over the long term]?
>
> *Mr. Friedman:* I find it hard to conceive of [such] circumstances . . . Our economy is one which has a strong tendency to grow. [We have before us a record of its growth over] the past 150 years. [People annually add to their capital,] so that . . . unless we make serious mistakes in our national policy we can look forward with great confidence to a growing economy.
>
> *Senator Bush:* The point I want to make though, is that [the prescription that there be a steady increase in the stock of money] is geared to this other [condition].

Mr. Friedman: And that they are related one to the other, so that unless there is a steady growth [in the stock of money,] obstacles are imposed upon the growth of the economy. And, of course, unless there is a growth of the economy, the steady growth of the stock of money would mean inflationary price rises.

As to the practicality of it, Senator Bush, it is unquestionably practicable. I think [Congress should] specify objectives for an agency that are within its competence. I would not favor your instructing the Federal Reserve Board that it stabilize the price level, because it may not be able to do so – that is not something over which it has direct control. It has only an indirect effect on the price level insofar as it affects the stock of money. On the other hand, the stock of money is what it does directly control.

By the "practicality of it," the senator has in mind, I think, not the possibility of the legislative agency's finding an effective strategy for successfully playing its part in the new "game." As the second advisor intimated, the personnel of the agency, by doing things they already are authorized and know how to do, would be able to keep the value of the variable λ_t within the narrow range prescribed for it. But would this be "practical"? That is, would they be permitted to continue doing so in the face of the adverse reactions that would be experienced by responsible persons toward the outcome of this new game's being played?

In turn, by "consequences," Professor Friedman has in mind, I think, natural consequences of an economic system's working under certain circumstances. The one cited, sharply rising interest rates, as an illustration of what is to be normally and resignedly expected in the event of certain other things happening, is among the ones, I suspect, that had occurred to the senator and induced in him the doubts about the "practicality" of the proposed change. And so as to have from this case of the practice of the science an illustration of the same point stressed in the previous section, let us suppose the recommended rule to have been adopted after all, and then the other things mentioned to have happened, thus bringing on the occurrence of the aforementioned consequences – which, in a rough and general way, is what much later actually happened. And let us then imagine the legislator of the previous section, or the second specialist advisor of this one, preparing his chart to show these consequences in order to demonstrate for his audience what he is adversely reacting to in the outcome of the altered system's working – and Professor Friedman responding as did Professor Schultz in the previous section: "This, therefore, is to say that this not an abnormal thing that one sees up there."

The stance that thus would have been assumed, and that seemed in fact to have been more or less assumed all along, is that of the clinical practitioner of an applied natural science. But again, as before, it is not a stance that quite fits the factual circumstances of this professional practice – which are essentially the ones postulated in simple form in the development of fair game theory (see Sections 3.4 and 3.5); so that all that was said in the preceding section in this regard is as applicable here too – in particular, with reference to the matter we used the problem of the Gambler's Ruin to illustrate: the very special meaning of *norm* in this context, in contrast to its meaning in the applied natural sciences – and what this implies with respect to how specialists in our field must proceed in finding out and describing instances of such norms (see Section 6.2).

I shall add just this respecting Professor Friedman's thought and method. In Section 2.5 we commented upon the work of Wesley Mitchell and his associates of the twenties and early thirties – holding it to have been on the right track but requiring for its further development a stochastic theory whose accessibility lay yet in the future. Professor Friedman, as I view his work, belongs with those discussed in that section. As a youth he was the preeminent pupil of Arthur F. Burns, who in his own youth had been the preeminent pupil of Wesley Mitchell – who, strange to say in this context, had been in his youth a much admiring student of Thorstein Veblen. The theory of the subject of Friedman's professional advising is not the Marshallian neoclassical economics with which he is commonly associated, and with which he associates himself, but rather is that that is commented upon in that section of Chapter 2 and the Appendix attached thereto.

3.8 Two exhibits of the practice of the profession

I present now the two exhibits. Our interst in them, as I have said, is exclusively conceptual. They are intended for the reader to exercise himself upon: in identifying, to repeat our earlier statement of his task, what the things and relations are that the talk is all about – what it is that is working and then what the other things are in whose properties the outcome of this working is manifested – and what suppositions are required for the intelligibility of the talk.

In forming the exhibits[14] I have deleted phrases and sentences

[14] Exhibit A: From *Hearings before the Joint Committee on the January 1955 Economic Report of the President,* 84th Congress, 1st Session, January 24 to February 16, 1955, pp. 624–32. (*cont.*)

that seem to me to be repetitive or superfluous, and at several places I have resorted to paraphrase – these deletions and alterations being indicated by the customary ellipsis dots and emendation brackets. So far as I can tell, however, I have not altered the sense and style of the remarks at all.

Exhibit A

Vice-Chairman Patman: . . . the Economic Report of the President . . . is saying . . . that the small-business man and the farmer are suffering more than any other group . . . however, I fail to find where any satisfactory solution has been offered.

I have prepared here a chart. Could I get someone over here, please, to move this chart so it can be seen? . . . There is a chart in (1) the Economic Report of the President that is very similar . . . It is on page 98, if you have the report . . . Now on all of these charts, like on page 42, chart 26, you will notice that the farm prices, raw material industrial prices, they go way down when the finished goods and semiprocessed materials, all administered prices go straight along, they do not fluctuate . . .

I just wonder if you members of the panel agree with me that (2) monetary actions affect the farmer more quickly and more . . . effectively than [they do] any other group . . . I will ask you if you agree with me that farm prices respond more quickly to monetary action than prices generally. Do we all agree on that? Dr. Schultz, do you agree on that?

Mr. Schultz: I am not going to take your next step, though. I will take this one, yes.

Vice-Chairman Patman: All right. [The panel agrees] that the farm prices are more responsive to monetary actions than other . . . prices . . . Now, then, if you will notice this chart here, the prices that the farmer has had to pay have not gone down much. In fact, in 1951, . . . when the so-called accord was agreed to and money was made hard and interest high, other prices did not respond too much, but farm prices responded very quickly. They took a nose-dive, . . . and in 1953, when the hard-money policy really got into high gear, the farm prices . . . went down further, but the prices paid by farmers not only leveled off, but got a little higher. Do we all agree on that?

(*Footnote 14, cont.*)
Exhibit B: From Joint Economic Committee of the 86th Congress. *Hearings on Employment, Growth, and Price Levels, Part 4, The Influence on Prices of Changes in the Supply of Money,* May 25, 1959, pp. 605–69; and Subcommittee on Domestic Finance of the Committee on Banking and Currency, House of Representatives, 88th Congress, 2nd Session. *Hearings on the Federal Reserve System After Fifty Years, Vol. 2,* February 25, 1964, pp. 970 et seq. (Testimony from the latter source begins with that of Rep. Reuss – ". . . Mr. Friedman, when you speak of the ability of the central bank . . ." – and ends with that of Mr. Mitchell – "Ignoring all other consequences, absolutely"; i.e., the exhibit is not strictly chronologically arranged.)

Mr. Benedict: No.

Vice-Chairman Patman: All right, what is your answer there?

Mr. Benedict: Well, I do not discount at all the importance of monetary management and interest-rate management, but . . . there were other factors that had in my opinion more to do with the easing off of farm prices than did the interest rates. I do not think the hard-money program had very much to do with that.

(3)

In part we are in a process of readjustment from a period of very high and very abnormal demand for farm products, and we have had a continued high productivity of farm products. It seems to me that the balance between supply and demand has affected farm prices rather more than the monetary policy [that has been] followed.

Vice-Chairman Patman: Well, . . . in one capacity or another, bankers have occupied bottleneck positions in monetary policies, and . . . while the bankers were doing so well and big business was doing so well, the President says in his report that the small-business man and the farmers hit an all-time postwar low . . . The prosperity is going more to the big man, and the little man is not only not getting any of the prosperity, . . . but the net effect is that he has been penalized.

(4)

What do you gentlemen think of that? Would you mind commenting briefly on it?

Mr. Schultz: Mr. Patman, . . . the point that I wanted to make, which runs off a bit from your general line, from your argument here, runs as follows: This is a judgment about the way the economy lay. If we could have an economy that was fully employed the next five years and if in that economy we could have steady general prices, neither inflation nor deflation . . . [notice that] I have put two conditional notions here . . . I am trying to avoid the effects of a rise in the general price level . . . or a drop in this . . . but if you had full employment and [stable prices] today in the American farm economy, the costs are such that if you took the old parity ratio, things would clear the market at about 85 to 90 percent of parity . . . the terms of trade reflected by the general costs and demands of 1910–13 have changed that much.

(5)

(6) This, therefore, is to say that this is not an abnormal thing that one sees up there.

Vice-Chairman Patman: You mean it is not abnormal for [farm and raw material] prices to continuously go down?

Mr. Schultz: Not down, but where they are 85 or 89 percent of parity in the old sense, that is getting to where the cost of these things really lies in our economy.

Vice-Chairman Patman: I know, but . . . you do not want one line to run one way and the other line the other.

Mr. Schultz: I am not interested in the lines, I am interested in how the economy is set. The economy is really set so that costs have come down in agriculture.

Vice-Chairman Patman: Come down?

Mr. Schultz: Yes, about 15 percent per unit of product, that is what [these lines mean].

Vice-Chairman Patman: Well, ... in February of 1953, when they were looking around to see who they could help, they did not see the little farmer ... [or] the little business man ... when two segments of our economy, the little business man and the small farmer, were screaming for help, ... all eyes were centered on helping the stock market. I think their eyes should be centered on agriculture and the small-business man. That is what I am trying to get at ... (7)

I particularly want to help the family-sized farmer. It has been suggested to me that we should consider giving the farmer who produces, we shall say, up to $7,500 a year ... a hundred percent of parity through the Brannan plan, or any other practicable way. In other words, just give him an opportunity to earn a living if he works for it; ... up to $7,500, give him a hundred percent, and all above that, up to say $15,000, give ... 75 percent or 50 percent, providing that for production above $15,000, we do not have any supports at all. (8)

What would you gentlemen say about that? ... Just start at the end of the table, if you will, and briefly state what your opinion would be on something like that. You see, that is for the family-sized farmer.

Mr. Welch: ... I do not know whether a person who produces a bale of cotton ... should be guaranteed a hundred percent of parity [while not doing this for] another person ... on an efficient producing unit ... whether you would want to penalize him there or not.

Vice-Chairman Patman: Well, I am looking at it from the standpoint of the family-sized farm and how to give them an opportunity to earn a living. I think out of about 6 million farmers, about 4 million are not farming as a business, they are farming as a mode of living. In fact, many of the farmers I have known ... have eked out an existence and finally sent their boys and girls to college and they have become fine men and women ... I just look with great disfavor and disappointment on the mode-of-life farmer going out. I just have a feeling that this great country of ours could at least make it possible for that little family to have a living if they went out there with their hands and worked for it and produced it. (9)

Mr. Welch: ... Mr. Congressman, it is difficult for me to see ... how you can get at that group ... [who] are really not commercial producers ... unless you do set aside certain groups and say that we will support you but this group over here, we won't. (10)

Vice-Chairman Patman: That is what I am saying. I am setting them aside and saying they ought to be supported in particular ...

Mr. Welch: I am all for encouraging the family-sized farm, ... but I do have some misgivings as to whether you can extend a support price for those groups and exclude your other producers who are also contributing to our total resources.

Vice-Chairman Patman: Well, I would do it as a matter of public policy. I would just say we want to encourage the man who lives on a farm and wants to make a living. If he is willing to work for it with his hands and produce enough he ought to have a living wage, and we are going to make it possible for him to have a living wage. If that is discriminating against anybody else, it is all right with me . . . (11)

Mr. Schultz: Congressman, I think the idea . . . is weak at the very point where you want it to be strong . . . There are a million farm families in the United States, full time in this business, able bodied, who had a cash income from all sources of less than $1,000 in 1949. These fellows are not helped by this kind of a proposal at all. They sell so little that we do not get to their poverty until we bring them more economic opportunity, which means they must have more resources to work with . . . we have really not [been] coming to grips with this low-income group in agriculture. We have thought we could do it with price supports, but the problem is deeper . . . (12)

Vice-Chairman Patman: You know, I do not agree with you just exactly there . . . In this competitive market there are disadvantages [to being a small farmer], but if you give them a guaranty: if you work for it and earn it on parity prices, we will give you up to – I am not exactly sold on $7,500 as the exact amount, but give them enough to assure them a decent living under decent conditions if they work for it.

Mr. Schultz: . . . This means you have to do more than parity prices. I am not afraid of [forward prices] which can be put before the farmer so he can make plans accordingly . . . Therefore, I am not against parity prices if these prices have real meaning . . . Then we can bring much greater certainty to farming as it deserves and there will be much greater efficiency. But let me repeat, the really small poor farmer, 1 million and more, we do not get at in prices . . . (13)

Vice-Chairman Patman: I hear what you say, but whenever you let them know they will get a certain price if they work for it, they will work their heads off . . .

Mr. Nicholls: I certainly agree with Congressman Patman on the objective of trying to help this small farmer, the only thing is I do not think his suggested solution is the right one or the effective one. I would call your attention to some tables that I have appended to my statement, . . . Page 1, appendix table 1 . . . Obviously, price-support programs . . . primarily benefit those larger farmers, and . . . they . . . need financial aid . . . least . . . On the other hand, . . . at the lower end of the scale, the end of the scale that you are speaking of, price support will simply not do much good . . . the solution of the low-income farmer's problem really lies outside of agriculture.

Vice-Chairman Patman: I am afraid you do not understand . . . I would let him grow anything of certain basic products at a parity price, he

(14) could mix them up. The main thing is to permit him and his family, if he works hard enough and produces, to be assisted in getting prices which would give him a good living . . .

Would you like to comment on [my proposal], Mr. Paarlberg?

Mr. Paarlberg: . . . We undertook a study of it, and one aspect of this proposal that came out of our studies was this. A program of this (15) sort could not be operated with the conventional system of price support and loans. It would have to be a payment program, . . . because if you endeavored to support the prices of these small farmers you would in effect hold an umbrella for the large farmers as well . . . the only means by which this program could operate would be through a payment program.

Vice-Chairman Patman: Thank you, sir. Mr. Chairman, I think I have taken up enough time.

Exhibit B

Senator Paul Douglas (D., Ill.): Mr. Friedman, I gathered from your final comments that you believe that the Federal Reserve policy should have a total money stock increase [at] approximately a constant rate roughly equal to . . . [that of the net national product in real terms] . . . and you don't think Reserve policy should be used as a short-run stabilizing factor . . . You think Federal Reserve policy should be used . . . for long-run stability, but not for short-run stability? . . . What are you going to do about the business cycle? The Federal Reserve Board thinks it should try to stabilize [or moderate] the cycle. You are saying it should not try to do so and, similarly, you say the Government should not try to do so. Who is going to do it?

Mr. Friedman: Senator Douglas, the question is what one thinks the major problem is and what one thinks has in fact been the effect of governmental policies in these areas in the past. The statement I made is based upon the conclusion that, despite intentions, the policy measures actually taken have historically been a destabilizing factor . . . The effect has been to destabilize the economy . . . As a matter of theory, obviously the sensible thing to do . . . is to try to be relatively tight in money and fiscal policy during a period of expansion and to be relatively easy during a period of contraction . . . But if one looks at . . . what in fact has occurred as a result of officials trying to follow such a policy, he will find that the effect has been just the opposite [of what was intended,] that in fact . . . the effects have been destabilizing. Why is this?

If monetary and fiscal policy were like a water tap so that as soon as you turned it on it ran and as soon as you turned it off it stopped, it is hard to believe that it could have the adverse effects I have suggested. But that isn't the case. Monetary and fiscal policy is rather like a water tap that when turned on only starts to run 6, 9,

12, 16 months later. It is because of this long lag in the reaction to policy that you have . . . an effect opposite to that intended.

Senator Douglas: That is said to be one of the difficulties in fiscal policy, . . . but is it a defect of monetary policy, which is supposed to work more immediately and not have such a time lag?

Mr. Friedman: I think we have to distinguish between two different problems: How fast you can change the money supply, and how fast the money supply changes economic activity. With respect to the first, the changes in the money supply, that can be brought about very rapidly . . . by open market operations . . . But the second, the time lag between the changes in the money supply and the changes in economic activity, is a different matter.

If one studies the chart [on display, showing changes in the money stock], you find that peaks in the rate of change of the money stock . . . precede the peaks in general business conditions by something like 16 months on the average, and the troughs precede the troughs in general business by something like 13 to 14 months on the average . . . What is even worse, the lag is [by no means invariable.] Thus you have a situation such that, when the Federal Reserve System takes action today, the effect of that action may on some occasions be felt 5 months from now and on other occasions 10 months from now, on other occasions 2 years from now. That is the major reason why it is so difficult . . . to know what measures one ought to take at any given time.

Senator Douglas: Therefore, do not do anything except keep the supply of money expanding at the [constant] rate?

Mr. Friedman: Senator Douglas, that would be quite a lot . . . It seems as if any fool could do better, but in fact very wise men have been unable to. If one goes back and examines the difference month by month between the actual behavior of the stock of money and the behavior under the alternative I suggest of a constant rate of increase, you will find that the actual behavior has been less consistent with what in retrospect you would have regarded as desirable than the alternative . . .

If you look back over the whole period from 1867 to date, the money supply has had a very strong upward trend and it has usually risen during contractions as well as expansions in business, but at a slower rate.

Senator Douglas: Is that true of 1929–33?

Mr. Friedman: Let me give the exceptions, because they are a very interesting series of dates . . . The only occasions on which the stock of money fell absolutely during the business cycle are 1873 to 1879, 1893 to 1894, 1907 to 1908, 1920 to 1921, 1929 to 1933, and 1937 to 1938. [N.B. Friedman is "speaking of money in the broader sense – currency plus demand deposits plus commercial bank time deposits."]

Senator Douglas: Those are periods of depression?

Mr. Friedman: Those are periods of great depression . . . The only occasion on which the money supply falls is in the great depressions. In every great depression, it has fallen.

My main point is really that an essential precondition for avoiding great depressions is that we keep the money supply growing at a steady and regular rate. To have kept prices stable during past periods would have required a rate of increase of the money supply of about 4 percent per year . . .

Senator Douglas: . . . I will ask you just one more question, Mr. Friedman . . . Do you think the money supply was allowed to increase adequately during the period from 1954 to 1957; the increase for the period as a whole . . . was only 4 percent, whereas on a 4-percent-per-year basis it would have been 12 percent?

Mr. Friedman: The number that one wants to use for the desirable rate of growth of the money supply depends critically upon the concept of money . . . used . . . [Also,] one has to be careful what date he starts from. But I would say that . . . if you had started from somewhere at the average level around 1952 or 1953, somewhere when you were not either at a trough or at a peak, and from then on had expanded the total of currency plus demand deposits, plus commercial bank time deposits, by something like 4 percent per year, you would have had a monetary policy better adapted to the fluctuations we have had than the policy actually followed. Such a constant rate of rise . . . would have meant a slower rate of rise than we actually had during 1955 and a faster rate of rise during 1956 and 1957. It would have meant a faster rate of rise during the period of the recession and a slower rate of rise since April 1958 [i.e., during the expansion] . . .

Representative Thomas Curtis (R., Mo.): Professor [Friedman], I was very interested in your recital of those periods before World War II of monetary contraction and then the fact that you did not list 1949–1950, and 1954–5, and 1957 and 1958, . . . [times that] people have called recessions . . . May I conclude . . . that you regard those three postwar recessions as of a different nature than those you recounted?

Mr. Friedman: Yes . . . I think that one can in fact distinguish historically among two different classes of depressions . . . – mild recessions and . . . deep depressions. The kinds . . . we have had since the end of World War II have been relatively mild . . . The kinds I was citing as occurring in 1920–21, 1929–33, and 1937 to 1938 were deep depressions.

I think that our studies establish an enormously strong case that in every deep depression monetary factors play a critical role. Monetary collapse has been a major source of deep depressions, and if I were being a bit more unguarded, I would say the primary source.

On the other hand, if one takes the minor recessions, such as 1948–49, 1953–54, 1957–58, the monetary factors may have contributed to them, . . . but . . . I am inclined to believe . . . that other factors played the main role.

Representative Curtis: Could we turn it around, though, and say that possibly wise monetary policies helped to prevent post–World War II recessions from becoming deeper?

Mr. Friedman: If by wise monetary policy you mean avoiding the kind of catastrophic mistakes . . . that were made in 1929 to 1933 and . . . 1920–21, yes. The behavior of the stock of money since World War II, and particularly since about 1950, has been very much more conducive to economic stability than it was in the earlier period, and it has been conducive to economic stability because it has come very much closer to the kind of straight line policy that I have been suggesting.

[Regarding the chart on display] if I may call your attention to it. Disregard the very rapid short-run movements in it because that is a question of mistakes in the figures . . . What I would like to call your attention to . . . are the longer swings. You will note that whenever you have a period when the swings are very sharp, we have had a period of great economic instability, and whenever the curve is relatively stable and the swing is rather small we have had economic stability. There is a stable period just before World War I and again in the 1920's . . . from 1922 to 1929–and again in the [post–World War II] period, and those are three periods which by common consent would be regarded as the most stable periods in economic activity . . .

Representative Curtis: Professor, in your prepared statement you state that "under present conditions in the United States, the Federal Reserve System essentially determines the total quantity of money," and then you go on to develop that. And in the concluding sentence of the same paragraph, you say: "There is no doubt that, if it wanted to, it has both the formal power and the actual technical capacity to control the total stock of money with a timelag measured in weeks". . .

Really that surprised me a bit . . . It led me to thinking that maybe my basic concepts of what you regard as money need correction. Am I correct in the assumption that the measurement which you use for quantity of money . . . [also reflects] the amount of credit that will be extended as well, or how do you relate credit and money? That is where my difficulty comes.

Mr. Friedman: I am very glad you asked that question because I think it is a very important question and one that is the center of much confusion . . .

By the stock of money, I mean literally the number of dollars people are carrying around in their pockets, the number of dollars they have to their credit at banks in the form of demand deposits, and also commercial bank time deposits. That is the stock of money at any moment of time.

The amount of credit, on the other hand, is [the amount of] loans outstanding [in one form or another] . . . With any given stock of money you can have widely different amounts of credit . . . The two are, of course, closely connected, [especially in our monetary system where] creation of money has been combined in commercial banks with the lending and investing of funds.

Representative Curtis: . . . I am among those who are confused on this subject . . . It seems to me that one of the big problems that faces us at the legislative level centers more around the question of credit than it does of money. . . . I guess it doesn't make . . . too much difference whether it is money or credit, as far as considering the amount of purchasing power . . . that is available.

Mr. Friedman: I think it does, Mr. Curtis. . . . It makes a great deal of difference. I think [so] from your point of view in particular, . . . particularly from your point of view for this reason: The Constitution gives Congress control over what money shall mean and what shall be used as money and as legal tender. Congress has the direct responsibility to specify what our monetary system shall be, so I think control over the amount of money, either directly, or indirectly through specifying the kind of monetary standard we shall have or the rules under which the stock of money shall be changed, is an inescapable part of the legislative responsibilities of Congress.

Control over credit, [however,] is in a very different area . . . I see no reason why we should . . . have any stringent control over the borrowing and lending activities of people. Credit is of many kinds. Most credit . . . does not derive from banks. It derives from personal loans . . . in the form of mortgages, . . . bonds, or . . . stocks. It derives from transactions [between borrowers and] financial intermediaries such as life insurance companies, investment trusts, and the like . . .

Representative Henry Reuss (D., Wisc.): . . . Mr. Friedman, when you speak of the ability of the central bank to control the money supply, they do that, do they not, by making available bank reserves and deposits which are the crucial part of the money supply here, but are only created if businessmen and others utilize that lending capacity of the banks? Is that not so?

In a time of real depression, the monetary authorities can create bank lending powers through increasing reserves, yet the money supply may not be much increased if businessmen are absolutely helpless and do not borrow money at any price. Is that not so?

Mr. Friedman: I do not believe so . . . The Reserve System can, if it wishes to, control the quantity of money. By altering the volume of reserves available for banks to hold, it can determine the quantity of money within very narrow limits and with very brief delay.

Representative Reuss: You believe that this country would be better off if Congress simply legislated a rule of conduct for the monetary authorities which said, "Increase the money supply, defined as currency outside banks and time and demand deposits, at the . . . rate of 4 percent per year"? You say 3 to 5 percent . . . Do you ever recommend a percentage increase for the narrower definition just including [demand deposits and currency]?

Mr. Friedman: Yes. 3 to 5 is about right for the broader definition. Somewhere between 2 and 4 is about right for the narrow definition.

Representative Reuss: Now which of the two would you select if we were writing the statute here? . . .

Mr. Friedman: I would take the broader, subject to the proviso that the present control over rates of interest on both demand deposits and time deposits is eliminated . . .

Representative Reuss: With this model statute we are constructing, I will recapitulate as follows: Congress says to the Fed: Make additions to the money supply at an annual rate of 4 percent, "money" being defined as currency outside banks and both time and demand deposits.

What instruments of monetary policy would you let the Fed use? Certainly open market operations?

Mr. Friedman: Yes. . . . My own preference . . . would be to eliminate discounting completely, . . . [and] I would also eliminate the ability to change reserve requirements so that I would leave the Fed with the one tool which is the most potent they have; namely, open market operations. . . . There is a sizable slip between the open market operation and the final money supply, first because part of the total money stock is held as currency and the public may change the proportion in which it wants to hold currency and deposits and, secondly, because the banks may change the ratio of reserves they want to hold. [But] I think the Federal Reserve would operate such a program very well . . . I think they are very good at these kinds of technical operations . . .

Representative Reuss: Back to your percentage again, should it be 3, 4, or 5? Have you considered anything like a formula-timing arrangement . . . whereby you can relate that percentage to such things as unemployment, degree of unused industrial capacity, so that in a year or a month or a week, at which we were running at 6 percent unemployed and 15 percent of the industrial capacity unused, maybe that week the money supply ought to be increased at a rate of 5 percent, whereas in a week when we get closer to capacity you ought to go down to 3 percent? Would that not be feasible? Is there anything wrong with considering that?

Mr. Friedman: There is obviously nothing wrong with considering it, . . . but I do not think it would be desirable at the present state of our knowledge . . . I do not think we could have reasonable confidence that such a formula would do good rather than harm. The reason . . . is precisely the point I have emphasized earlier; namely, the time which it takes for monetary changes to have their effect. We cannot even measure what unemployment is now. We can measure only what unemployment was a month or more back. More important, what we do now will affect not the unemployment of today, . . . but maybe the unemployment of 5 months from now or 6 months from now or a year from now . . . I do not believe that we know enough now to set up a formula of this kind which would do more good than harm.

Representative Reuss: Strangely enough, I have more fears about your . . . proposal on the inflationary side than I do on the deflationary side . . . That is so for this reason. If you set your percentage figure of money increase each year at, say 5 percent, I would really have no fears about it being inadequate . . . However, on the inflationary side, if you speak in terms of the Continent of Europe, of the full employment of men and factories, I tend to shy away a bit from creating 4 percent additions to the money supply [during such times]. I will let you get by without putting an accelerator on this, but could you not put a brake on it?

Mr. Friedman: I think it would be very undesirable to do so. In point of fact, I personally do not know of any inflationary episode in any country in which the money supply has increased as little as 4 or 5 percent a year. The only way, I believe, that you get the kind of dangerous inflationary conditions that you are conceiving of would be by having a more rapid rate of increase in the money supply than would be specified in the rule.

This is certainly true of the American experience. I have not examined equally carefully the experience of all other countries, but I do not know offhand of any example in which there has been substantial inflation without a substantial rate of rise in the money supply, by which I mean a rise of more than 4 or 5 percent a year . . .

Representative Reuss: [addressing Federal Reserve Board member George Mitchell]: . . . While I want to make it clear that I am by no means a "Friedmanite" and am not prepared to buy lock, stock, and barrel his proposition, I am not persuaded that you refuted him this morning, and I would like to pursue this a bit with you. It is a fact, is it not, that the Federal Reserve System can control the money supply whereas it cannot, nor can any other governmental agency except very, very indirectly, control industrial production and employment and gross national product? . . . That is true; is it not? . . .

Mr. Mitchell: Well, let me say first that the purpose or the objective of both fiscal and monetary policy is to effect the growth of the economy and . . . to minimize cyclical fluctuation. So we are trying to effect the things you say we cannot effect with our policies.

Representative Reuss: Yet, in your wildest, most euphoric moment, you do not claim that you can, all by yourself, bring about full employment without inflation?

Mr. Mitchell: All I am saying, Mr. Reuss, is that the point about fiscal and monetary policy is that it is attempting to do the very thing that you say it cannot do . . . I think monetary policy can make a contribution in this direction; yes.

Representative Reuss: Agreed. Is it not also true that monetary policy can control the money supply? Whether that, in turn, will produce the beneficent results on employment and production that we all want is another matter, but you can control the money supply, can you not?

Mr. Mitchell: Well, it is at times difficult. The money supply grows in a very lumpy fashion, and this is because the initial action which we take, in providing reserves, does require a response from the banking system from individuals . . . You can eventually do something with the money supply but in the course of doing this you may cause some things to happen that you believe are undesirable and, therefore, the goal of just making the money supply move [i.e., at some fixed rate of increase], if followed relentlessly, could have an impact upon credit conditions and expectations that might be totally undesirable.

Representative Reuss: Yes, but you must answer my question, which was . . . not whether it is good to make changes in the money supply the sole goal of monetary policy. There you have indicated you disagreed with Friedman, who says it is, but my question is whether . . . you can change the money supply. No doubt about that?

Mr. Mitchell: Ignoring all other consequences, absolutely.

Senator Bush: Professor Friedman, I want to go back to something you said a little while ago regarding the Federal Reserve Board and the possibility that it might contribute to instability by its monetary policy. We have frequently heard the Federal Reserve express their policy as one of leaning against the wind, so to speak, and I would like you to comment on that policy if you understand what is meant by it, [which] I am sure you do . . . What should the Federal Reserve Board do with demands for credit increasing? Prior to the most recent recession, we had tremendous increases in the use of installment credit. In fact, there are some pretty reliable opinions that it was overuse of credit by consumers . . . that brought about this recession . . . , because it stimulated the purchase of goods beyond the year in which they should be buying them . . . What is your general observation about that?

Mr. Friedman: May I first call your attention . . . to a feature of [another chart on display], which I think is . . . important. The Federal Reserve System was introduced in the year 1914 . . . This is on a ratio scale so that equal distances mean equal percentage changes. I think you will agree that the striking thing about this chart is that [it shows the money stock to be] a much more stable thing before the Federal Reserve System than it is afterward . . . If you take the whole period from 1869 to 1914, there is nothing like the instability that prevailed in the period after 1914, . . . even if you take out the two wars. Therefore, the Federal Reserve System, established partly with the object of promoting greater stability in the stock of money, has had the result of promoting less . . . So far as the more recent period is concerned [and the Board's] policy of leaning against the wind, . . . the problem is to know which way the wind is blowing, not when you act but when your action is effective. If what I do today has effects maybe 5 months from now, or 10 months from now, or maybe 15 months from now, then I have to know which way the wind is going to blow 5, 10, or 15 months from now. That we do not know, so in practice [Board policy amounts to trying] to lean against the wind when one doesn't know which way it is blowing.

Senator Bush: Are you saying, then, that because of the difficulty involved there should be no attempt to do it?

Mr. Friedman: Yes, sir. I am saying that it would be preferable . . . for the Federal Reserve System to say to itself, or indeed for Congress to instruct it to act in this way, that instead of trying to vary its policy behavior from day to day, instead of looking at credit conditions and the like, it would limit itself to seeing to it that the stock of money grew at a perfectly steady rate month in and month out, year in and year out. This would provide a stable background for the other fluctuations.

Senator Bush: This assumes, I presume, that the economy would also grow at a stable rate. Is that not so?

Mr. Friedman: It would not grow at a perfectly stable rate.

Senator Bush: Would you want the stock of money to increase at a stable rate, of 3 or 4 percent a year, regardless of which way the economy was going?

Mr. Friedman: Yes, sir–because . . . if the economy was tending to go down, this would tend to pull it back up. If it was tending to go too far up, this would tend to pull it back down. It would have the effect of a thermostatic reaction . . .

Senator Bush: I thought you said a little while ago that the stock of money really didn't affect the upward or downward movement very much.

Mr. Friedman: No, sir . . . I didn't intend to say that. I think the stock of money is extraordinarily important in its effect, but what is important about it is the instability in its behavior.

Take the 1929–33 depression, which is [one of] the two greatest depressions in our history . . . I think there is no doubt whatsoever that the depression would have come to a close at the latest in 1931 if the Federal Reserve System at that time had not allowed the money stock to decline catastrophically. If I may go back to [one of the charts] and refer to the money stock again, the policy I am suggesting would have had the money stock growing steadily from 1929 on instead of declining sharply. If it had done so, we would never have had the depressions of 1929–33 . . . It might have been something like the 1957–58 recession. My guess is that it would have been over either in late 1930 or the spring of 1931.

Senator Bush: Would you say that the money stock was inadequate all during the thirties? . . .

Mr. Friedman: . . . The inadequacy or adequacy of the money stock depends upon its preceding level . . . By comparison with 1928–29, the money supply was inadequate throughout the thirties, yes.

Senator Bush: I would like to turn to another line of questioning for a moment. How do you feel about the question of giving the Federal Reserve Board a little more control over credit, . . . particularly . . . consumer installment credit?

Mr. Friedman: I think it would be a very bad thing to do. I think the Federal Reserve System now has too many powers, not too few. It is doing things that it ought not to be doing.

. . . As I was saying, Congress and its agencies have a definite responsibility about money. So far as credit is concerned, free enterprise is just as good for credit as it is for shoes, hats, and anything else. The objective of our policy ought to be to allow credit to adjust in a free market, provided we maintain a stable monetary background. Consequently, I think it is inappropriate for the Federal Reserve System to have powers over consumer credit . . . Its present powers over margin requirements are equally inappropriate . . . For the purposes of monetary policy, that is to say, controlling the stock of money, it is unnecessary for the Federal Reserve to have any powers over consumer installment credit, over stock market credit, or over any other type of credit directly.

Senator Bush: In your opinion, does our current adverse balance of payments call for corrective monetary policy meaures?

Mr. Friedman: No, sir. Our adverse balance of payments, which involves a gold outflow, is fundamentally a consequence of a whole pattern of policies including as a very major policy our foreign aid policy. Given our foreign aid policy, it seems to me eminently desirable for the United States that a large part of it should take the form of an outflow of gold rather than of goods . . .

Senator Bush: You are not particularly concerned at the moment about the trend of our balance of payments?

Mr. Friedman: No, sir. The crucial question relates to gold, . . . [which is] very difficult and complicated, but one of great importance . . . If we could have a real honest-to-goodness gold standard, I think there would be much to be said for it. I don't see any prospect whatsoever that we are going to have one . . . Our present gold policy is comparable to our present wheat policy. We have a price support program for gold, with the one exception that we offer the support price to foreigners as well as to domestic producers . . . From this point of view it is highly desirable that we get rid of a large part of our gold surplus . . . We tried to prevent that gold from influencing our monetary policy when it came in. It would be a serious mistake to let it influence our monetary policy when it goes out . . .

Senator Bush: We have on the order of $20 billion worth in our gold supply, but my recollection is . . . nearly $13 billion . . . is subject to recall by other governments, by other peoples, which would leave our supply at $7 to $8 billion. Does that seem adequate to you in view of conditions in the world today?

Mr. Friedman: Yes, Senator Bush . . . Foreigners are inevitably going to hold dollar balances here for a variety of purposes, and there is no immediate chance that the claim against gold will be exercised, but if they were, I would personally think it a serious mistake for us to promote a major deflationary movement within this country to prevent the gold from flowing out . . . The better course of policy would be to let it flow out. Indeed, and this is more extreme, I think it would be the better course of policy to permit the price of gold to become a free market price instead of a controlled price . . .

Senator Bush: . . . One of the principle objects of this committee's work this year is to try to find out the relationship between the maintenance of employment and price stability. I would like you to comment on that . . . Do you think those are mutually conflicting or not? . . .

Mr. Friedman: I do not believe they are mutually conflicting. I summarized some of the historical record on this question in one of the papers that was . . . published in the compendium last year. Let's take just the American experience, if I may.

In [a chart on display] real income shows a very rapid growth throughout the period from 1880 to the First World War, except for the sharp depression in the early nineties. The earlier period (before [the] 1890's) was a period during which prices were falling at the rate of 2 percent a year. The later period was a period during which prices were rising at the rate of 2 percent a year. The period of the twenties, which was also a period of rapid growth, about 1923 to 1929, was a period in which prices were almost exactly stable.

My conclusion is that what is important for economic growth and economic stability is that prices behave in a regular way, that they not display large fluctuations. The important thing is reasonably stable behavior of prices . . .

Senator Bush: Would you think then, in view of that, that it would be wise for us to amend the Employment Act of 1946 so as to state in the law that price stability is a condition, or requirement, or assist to full employment?

Mr. Friedman: I think it would be desirable to amend the act to state that a reasonably stable price level is one of the objectives to be sought . . . I should also say . . . that I find it hard to believe that this would be of major practical importance, by comparison with the adoption of measures such as a reasonably stable rate of growth in the monetary supply, that would have the effect of giving us price stability . . .

Representative Widnall: It is not clear to me how you arrived at that figure of 3 percent. What is that based on? . . .

Mr. Friedman: It is based on past history. Suppose we take the experience in the United States over an 85-year period from 1871 to 1955 . . . That is the period covered roughly by these charts. Over that period, taking it all as an average . . . and not looking at the fluctuations within it, the stock of money . . . has risen by about 5¾ percent a year. That is the average.

One and three-quarters percentage points has represented population increase. About 2 percentage points has represented an increase each year in average per capita real income. About 1 percentage point has been absorbed by . . . a growth in the amount of money people want to hold [as cash balances] in real terms, and finally, on the average over this 85-year period, about 1 percentage point has been absorbed by price rises.

If we take the 85-year period as a whole, it would seem that over that period it would have taken something like a 4 or 4½ percent per year rise in the stock of money . . . to have kept prices stable . . . This is for the particular definition of money I have used. You would get a different number if you used a different definition.

Under present circumstances, the rate of growth of population is perhaps a bit less than it was over this period because these were the periods of great immigration. If one allows for what seems a reasonable expectation of what is likely to happen, about 3 percent would be required on the average to offset growth in total output, allowing for growth in both per capita output and population. The question then becomes, what to do about the secular trend in velocity [i.e., the growth of the size of the cash balances that individuals and firms desire to hold on the average]. If we take this figure for the past 85 years and assume that it will apply to the future, we get about 4 percent as the annual rate of growth in the money stock required for price stability.

My own feeling is that what is really important is to pick a number and stick to it and that it isn't nearly so important whether that number is 3 percent, 3½ percent, 4 percent, 4½ percent, so long as it is somewhere within that range. Suppose you picked a slightly wrong number. The result would simply be to have a slight tendency for prices either to decline very slightly or rise very slightly, and on the average you would come out about right. The important thing is to provide a background of certainty in terms of which people can make their plans and in terms of which the system can operate . . .

Senator Bush: If Mr. Widnall will permit me just to ask a question, the thing that troubles me about your plan is the practicality of it. You thought, of course, a lot about this and you believe it is perfectly practical for the Federal Reserve to step up that stock of money each year at an even rate?

Mr. Friedman: Oh, yes.

Senator Bush: Regardless of what the economic conditions may be, or the demand of the Treasury may be, fiscal policy influences may be. That can still be done practically, in your judgment;

Mr. Friedman: It is perfectly practical. This doesn't mean of course, that there won't be some consequences. If you otherwise have strong inflationary pressure or strong upward pressure in a boom, following this policy would mean that the interest rates will rise sharply and the Government will have to pay a higher price for its money the same way everybody else does.

Senator Bush: It is based on a confidence of a gradually rising gross national product?

Mr. Friedman: Yes, sir . . .

Senator Bush: You would not advocate it if you looked for a rather stable action of the gross national product?

Mr. Friedman: . . . I find it hard to conceive of the circumstances that would produce a stable gross national product . . . Our economy is one which has a strong tendency to grow, that it has grown for 150 years . . . People [exhibit a] willingness to save some part of their annual income to add to capital, so that . . . unless we make serious mistakes in our national policy we can look forward with great confidence to a growing economy.

Senator Bush: That is the point I wanted to make though, that the steady increase in the stock of money is geared to this other specification.

Mr. Friedman: And that they are related one to the other, that unless you have a steady growth [in the stock of money] you may impose obstacles in the way of a growth in the economy, and of course, unless you have growth in the economy, the steady growth in the stock of money would mean price rises.

As to the practicality of it, Senator Bush, I think that it is unquestionably practicable. I think [Congress should] specify objectives for an agency that are within its competence . . . I am not myself in favor of your instructing the Federal Reserve Board to stabilize the price level, because it may not be able to do so. That is not something over which it has direct control. It has only an indirect effect on the price level insofar as it affects the stock of money. On the other hand, the stock of money is exactly what it does control.

Representative Widnall: Did I understand you to say that savings reduce the velocity of money?

Mr. Friedman: No, no. [I did not intend to say that.] . . . Increase in real cash balances, yes.

Insofar as people save, they add to their wealth. Insofar as they are adding to their wealth, they keep some part in the form of money. If they kept in the form of money only the same percentage compared to their income [as in former years], velocity would be unchanged. Historically, they have done more than that . . . As people's income has gone up by 1 percent in real terms, that is, in terms of goods and services – they have tended to increase the amount of money they held by something like $1\frac{3}{4}$ percent, and this has meant a decline in velocity.

Do I get at your point? I am not sure I do. Velocity is a confusing notion. In many ways I think it would be better if we turned it upside down and used its reciprocal. Let me see if I can put it this way: . . . People are holding in the form of money an amount equal to about 7 months' income. If you go back a hundred years, they were holding in the form of money an amount equal to about 2 months' income. That is what has happened over 100 years. That is what 1 percent a year amounts to over 100 years. It has gone from about 2 months to something like . . . 7 months . . .

As people have gotten richer in terms of their income and their wealth, they have increased the number of months' income which they hold in the form of cash or deposits. That is what a decline in velocity means, when translated into terms that I think are perhaps more meaningful . . . So that an accumulation of savings, insofar as it increases wealth and insofar as it is held in cash, does lower velocity. Does this answer your question?

Representative Widnall: Yes, sir. Thank you.

PART II

A nation's economy in geographic space and time: on the task of specifying norms of various aspects of it

CHAPTER 4

On constructing a small-scale model of a nation's population of people

4.1 An introductory statement of the descriptive task undertaken

For a general introduction to the chapters of this Part II, I refer the reader to Sections 1.4 and 1.5; and with this reference, I shall proceed to the work at hand.

We have interpreted certain of Professor Schultz's remarks, recorded in Exhibit A at the end of the preceding chapter, as an invitation that his audience raise to mind a visualization of an economy developing over a time span of some five years while fully employed and in a state of price stability. Whatever this specialist advisor may have consciously had in mind, we shall take this as a request that the idealized states of these two aspects of the economy be tentatively specified and depicted – states of things that choosers of the law can be brought by rational discourse to agree upon as states not reasonably reacted adversely to. And it shall be our task to try to find sensible steps that practitioners of our science might tentatively take toward constructing what we shall call *standard forms* that depict such norms. To describe what a population or process of events looks like in fact as it develops over time is a straightforward problem with which anyone is familiar. To describe what those factual features of it are that are conveying to responsible choosers of the law a sense of dubious performance of a currently operating economic system is a somewhat more involved problem. To describe what those features of it would look like were they such as would not induce a rationally arrived at sense of disapprobation is yet more involved. And our efforts at this task are deliberately experimental – the intention being, as we have said, to try to clarify what would seem to be important insights of Knight pertaining to the peculiarities of economics as a descriptive science.

In the remaining sections of this chapter we shall have recourse to a literature in which demographic geographers are informative about how a large nation's population is typically arranged over the geographic area that contains it – that is, about what one might expect to find were he to examine the spatial distribution of a nation's population at each of a succession of moments in time. When the labor force of this population is said to be fully employed, some proportion of its members nonetheless are unemployed at any moment, just as a minimally congested flow of vehicular traffic contains at any moment some vehicles waiting for passage; and this proportion, corresponding to the minimally unemployed population, is a "global" measure of the density of these temporarily unemployed members among all members of the labor force. The population having arranged itself over the national area so as to form a spatial distribution of variously sized urban concentrations, there is a comparable measure of the density of unemployed members corresponding to each of these local subpopulations. And we shall undertake in Chapter 5 rudimentary empirical inquiries to determine provisionally the typical or "normally expected" variation over geographic space of the density of unemployed members of what is generally looked upon as a fully employed national population.

It is a physical model of a human population that we shall imagine being constructed, each member momentarily located and tracing out as time progresses such "paths of motion" as those of the checks that drew Knight's scorn (see Section 3.3). And for this we imagine the information upon this expected variation of the density of the unemployed to be applied in the preparation of a map to represent the model at time $t = 0$ – the elements of the population being represented by small objects placed on the map, each being differentiated to show employment status, and with the spatial variation of the density of unemployed members conforming with what our studies tentatively indicate as "normally to be expected" for a fully employed population. The measured densities (unemployment rates) respectively corresponding to the subpopulations are taken as indicants of the employment states of these local population concentrations. As time passes, individuals make transitions from employment state to employment state, so that after a lapse of time t the employment states of the local subpopulations will have been altered. And having in mind an imagined construction of a map to represent the subsequent population at time t, we undertake additional rudimentary empirical inquiries for numerically specifying the cells and margins of a table showing a bivariate frequency distribution of the N subpopulations of the nation classified by unemployment rate at time 0 and also at time t. These studies lead to a rule, describing an apparent statistical regularity, that anyone might apply to fill in the cells and margins of the table, given only (a) the value of the measure of the global density of unemployed members – that is, the national rate of unemployment – and (b) the length of time t during which the national rate remains constant at this value. The information contained in this table pertains (1) to what we shall tentatively interpret as the typical or normally expected spatial distribution of the minimal number of unemployed members of a population that is said to be fully employed and (2) to what we shall provisionally label as normally expected transitions from employment state to employment state that the regional subpopulations make with the passage of time. And upon the basis of these data, we shall contemplate the possibility of the construction of a physical model that depicts tentatively these specific details of the development of a spatially distributed national population of people during a time when it would have been generally said to be in a state of full employment. Once constructed as a visual aid to one's intuition, detail may be added to it – for example, relative to the degree of concentration of unemployed members within one or another class (age, race, sex, education, income class, income class of father, etc.) of individuals and thus to the degree of inequality among defined classes with respect to the incidence of the minimal unemployment. And accompanying the addition of detail to which attention would thus be called, there would of course be a continuing review of what this idealized employment state of a population may reasonably be conceived to be.

As I think about the thing, I waver in my interpretation of it. The idea of this figure certainly does appear to me to be implicit in legislative deliberations in which discussants communicate with one another about what they see and adversely react to as the state of the employment of the nation's population. We begin by speaking of the imagined configuration as a standard form of an aspect of the economy π_t when its state is not "abnormal" – that is, when responsible choosers of the law would agree that nothing much may be said to be wrong with it. But perhaps another statement of this would better conform with the factual circumstances of the unique kind of discussion that we are studying. Wesley Mitchell, in a work to which we earlier referred (see Section 2.5), used the term *phase* as a name for one or another state of the economy that he undertook to describe – and one such phase he singled out as being generally looked upon as "most conducive to social welfare." It is a state that the actual economy π_t may be observed to pass into, stay in for a while, and then pass out of. As with the phase, so too with the idealized employment state of the nation's population that Schultz asked his listeners to visualize: The length of time that the real population remains in that state, having made a passage into it, is a variable with an expected value presumed to be dependent upon conditions that might conceivably be identified and altered by legislative design. Once it leaves the state, it stays out for a while before returning; and the extent of its departure and the length of time a departure covers are also variables with expected values presumed to be dependent upon modifiable statutory law. It is generally looked upon as well that the first expected value be relatively large and the latter two relatively small. These three expected values qualify as likely components of the performance vector β_t specifying the operating characteristics of the modifiable economic system $\{\theta, S\}$. The defining of the performance variables, in terms of which this population's development over time may appear well or ill to choosers of the law, involves specifying the idealized state as a norm.

I can readily understand the reader growing weary with my dwelling upon the details of this particular descriptive problem. I am drawn to do so, I think, in an effort to refine a statement of it to serve as an aid to one's intuition as he ponders the problem of describing some other aspect of an economy that while no less real may be not so easily visualized. Whatever the difficulties of one's obtaining accurate and comprehensive observations upon it, and however overwhelming one may find the problem of organizing a description of so complex a thing, the entity a state of which it shall be our first task to depict is as concrete and real as anything can be: a population of differentiated elements distributed over geographic space and developing over time. When an observer declares a real economy to be in a state of full employment, or in some respect and degree to have departed from this state, the specific thing, for the main part, whose state is being referred to is this population of physical beings. One may despair of ever having accurate counts upon it, of classifiers and enumerators ever being able to recognize consistently the respective employment statuses of its constituent members as these statuses will have been defined in their instructions – of even ever being very clear in his thought about the meaning of accuracy in this context, that is, of the accuracy of the formulation of the instructions themselves. But he can at least hold in his mind's eye a clear conception of the general form of what the observations are supposed to have been upon – and adapt the data available to him as best he might for a tentative filling in of details.

4.2 Steps in the first stage of a doing of this task

We shall now proceed with the first part of this task. Let P be the aggregate number of people constituting the population of a nation covering a large contiguous area such as the one over which most of our own is dispersed. Suppose that we already know what *urban* and *rural* mean, in the sense of being able to recognize a location as being either one or the other; and let P_u and P_R be the aggregate sizes, that is, counts of the respective numbers of members, of the urban and rural populations. Suppose also that knowing what *urban* means is to know what a *city* is, in the sense of being able to identify the members of the population of any city. Let P_i be the size of the population of the ith city, and denote by N the number of cities, so that $P = P_R + \Sigma_1^N P_i$. What we presently seek to find is a set of instructions for arranging P small disks, each to represent a member of a national population of people of size P, upon a large map representing the area covered by the nation, the resulting configuration to be interpretable as a small-scale model of a spatially dispersed national population of this size. We shall think of the operation as involving several successive steps: first, determining P_R as a function of P, and perhaps of some index of the technological state of the economy at the time in question, and spatially distributing this number of disks over the area of the map; second, partitioning the remaining P_u disks into N subpopulations, N being a function of P, and the ith subpopulation being the population of a city of size P_i; third, spatially distributing these N subpopulations, the ith of them being represented on the map by a column of P_i small disks; and, finally, spatially distributing the disks in each of these N columns to form the "shape" of a city of its size. We shall consider first the last of these steps.

4.3 A city viewed as a detail in a population density configuration

I shall suppose that any reader who is observant and well-traveled will be told much about the physical characteristics of a city if told only the city's size – that is, he will grant that there is much information in the statistic P_i, cities of similar size sharing many properties in common. Cities are similarly shaped when viewed from high above, and the size of a city's population affords one a fair estimate of the size of the area covered by its shape. They are also similarly shaped when viewed in profile – high[1] at the center and sloping off toward the edge – and, again, information on the size of the city's population, or the size of the area that it covers, affords a basis for one's estimating how high at the center and at what rate the sloping off takes place. Upon the area covered by any city there is superposed a network of passageways through which there is a continual flow of traffic; and this network and the traffic flowing through it have properties that are similar for cities of similar size. The members of the population of any city have occupations, and the "occupational structures" of the cities of similar size have a good bit in common. A city is the origin of much traffic moving outward and the destination of much traffic moving inward; and the aggregate volumes, commodity compositions, and the spatial distributions of the destination points of the outward flow and of the departure points of the inward flow are all respectively similar for cities of a similar size.

In asserting that information upon the size of a city's population affords a basis for one's estimating the size of the area covered by the city, I intend merely to state that there is a usefully high correlation between these variables – that the larger the P_i, the larger the expected value of A_i. The authors whose estimates of the numerical specifications that we shall now present will have simply undertaken to systematize and make quantitatively explicit such general statements of relationships as these that are more or less taken for granted by experienced and perceptive travelers. And our task at the moment is the quite restricted one that we stated: on the basis of quantitative statements made by students of the "physical structures of cities," to compile a set of instructions for one's spatially distributing P_i small disks, representing the members of a city's population, so as to form a model density configuration having a shape and form resembling those of a city of size P_i.[2]

We shall begin by imagining a map representing the terrain covered by a city and its immediate environs; and we shall suppose that upon this map there is superposed a grid corresponding to a typical network of streets and passageways. This grid would partition the area representing the terrain covered by the city into sub-

[1] In terms, say, of density of buildings, and during busy hours of the day, of population and traffic.

[2] There have been many empirical studies upon which one may draw in devising a set of provisional instructions for this purpose; and what would appear to be a comprehensive collection of references to such studies may be found in the work of Berry and Horton (1970*a*; 1970*b*). In the latter (1970*b*) they reproduce a series of figures (12-4 through 12-10, pp. 451–5) that afford visual representations of the kind of physical model that would be constructed.

areas, approximately square in shape and with sides of about 250 feet.

When viewed from above, a city has a fairly evident "edge," and this edge traces out a shape that seems typically to be roughly circular or else, if it lies in a narrow valley or along a coast, elliptical or semielliptical (Steward 1953: 576). The total area of A_i of this shape is said (Stewart and Warntz 1968: 131; Stewart 1948) to be given approximately by $A_i = CP_i^c$, in which C is a parameter that changes slowly with time, and c, for practical intents and purposes, is a constant whose value is estimated to be about ¾. The values of C and c were estimated by elementary regression methods that any student might apply; and using 1940 census date, the author whom we now quote estimated C for the United States and for that era to be about 1/357. This estimate refers to the area within the political bounds of the city and thus is likely to be smaller than a value of C corresponding to the usually larger "urbanized area" enclosed by the edge that one may see from high above.

For the typical case, in which the shape covered is bounded by an edge resembling a randomly distorted circle, the expected value of the distance R_i from the center to this outer bound is taken to be approximately $R_i = (A_i/\pi)^{1/2}$, the value of A_i being calculated from the foregoing formula. The "edge density" of population, denoted by D', is not independent of P_i but is generally said to be in the neighborhood of 2,000 per square mile for a sizeable urban concentration. The density D_0 per square mile in the immediate neighborhood of the center of the city, and we speak now not of the residences of the people but of the people themselves at some moment during the busy hours of a day, is said (Stewart and Warntz 1968: 132) to be estimable as a function of P_i, namely, $D_0 = 75P_i^{1/2}$. And the expected density D_r per square mile at points r miles from the center is given approximately (Stewart and Warntz 1968: 131, 145; Clark 1951: 490–6) by $D_r = D_0e^{-r/b}$. The value of the parameter b, which measures the rate at which the expected density D_r declines from the center to the edge as r increases, is also said to be estimable as a function of P_i, and this estimated value is obtained in the following manner (Stewart and Warntz 1968: 145).

The population within a circular band having a small width Δr and whose bounds have an average radius r is given approximately by $2\pi rD_0e^{-r/b}\Delta r$. The total population P_i is thus given approximately by the expression

$$2\pi D_0 \int_0^{R_i} re^{-r/b}\,dr = 2\pi[b^2D_0 - b(R_i + b)D']$$

With D' being a function of R_i, and R_i and D_0 being functions of P_i, then b is also a function of P_i.

Though a cumbersome operation, it would now be a routine matter to distribute a population of small objects in accordance with the foregoing specifications. We may imagine the task being undertaken for, say, a city of size $P_i = 100{,}000$. This number of small disks would be distributed over an approximately circular area of size A_i. The superposed grid would partition this total area into subareas of size a. There would be A_i/a of these subareas, and we suppose these to be arbitrarily numbered 1, 2, 3, . . . The assignment of the disks to the subareas would be done randomly by some such procedure as one that involves the use of an urn-and-ball schema, a ball to be drawn for each disk, with replacement, and the disk to be assigned to the subarea whose number is on the ball. If subarea densities were uniformly distributed over the total area, the composition of the urn would be such that the number of balls corresponding to each subarea would be the same for all; and on each draw the probability of any given subarea being drawn would be

$$\frac{a(P_i/A_i)}{P_i} = \frac{a}{A_i}$$

But the "normal" case is not described by a uniform distribution, and the proportion of balls corresponding to each subarea would be made to depend upon the distance of the subarea from the center. A circular band with average radius r and width Δr contains $2\pi r\Delta r/a$ subareas and an expected population of $2\pi r D_0 e^{-r/b}\Delta r$ persons. The expected population per subarea is thus $aD_0e^{-r/b}$; and the proportion of the balls in the urn corresponding to a subarea r miles from the center will be $aD_0e^{-r/b}/P_i$, rather than the uniform

$$\frac{a(P_i/A_i)}{P_i}$$

The figures to which we referred in a previous footnote convey, in a general way, a visual impression of what I suppose a physical model would look like were it constructed in accordance with these specifications – except that these published figures depict the physical form of an actual large city located along a coast, and whose edge is thus not circular but semielliptical. They are photographs, apparently, of three-dimensional models of the spatial arrangements of the population of Chicago, of the floor area of that city's buildings, and of the destinations of the intracity trips that members of its population made during a sampled time period.[3] The difference between what such photographs would depict for a more typical "circular" case and what our physical model would represent seems to me to be essentially similar to the difference between an observed bivariate frequency distribution and a fitted "theoretical" bivariate density function, the form of this latter having been roughly approximated by Monte Carlo procedures.

4.4 The density configuration of which a city is a detail

The authors whom we have quoted in the preceding section called the configuration which they specified the *standard form* of a city of size P_i (Stewart and Warntz 1968: 130). Let us now understand i to be the rank of the city in an ordering, by size of population, of all the N cities contained within the bounds of a large nation like our own – that is, there are i cities among the N that are at least as large as P_i. The aggregate urban population is $P_u = P_1 + P_2 + \cdots + P_N$, the Nth being the smallest population concentration recognized as urban. Our next task is that of partitioning an aggregate population of P_u small disks into N subpopulations and then distributing these subpopulations over the area represented by our map, thus to construct a standard form of the spatial arrangement of a large nation's cities and towns.

We shall do as we did earlier and devise our set of instructions on the basis of quantitative statements by students of the spatial distributions of human populations. These statements mainly have to do with the stability of form of the size distribution of urban concentrations and of the pattern manifested in the spatial arrangement of these variously sized urban centers. One need not take too much to heart and get vexed over our referring to what the result-

[3] The models and figures were prepared by Berry (1959) for the *Chicago Area Transportation Study, Final Report, Vol. I, Survey Findings.* They are reproduced in Berry and Horton (1970*b*: 451–5).

I shall mention in passing one other author's mode of specifying the density configuration formed by the spacing of a city's population. Sherratt (1960) uses the right half of the normal probability density function $D = D_0e^{-r^2/2\sigma^2}$, rather than the $D = D_0e^{-r/b}$ used by the authors whom we have quoted; and he assumes that the variance σ^2 is itself a variable and a function of the angle of direction from the center of the city. The three-dimensional configuration that Sherratt would construct would thus be asymmetrical, and he reports that such a configuration fits the population distribution of the actual city that was the subject of his studies (Sydney, Australia). In deriving a variety of relationships – for deducing information upon which to base the planning of the city's growing network of streets, pipelines, and the like – he replaces this variable σ^2 with its mean value and thus, in effect, works with a symmetrical bivariate normal distribution of the same sized population.

ing density configuration would depict as a "normal expectation." It is submitted only as a tentative start – as an experimental step in the identifying of elements of pattern. Anyone could devise a way of spatially arranging P_u small objects such that the result would be immediately rejected by any observant person as a representation of a credible spatial distribution of a nation's urban population. Dozens of ways readily come to mind for forming spatial distributions that almost anyone would reject without a second thought. What we shall strive to do is to arrive at a specification possessing a modicum of credibility, in the sense that a knowledgeable person would not reject it on its face as a representation of the spatial arrangement of a real human population. If the reader will grant this – that there are spatial distributions that are definitely inadmissible for such a representation, and also spatial distributions that conform in certain respects to what one has become used to seeing – then, as it seems to me, he accepts the supposition that there are elemental "expectations." And we are presently trying to identify provisionally what elements of stable pattern there are that may be said to exist.

P_i is the number of people within the area that one may see from high above as being covered by the shape of the *i*th largest city; and among the several population counts for each city that are reported by the Census Bureau, the count of the population located within what it calls the urbanized area would seem to be the nearest to what we intend P_i to represent. For these reported data, one who has not tried it would perhaps be surprised by the closeness with which he may estimate the size of the *i*th largest city by dividing P_1, the size of the largest city, by i. This formula is the so-called rank-size rule $P_i = P_1/i$. A generalized form of the inverse of this relation is the distribution function that is called the Pareto distribution, which is a limiting form of what is now beginning to be known as the Yule distribution.[4] In the following section we shall illustrate and comment upon certain probabilistic models, that is, statistical mechanisms, that when set in operation generate the kind of variation described by it; but for the present we shall pursue our task on the assumption that the simplest version of this rank-size rule is applicable.[5]

On this basis we may write

[4] For the reader who may be interested, the following provide samples of studies and discussions of the Yule and Pareto distributions: Simon (1957: 145–64); Yule (1924: 33–64); Parzen (1962: 296–8); Simon and Van Wormer (1963); Mandelbrot (1963); Haran and Vining, Jr. (1973*a*; 1973*b*); D.R. Vining, Jr. (1974; 1976).

[5] The statements that we make in this section about the size distribution of cities are based upon an article by Stewart (1947). More recent references may be found in

$$P_u = \sum_1^N P_i = P_1 \cdot \sum_1^N \frac{1}{i}$$

for which there is a ready approximation formula (Stewart 1947: 464): $P_u \doteq P_1 \cdot (\log_e N)$.

With a value assigned to P_N, the size of the smallest concentration of population that is to be recognized as a town, and inasmuch as $P_1 = P_N \cdot N$, this formula provides a relation between P_u and N. The author from whom we are now drawing submits an empirical rule by which he relates N, the total number of cities and towns, with the proportion of total population that is urban. This relation as he offers it is $N = 10{,}450(P_u/P)^2$ or $P_u = P\sqrt{N}/102$; and he maintains that it has held well enough for all the census enumerations available to him (Stewart 1947: 468–9). Thus, with P given, P_u is determined – and then N and P_1 and hence all the values of P_i (Stewart 1947: 469–70).

We have now the final step: to assign locations to the P_R disks representing the individuals who do not live in cities or towns and to the N columns of disks representing the cities and towns containing the urban populations of P_u individuals. With respect to this task, I shall be brief. Having canvased the literature on the subject,[6] I conclude that one can do scarcely better presently than to distribute randomly the P_R disks and then in turn the N columns of disks over the area of our large map, in such a manner as to have each point in the area as likely a location as any other for the center of each of the objects to be located. Some day students of populations may know enough to be more realistic at this, making some places more likely locations than others; but I am aware of no discussion of how this would be realistically done now.[7] The simple random procedure

Berry and Horton (1970*c*). The earlier article, however, seems to me better suited for my present purposes.

The rank-size rule is an empirically determined relation that appears to hold only for the larger cities – say the 150 or so that have urbanized-area populations in excess of 100,000. It overestimates the sizes of smaller cities. Although I have not tried it, I am inclined to suspect that the Yule distribution, only the tail of which is approximated by the rank-size rule, would provide a fit including the smaller cities – this being a surmise from a perusal of the charts on pages 45–49 of the Yule article cited earlier. But for our present illustrative intent, we shall assume, as Stewart does, that the rank-size rule holds for the smaller cities too.

[6] See Lösch (1954: 389–94), Dacey (1968), Matui (1968), and King (1968). Suggested mapping and an extensive bibliography may be found in Berry and Horton (1970*d*).

[7] Elsewhere (R. Vining 1964: 35–7) I have discussed in general terms the problem of simulating a normal spatial distribution of natural resources and thus a representation of an expected variation of resource endowment among subareas. In an article cited earlier, Mandelbrot (1963) mentions several times an unpublished paper of his: "Statistics of Natural Resources and the Law of Pareto."

would result in the distributions of distances between cities and their nearest neighbors of comparable size being not flagrantly out of line with observations.[8] Also, for a large subarea there would be the mixture of small and large cities and towns, so spaced as to lend an observer the impression of a hierarchical arrangement of the kind that has been so much discussed in the literature.[9]

4.5 The development over time of this density configuration

Let P_0 be the size of the nation's population at time $t = 0$ – the sizes of the rural population, the urban population, and the *i*th largest city at that origin moment in time being $P_{R,0}$, $P_{u,0}$, and $P_{i,0}$, respectively. A census enumeration at this initial moment would provide the data required for constructing a small-scale physical model depicting the real and actual thing of which the model resulting from our rules purports to be a provisional expectation – that is, what students of the thing have said it would look like, in certain of its general features of form, at some time in the era of the 1940s.

A sequence of census enumerations at imaginably short intervals, for $t = 0, 1, 2, 3, \ldots$, would yield the data for constructing a sequence of such physical models that would depict the actual development over time of this spatially dispersed population – showing its growth at different and varying rates in its different parts as the whole is growing in the aggregate. There is nothing in the literature of which I am aware on the basis of which rules such as those set forth in the preceding sections might be readily extended for a construction of expectations of this real development over time. But I shall comment upon certain recently published work that seems to me to be promising for the purpose of such an extension.

N_0 is the number of cities or towns that the census enumerators would find and count at the initial time $t = 0$; and the populations of these urban concentrations, together with the one rural population, would constitute $N + 1$ subpopulations by which the

$$P_0 = P_{R,0} + \sum_{1}^{N_0} P_{i,0}$$

[8] Theoretical distributions are fitted to observed distributions in the references cited in footnote 6.

[9] This literature originates, I suppose it may be said, with W. Christaller's *The Central Places of Southern Germany* (1966; originally published 1933) and with Part II of A. Lösch's *The Economics of Location* (1954; originally published 1939). See also Berry and Pred (1961).

members of the aggregate national population would be classified at that time. For identifying an urban concentration – that is, for telling whether or not a collection of people within some particular area is to be counted as a city – the enumerators would have been provided with a size criterion; so that at the time of the enumeration, in addition to the isolated rural families there would have been many hamlets so small in size as not to be counted among the N_0 urban concentrations.

The size of each city or town, as well as the size of the rural population and of each rural hamlet within it, is subject to change with the passage of time as a result of births, deaths, immigrations, and emigrations. And if the relevant events that occur during the elapsed time were enumerated and recorded – that is, the births, deaths, immigrations, and emigrations for each urban place that exists during that time, as well as for each rural hamlet and the rest of the rural population – one could of course matter-of-factly transform a physical model depicting the nation's spatially dispersed population at $t = 0$ into a similar model representing this population at $t = 1$. Or if the rates at which these events in fact occur are stable in some sense, and dependent upon or deducible from the factual circumstances represented in the model for $t = 0$, one might in like manner construct the model for $t = 1$, and thus for $t = 2, 3$, and so on, without census enumerations of these events actually being made.

This second way of forming a sequence of small-scale representations of the population at successive moments in time is what I have in mind as a prospective extension of our rules. And it is to this, I think, that the authors are contributing to whose work we shall now refer. What is spoken of as a "model" in this work is not the physical representation of the spatially dispersed population that we have been contemplating. Rather, the thing that these authors call a model (Haran and Vining, Jr. 1973*a*: 421–37) – in particular, the Yule – Simon model – is what we have earlier called a "statistical generating mechanism" or a probabilistic "conceptual experiment" (see Sections 1.6, 1.7, 2.4, 2.5, and especially the Appendix to Section 2.5). It consists of a set of rules or instructions whereby one might experimentally generate a collection of subpopulations that grow and develop, as it were, as a result of random occurrences of just such events as the ones we have listed.

In the most rudimentary version of this Yule – Simon model, and as it is applied for simulating something that in certain respects looks like the growth and development of a human population, the assumptions are very restrictive indeed. It is assumed that new towns appear – are newly born, so to speak – randomly in time at a constant rate. This occurrence of a birth of a new town corresponds to a rural hamlet's having attained in its growth the minimum size required for its being counted as an urban town. Once the town has come into being, it is assumed to grow as a result of an excess of births over deaths of individual members of its population – and also by a net in-migration from the rural population. This latter is treated, in substance, as having the same effect as an increase of the birth rate relative to the death rate in these urban subpopulations. It is further assumed, in effect, that city-to-city migrations are mutually offsetting and are not a factor affecting the growths of city sizes. The growth of the ith city's population is thus assumed to be independent of the growths of the populations of other cities, and the rate at which individuals are randomly added to it is assumed to be proportional to the number of individuals of which it presently consists.[10]

This mechanism, when set in operation, as it is said, generates a collection of populations whose sizes after so long a time conform with Pareto's law, that is, the rank-size rule – which in the previous sections we applied in specifying our physical model of a spatially dispersed urban population at time $t = 0$. This rudimentary version of the apparatus is the point of departure for the experimentation pursued by Simon and his associates. It is shown first that one may make the assumptions less restrictive, more in accord with what would seem to be the case in fact, and yet have a mechanism that generates a collection of populations whose sizes conform with this same statistical law. And thus one might work out a way, using a mechanism based upon less unrealistic assumptions, to transform our physical model of the population at $t = 0$ into one representing it at $t = 1$, with the growth of the urban population being made what seems likely, and with the size distribution of the cities retaining the Pareto form.

But for the purpose of this extension of our rules, the promise of this work with the Yule–Simon model, as it now seems to me, lies in

[10] The size of a city, as this elementary version of the model has it, would be called in the literature of the theory of stochastic processes a "birth process with linear birthrate" and also a "Yule process" – λ being the excess of the birthrate over the death rate and n the size of the city's population; individuals are added to the population randomly in time at a rate $n\lambda$. See Cox and Miller (1965: 156) and Parzen (1962: 296–8). At time t there would be a collection of such growing populations; and the expected number of them having exactly n members would be given by what is called the Yule distribution, a limiting form of which is Pareto's law. To me, with the mathematical limitations that I have, the most readily understandable account of the derivation of this distribution is afforded by the combination of Yule's original article (Yule 1924) and Parzen's book (Parzen 1962).

the experimentation that is being done with one or another variant of this mechanism. In the recent study to which we referred, the authors note that whereas the Pareto distribution has apparently fitted well enough the observed size distributions of the largest urban concentrations of this nation for the censuses through 1950,[11] the conformances are not so good for 1960 and 1970 – something seems to have happened, and perhaps still be happening, to the real mechanism that is generating the variation in these city sizes that is being observed and recorded.[12] They further note that for certain large nations whose aggregate urban populations are growing slowly or not at all, there appears to be the same kind of discrepancy betwen the shape of the Pareto distribution and the shape of the distribution that is actually observed. And it occurred to them to consider that what has been happening to this real mechanism may perhaps be traced to this: that the rate of migration into the urban subpopulations from the source external to this collection – that is, from the rural population in the midst of which these urban concentrations are set – has been becoming progressively smaller, so that city-to-city migrations are now more prominent than was earlier the case among the events effecting growths and declines in city sizes. These authors have accordingly tried to modify the Yule–Simon mechanism so as to incorporate these new conditions into it that seem now to prevail.

By Monte Carlo methods they have investigated the properties of several variants of the Yule–Simon model; and this experimentation has had mainly to do with what happens when this external source of urban population growth – the net flow from the rural population into the existent cities and towns and the "births" occurring randomly in time of new urban towns – is allowed to become exhausted: so that for each subpopulation in the collection the in-migrations and out-migrations of a presently existing urban population are the predominant or sole source of change from one moment to the next in the size of that subpopulation. When there is this external source of growth of the number of cities and towns and of the average size of their populations, there is generated a steady-state size distribution having the Yule or Pareto form and whose parameters have values that are functions of time. To the extent that I read correctly these authors' reports, they are not yet prepared to say much about conditions to be satisfied in order that one may expect some new

[11] For charts showing the extent of this conformance through the censuses up to 1950, see R. Vining (1955: 152–3, Figures 1 and 2).

[12] Haran and Vining, Jr. (1973*a*; 1973*b*: 296–308); D.R. Vining, Jr. (1974; 1976).

form of statistical equilibrium. But the size distributions that result from the operation of their modified version of the mechanism diverge from the Yule or Pareto form in a way that looks similar to the divergence of recently observed city size distributions from this form.

This work aptly illustrates the kind of statistical problem discussed in the Appendix to Chapter 2 as being peculiarly economic; and in certain respects it is remindful of a remark by Schumpeter, prior to the time of the Yule–Simon model, upon the significance of Pareto's law:

> We must confine ourselves here to noticing the two classes of problems which it raises. There is first the question of "fit.". . . But there is second the question of interpretation . . . Few if any economists seem to have realized the possibilities that such invariants hold out for the future of our science. *In particular, nobody seems to have realized that the hunt for, and the interpretation of, invariants of this type might lay the foundations of an entirely novel type of theory. Viewed from this standpoint, Pareto's "Law" is path-breaking in the literal sense even though in the end nothing whatever is left of its particular form* [Schumpeter 1949: 155–6; italics added].

An Appendix to Section 4.5 in which correspondences are considered between the growth and developmental properties of a nation's population of people and the similar properties of a nation's stock of money: on the use of the Yule–Simon model for the study and analysis of these statistical properties

In Exhibit B at the end of Chapter 3, the subject of the discourse is the monetary system that was in operation at the time – what may be said to be wrong with the way it had been working and what changes legislators might be well advised to make in it. A critical part of the discussion pertains to what had been happening to the size of the stock of money that existed in the nation – what the growth rates of this size had been over selected periods of time and what these growth rates would have better been for the better working of the economic system.

Let M_t denote the aggregate size of the stock of money that is under consideration, and suppose that the data-gathering agency that is responsible for the forming and maintenance of a numerical record of what happens to M_t is the same agency that does this for the size P_t of the nation's population of people, or for the size of its population of firms or of its manufacturing establishments or of farms or the like – that is, census enumerators count and compile a measure of the one along with their counting and compiling of measures of the others. Just as the enumerators and classifiers of people would have been provided with instructions upon how to tell whether or not a collection of people within a particular area is to be counted as a town, and upon what people are to be counted for a measure of the size of the town, so these enumerators would have been instructed upon how to recognize what to count as a unit of money for a measure of the size of the stock of money. And suppose they would also have been instructed to retain in their tabulations the information upon where the enumerated units of money are located at the time of the counting – being provided, of course, with some rule to follow for assigning these locations – so that to correspond with the $P_{R,t}$ and

$$P_{u,t} = \sum_{1}^{N_t} P_{it}$$

in the case of the enumeration and classification of the nation's population of people, we would have in this case a numerical record upon $M_{R,t}$ and

$$M_{u,t} = \sum_{1}^{N_t} M_{it}$$

the N_t being the number of cities and towns for which the sizes of the substocks of money are to be compiled. The aggregate size of the nation's stock of money would thus be given, as in the other case, by

$$M_t = M_{R,t} + \sum_{1}^{N_t} M_{it}$$

for each of the times the counts are made.

This identification of a measurable amount of money with a population of countable objects may present difficulties to the reader – as it also does to me in the begging of the question of what the classifiers' and enumerators' instructions are to be. But I think an experimental descriptive inquiry such as this can be an aid to one's thought about what these instructions might appropriately be. We shall thus proceed with it, misgivings notwithstanding. Were our attention confined to that part of the conventional designation of the stock of money that consists of currency, we would, of course, be dealing with elements of a spatially dispersed population strictly conceived. Each would evidently have a geographic location at any specific moment in time. But so, too, could some plausible rule be found for assigning locations to the units of the other part of this conventional designation, the bank deposits. An elementary, localized substock of money, subject to disposal by some individual or agency, and being a component of what is called the "financial funds" or "liquid balances" that are contained within a region, may be transferred from one subarea to another. Such movements assume the form of flows over geographic space that vary in volume and direction as time goes on. Each day each bank in any city has checks drawn upon it payable to persons or agencies located in other cities – and checks deposited in it that will have been drawn upon deposits in other cities. There is a pattern of destinations of these units that originate within the subarea covered by a city, and a pattern of originations of the units that have their destination in this same subarea. And although I do not have any at hand, I would be surprised if studies of these patterns have not been made – comparable to those, for example, of the originations and destinations of railroad carload lots of merchandise and commodities.[13] The so-called stock in question is in relevant respects something like a population: each of whose "members" will have been "born," is subject to being moved about from subarea to subarea, and in the course of time will "die."

It is important, I think, that a student of the development over time of a national or multinational stock of money make some effort to think in these terms of a population process – a spatially dispersed collection of elements that is evolving and growing at different rates in its different parts as time progresses – inasmuch as crucial issues in legislative discussions of the performance of a currently operating monetary system not infrequently turn upon what responsible observers interpret as dubious properties of the spatial aspects of the development over time of the stock of money. It is evidently the case in discussions of the operating properties of a multinational monetary system. Not only do discussants expect of a system that it generate in its operation an appropriate growth of the aggregate world stock of money; the system is also called upon to generate in its operation geographic concentrations that are not excessive in degree.[14] And if

[13] There are quite remarkable statistical uniformities and regularities that may be noted in arrangements of geographic origination and destination data. Some years back I reviewed and discussed certain graphic representations of some of these regularities (R. Vining 1953: 57–64). From casual observations I am led to suspect that similar arrangements of originations and destinations of money payments would show similar regularity and stability.

[14] See, e.g., *International Monetary Arrangements: The Problem of Choice – Report on the Deliberations of an International Study Group of 32 Economists,* Princeton University Press, Princeton N.J., 1964.

one looks for it, he will find that this degree of geographic concentration has been a crucial topic of discussion in legislative deliberations upon the performances of national monetary systems.

Two old but sharply drawn cases come immediately to mind that could easily be adapted as exhibits of legislative deliberations upon this matter: the discussions among the members and professional staff of the National Monetary Commission in its designing of the original version of the Federal Reserve System as a proposed modification of the monetary system then in operation;[15] and the discussions recorded a few years later among members of and witnesses before a joint congressional commission of inquiry in its critical review of the performance of the newly modified system during the trying first six years of its operation.[16] In each of these reported deliberations, one may note that a principal point of issue is made of what some observers interpreted to be a periodic tendency for the national stock of money to become geographically concentrated to an excessive degree. To some extent, efforts were made to describe directly what this aspect of the stock of money's development looked like; but mainly this supposed tendency to periodic excessiveness in the degree of geographic concentration was talked about as being reflected in the heavy geographic concentrations of bank and other business failures during the periodic times of financial stress – and especially in the outlandishly large regional variation of interest rates charged by banks during these times.

The size P_i of the ith urban concentration of people changes over time as a result of occurrences of births, deaths, emigrations, and immigrations. And the size M_i of the ith substock of money changes over time as a result of occurrences of events that seem closely similar. Units of money are "born" with the act of the making of a new bank loan. Units of money "die" with the act of a redemption of an old bank loan. There is "emigration" of money units when a check drawn upon a component of this ith substock is paid into some other substock; and when the opposite occurs, there is "immigration."

Consider now the Yule–Simon model as it is applied in the study of the development over time of a nation's population of people. The assumptions that go into the makeup of this statistical mechanism are such as to have new towns being born randomly in time at a rate γ that

[15] See the report of the National Monetary Commission (1912) and also the monographs prepared for that commission by its specialist advisors (in particular, the one by Kemmerer upon the variation of interest rates). See also Warburg (1930).
[16] See Part 13 of the *Hearings before the Joint Commission of Agricultural Inquiry*, 67th Congress, 1921.

is some function of time. This comes, as the rationale of this application has it, from an excess of births over deaths in the rural population such that from time to time there is an occurrence of a rural hamlet's attainment of the minimum size for its being counted as an urban town. The assumptions are also such as to have the size P_{it} of any town, once it has come into being, to be what probabilists call a Yule process or "birth process with linear birthrate" (see footnote 10 in this chapter) – that is, with λ being the rate per member at which members are added to this *i*th subpopulation, P_{it} grows randomly in time at a rate proportional to the population's size, namely, at a rate λP_{it}. The rationale for this interpretation of P_{it} as an independent Yule process involves two simplifying assumptions: first, that intercity migrations are mutually offsetting, so that a city's growth is independent of the growths of other cities; second, that the migration into each existent city, from the rural population dispersed about it, is at such a rate that a stable value λ can be assigned to the excess of the birthrate over the death rate in that city to represent the rate per member at which new members are being added randomly in time to its population. But the unrealistic restrictiveness of these simplifying assumptions is substantially reduced in the modifications of the model that Simon and his associates have made. The rate λ_i per member at which members are added to the *i*th subpopulation is itself made into a random variable, with λ being its expected value; and conditions are assumed that set bounds to the number of intercity migrations that occur.[17] This somewhat more realistically constructed mechanism, just as the simple original of which it is a modification, when set in operation, generates a collection of subpopulations the variations of the sizes of which, after it has run for so long a time, conform with Pareto's law, that is, the rank-size rule.

Apart from the writing of M_t, the size of the aggregate stock of money, in place of P_t, the size of the aggregate urban population of people, and of $M_{i,t}$, the size of the *i*th substock of money, in place of P_{it}, the size of the *i*th urban subpopulation – that is,

$$M_t = \sum_{1}^{N_t} M_{i,t}$$

in place of

$$P_{u,t} = \sum_{1}^{N_t} P_{it}$$

[17] See D. R. Vining, Jr. (1974: 318–20) and Haran and Vining, Jr. (1973*a*).

there is only the one shift of interpretation that is required for adapting this model for an application to the study of the development over time of a nation's stock of money; and that shift seems to me to reduce also to a mere matter of giving other names to things. It pertains to the identifying of the external source of the growth in question. In the case of the urban population of people, the external source of added members is the rural population. The λ is the growth rate of the aggregate urban population and the expected value of the variable growth rate λ_i of the ith subpopulation; and its positive and stable value is attributed to a steady rural-to-urban migration. In the case of the nation's stock of money, the external source of the growth is the monetary authority. The λ, in this application, becomes the growth rate of the size M_t of the aggregate stock of money and the expected value of the variable growth rate λ_i of the ith substock of money. To the extent that real conditions – including the facts regarding intercity balances of payments – are similar to the assumed conditions of Simon's modification of Yule's model (see footnote 17 in this chapter), one may be led to expect that the factual urban substocks of money, those that are in fact generated by the working of the real monetary system during a time when λ is relatively stable in its value, will show sizes the variation among which conforms with Pareto's law.

I shall not here present but only report an arrangement of data that seems suggestive of and tends to support this expectation – at least for that predominant component of the conventionally designated stock of money consisting of bank deposits. The Federal Deposit Insurance Corporation (FDIC) publishes biennially the respective aggregate amounts of demand deposits held by individuals and firms for each of the standard metropolitan areas of this nation.[18] λ_t denotes for us the percentage change of the nation's aggregate stock of money from one point in time to the next. From June of 1966 to June of 1968 this percentage change was about 10 percent, and from June of 1968 to June of 1970 it was about 12 percent – something on the order of 5 percent per year. These FDIC data provide rough and approximate fixes upon some 233 values of λ_{it} for each of these two periods – and thus an impression of the order of magnitude of the variation of the λ_{it} values – over time for each and among all at any moment. For each of these two times, the $\lambda_{i,t}$ values are found to be approximately normally distributed, with mean values

[18] Federal Deposit Insurance Corporation. *National Summary of Accounts and Deposits in All Commercial Banks,* June 29, 1968, Table 4.2, pp. 103–22; June 30, 1970, Table 4.2, pp. 75–95.

that are not far off the value of λ_t, and with standard deviations of about 7.5 percent or about .6 the size of the mean value. Whatever the degree of stability of the λ_t, the rate of growth of the nation's aggregate stock of money, there are variations of the $\lambda_{i,t}$ values, the respective rates of growth of the substocks of money of which the nation's aggregate stock consists. But upon the meager basis of what these data show, our conjecture is that these variations are subject to a relatively stable statistical law.

Next, for each of the three dates, the Junes of 1966, 1968, and 1970, we arranged these 230-odd substocks of money by order of size; and then for each of these substocks the size was plotted on double-log graph paper against its rank in size. The plot for each of these times of observation was found to be fitted approximately by a downward-sloping straight line – not so well as for the case of city sizes in 1940 and 1950, but the impression conveyed is that of approximate linearity. This is the implication of the rank-size rule of Pareto's law: $M_{i,t} = M_{it}/i^{\alpha}$, with i now the substock's rank in size and with α the measure of the downward slope. Whereas in the case of the urban subpopulations of people, the value of α is approximately unity, its value in this case, as roughly estimated from these three observations, is in the neighborhood of 1.05. In Simon's interpretation, α is a measure of the degree of concentration – so that in this application one would say that the elements of the nation's stock of money are somewhat more geograpically concentrated than are those of the population of people. The impression that I get from the graphs is to this effect: that this predominantly large component of the nation's money stock can at least sometimes be shown as a downward-sloping straight line that shifts parallel to the right as the aggregate size of the money stock grows with time – which is what the operating properties of the Yule–Simon model lead one to expect, given that λ_t has been stable in its value over a sufficiently long interval of time.

I shall ask now that the reader refer back to Exhibit B at the end of Chapter 3. The legislators have put questions, and the advising specialist is responding to them:

> . . . the question [turns upon] what one thinks . . . has in fact been the effect of [policies] in the past. The statement I made is based upon my conclusion that, despite intentions, the policy measures actually taken have historically been a destabilizing factor . . . The effect has been to destabilize the economy. [On the face of things, it would seem] that the sensible thing to do [if you can] is to try to be relatively tight in money . . . during a period of expansion and to be relatively easy during a period of contraction . . . But if

one looks at [the practice and asks] what in fact has occurred as a result of officials trying to follow such a policy, he will find that the effect has been just the opposite [of what was intended,] that in fact the effects have been destabilizing.

And then later:

Yes, sir. I am saying that it would be preferable . . . for Congress to instruct [the Federal Reserve authorities] to act in this way, that instead of trying to vary its actions from day to day, looking at credit conditions and the like and trying to react to them, it would limit itself to seeing to it that the stock of money grows at a steady rate month in and month out, year in and year out. This would provide a stable background for the other fluctuations.

These "other fluctuations" – what certain of them look like in fact and what they would look like were they such as not to arouse a responsible observer's concern – are the subject of the chapters of this Part II. In discussions of the kind of which the exhibit is an instance, they are almost invariably referred to and described in terms of numbers; but the numbers so used can have no other sense than as measures defined upon something real. There simply has to be some reality upon which variables are defined for the forming of a numerical record – and this reality, in any case of responsible discussants undertaking its description, will be found to be either a population of identifiable things or else a process of events occurring in time and geographic space. The "fluctuations" that are measured and recorded pertain to the variation at any moment among the states of individual elements of the population in question and the transitions of these elements from state to state over the course of time. In referring to them, this specialist advisor evidently has in mind, not fluctuations of just any random character, but rather those in particular the statistical properties of which are such that rational choosers of the law can be brought by reason to take for granted as "normally to be expected" – that is, not such as can reasonably be adversely reacted to by persons responsible for the working of the economic system.

With this understanding, the reference to the "other fluctuations" is a reference to populations and processes of events developing over time while in states that are stochastically stationary, the variations of and among individual elements conforming to stable statistical laws. And for one who would view a nation's stock of money, its evolution and development over time, as we have proposed here to view it – as a population process – a "monetary background" or "monetary environment" is stable or unstable in this same stochastic sense of stability. Thus, the stability of a monetary background or monetary environment is not to be identified with a constancy of the value of λ_t, the rate of growth of the size of the aggregate stock of money, but rather with the stationary states to which this and other populations and processes are said to tend when λ_t is maintained at a constant value. One of the properties of this quasi-stationary state of the economy, were such to be the concomitant of a steadily growing national stock of money, would be described by the steady-state size distribution of the substocks of money. And during a time when this quasi-population may be said to be in this stationary state, and when the variation among the sizes of the substocks is described by this steady-state size distribution, the sizes and ranks in size and the rates of growth $\lambda_{i,t}$ of the substocks will be constantly fluctuating – but in conformance with statistical laws that are stable. It is this conformance to stable statistical laws of which a stable monetary environment would consist, not the constancy over time of the aggregate growth rate λ_t per se.

It occurs to me that a confusion between these two things – a constancy of λ_t as a stipulated condition in a specification of a statistical mechanism, and a constancy of λ_t as a description of a statistical property of a stationary state of a quasi-population – may be at the base of the controversy to which the advisor alluded in his remark that we have just quoted. For it is by no means a settled matter that the working of a mechanism that satisfies this one condition – λ_t being kept constant over time – will in fact result in a stable monetary environment in this sense of a stationary state of a nation's stock of money as it develops over time. And skillful experimentation with variants of the Yule–Simon model might at least contribute to a clarification of what the controversy is about.

To the extent that the facts of intercity balances of payments (the analogue of city-to-city migrations of people) and of the variations of and among the substock growth rates (the analogue of the variable growth rates of cities) conform with the assumptions of the Simon model (see footnote 17 in this chapter), and to the extent that in fact λ_t is kept at a constant value, the steadily growing national stock of money will in the course of time attain a state of statistical equilibrium; and the steady-state size distribution of the substocks of money will be of the Pareto form. One is led to this expectation by the properties of the Simon model. A mechanism of this kind might readily be constructed and set in operation in a laboratory, so that one could literally see it generate a collection of substocks the respective growth rates of which would be constantly varying and whose respective ranks in size would be constantly changing, but such that all the while the form of the size distribution would remain unchanged. The transitions that the substocks continuously make from size class to size class would be equilibrating, the aggregate stock growing steadily in size while in a state of statistical equilibrium. And having watched these equilibrating size transitions of the substocks when λ_t is kept constant, one might then reduce the value of λ_t, making its value gradually approach zero or less – to correspond with conditions that have prevailed on certain historical occasions – or making its value vary over time, upward and downward, thus demonstrating what these size transitions are like when they are disequilibrating and when the size distribution is not stable in form but oscillates perhaps between limiting unstable forms.

But the mechanism that would have been used in this demonstration is constructed upon Simon's assumptions, and how these compare with the facts of the real and actual mechanism is not known. I should think that an inquiry similar to the one reported in the work cited earlier (see footnote 17 in this chapter) might be illuminating regarding whether or not a nation's stock of money does in fact tend to a state of equilibrium when λ_t is constant over time – whether or not the facts of intercity payments and of variations among the $\lambda_{i,t}$ values are such that the substock transitions from size class to size class are in fact equilibrating when this condition is satisfied.

Any aggregate is, of course, a sum of some set of subaggregates: The size of the U.S. stock of money is the sum of the money stocks within the respective bounds of the 12 Federal Reserve Districts; the total stock of money within the bounds of the United States, Canada, and Mexico is the simple sum of the respective stocks of money within the three nations. The maintenance of a constant rate of growth for an aggregate has implications regarding the variations of and among the respective rates of growth of the subaggregates of which the total is a sum; and I am not aware of satisfying studies of what these implications might be. I shall say again, as I said at the end of Chapter 2, that I cannot vouch for having correctly reported the thought and method of the authors quoted; but these methods of Simon and his associates, as I understand them, would seem to me to be applicable for one's pursuit of these implications. And I bid any interested reader that he himself consult the articles cited.

CHAPTER 5

A provisional description of a nation's population developing over time while in a state of full employment

5.1 The unemployment rate as a measure of a physical property of a spatially dispersed population

We are set upon the task of devising a way of visualizing a small-scale physical model of a nation's population of people, showing its spatial arrangement at each of a succession of moments in time, and thus something about how a thing of this kind develops and evolves over the course of time. In this model, as we have imagined it to be, each member of the population would be represented by a small, thin disk that is initially undifferentiated. We are now to consider what this developing configuration may be supposed to look like when the disks representing the members of the population are differentiated so as to show their respective momentary employment statuses. We shall think of this differentiation as being done by color: a transparent disk representing a person who is not at the moment a member of the labor force; a green disk if the represented person is an employed member at that time; and a red disk if the person is an unemployed member.

If one can bring himself to suppose that these three categories – nonmember, employed member, and unemployed member – can be well enough defined so that census enumerators would be adequately instructed upon how to classify the real people constituting the nation's population at any moment, he may at least imagine having at hand the requisite data for constructing a model sequence showing what this component of the economy π_t will have looked like in fact, developing as it actually did develop during some selected period of time. It would be a device for scaling something that is vastly too large for one to visually comprehend down to a size small enough to see. The physical reality exists, of course, whether or not the classifying and counting are done; and were they done, the construction of the model sequence would amount merely to a placing and coloring of P_t small disks.

With such a thing in view, think next of the matter of organizing a description of it – of specifying the properties of it that persons whom economists are called upon to advise pay especial attention to. We shall ignore for the present the transparent disks and confine our thought to those that are either green or red – that is, to the ones representing the people who will have been classified and counted as members of the nation's labor force. Let the total number of these at time t be n_t; and let the number of them contained within the subarea centered upon the ith urban concentration be n_{it} – so that $n_t = \Sigma_1^{N_t} n_{it}$, with N_t, as in the preceding chapter, denoting the number of urban places that census enumerators are instructed to classify and count as such.

The size at the time t of that portion of the nation's labor force that lies within the subarea centered upon the ith urban concentration is n_{it}; and now let X_{jt} be a variable defined upon the jth member of this ith subpopulation, its value being 0 if the person is an employed member and 1 if an unemployed member. The mean value

$$\overline{X}_{it} = \sum_{1}^{n_{it}} X_{jt} \Big/ n_{it}$$

is thus the familiar unemployment rate as it would be calculated for this ith subpopulation. And let $\overline{X}_t$ be the weighted mean of the N_t values of $\overline{X}_{it}$ – that is,

$$\overline{X}_t = \sum_{1}^{N_t} n_{it}\overline{X}_{it} \Big/ n_t$$

So defined, $\overline{X}_t$ is the yet more familiar unemployment rate as it would be calculated for the nation's labor force as a whole – the simple ratio of the number of all the unemployed to the number of all members of the labor force. Note that the definition of this variable X_{jt} upon the elements of the population consists of the classification and counting instructions with which the enumerators are provided – so that given the employment statuses of the members of an actual population of people at time t, as these would be directly perceived by an independent observer, the values that are assigned to the n_{it} variables, and the resulting values of the functions $\overline{X}_{it}$ and $\overline{X}_t$, depend upon this set of instructions.

$\overline{X}_t$ is an index of the employment state of the nation's population as a whole – a measure of the "global" density of the unemployed as these would be represented upon the map in our model sequence for time t. $\overline{X}_{it}$ is an index of the employment state of the subpopulation in the subarea centered upon the nation's ith urban concentration – a measure of the "local" density of the unemployed in that *i*th subpopulation that would be shown upon the map. There are N_t of these values at any moment, and the variation among them appears to be dependent upon the magnitude of the global density – in the sense that the value of $\overline{X}_t$ determines approximately the proportion of the values of $\overline{X}_{it}$ that lie within any stated interval. That is to say, given the employment state $\overline{X}_t$ of the nation's population as a whole, there is apparently a typical or "normal" variation among the employment states $\overline{X}_{it}$ of the populations of the N_t subareas into which the national area will have been partitioned; and our first step will be that of doing what we can toward specifying this feature of the outcome of the working of an economic system.

5.2 The variation of this physical property over geographic space

I mentioned earlier the appeal to me of the probabilist's concept of a description of a random variable: A *description* consists of a specification of its distribution function – which tells one the relative frequency with which the values of the variable lie within any given interval of the range of its variation. In our present case, to put it briefly and without its qualifications at the outset, the variable $\overline{X}_{it}$ is thus described by a lognormal frequency function,[1] one of whose two parameters having a value that is stable over time and the other a value that is given approximately as a function of $\overline{X}_t$. This statement is illustrated by the observed and fitted distributions shown in Figure 5.1, the fitted distribution in each case having been completely determined by the size of the national unemployment rate $\overline{X}_t$.[2]

A random variable x is said to be lognormally distributed if $y = \log_e x$ is normally distributed. Hence, the probability density function of y is given by

[1] This is not to say that $\overline{X}_{it}$ is a lognormally distributed random variable, in the sense that it is that particular kind of statistical mechanism that generates its variation, but only that, whatever kind of variable it is in that exact sense, the lognormal frequency function affords an approximate description of its variation – just as the normal distribution affords an approximation of the distribution of any of no end of variables the exact form of whose distribution is quite something else, e.g., the binomial or Poisson. This is an important distinction, I think, in that ultimately, for the primary purpose of the description to be met, it is the exact form of the distribution that is wanted. See the Appendix to Section 2.5 at the end of Chapter 2.

[2] The figures and tables and much of the discussion in this section are from a previously published article in the *Journal of Political Economy* (Vining 1969: 205–12).

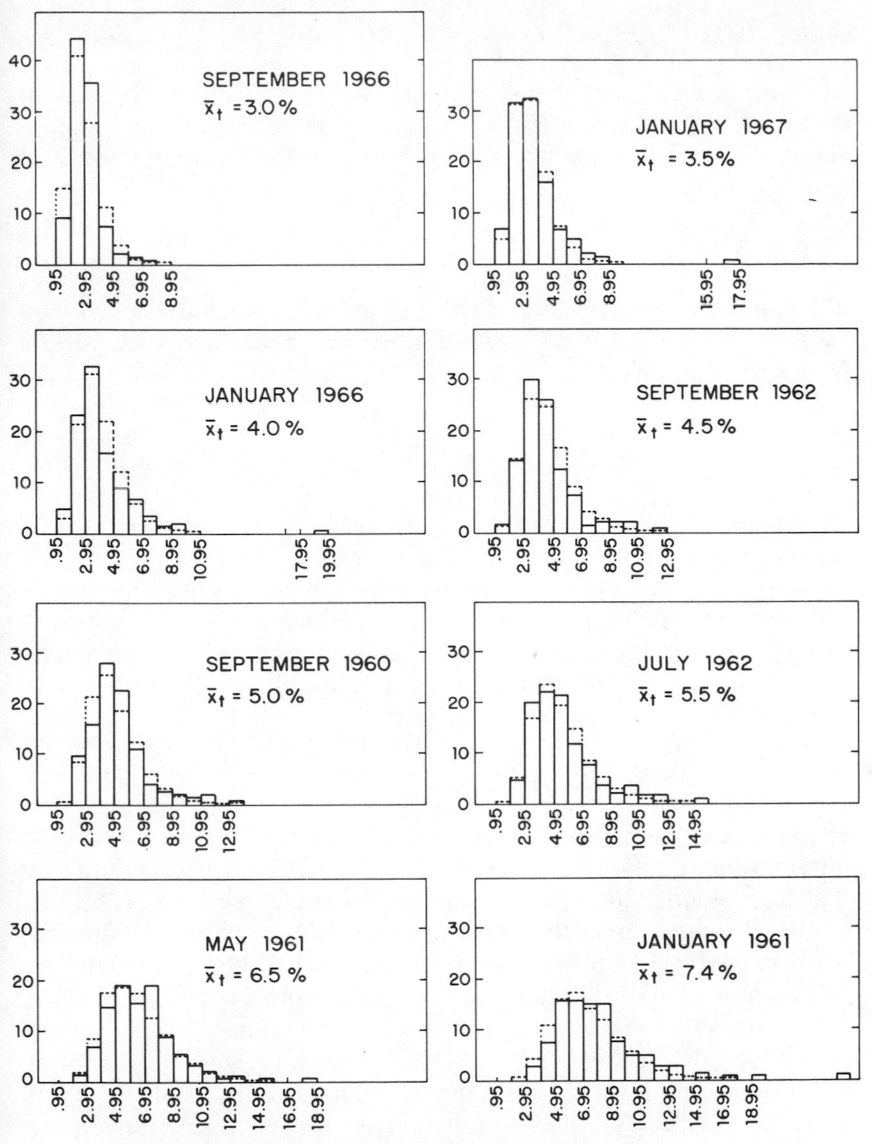

Figure 5.1. Observed and fitted lognormal frequency distributions of 146 labor market areas classified by size of unemployment rate (solid line, observed; dash line, fitted). $\overline{X}_t$ = unemployment rate in total labor force.

$$f(y) = \frac{1}{\sigma\sqrt{2\pi}}\exp\left[-\frac{1}{2}\left(\frac{y-\mu}{\sigma}\right)^{\frac{1}{2}}\right]$$

in which μ and σ are respectively the expected value and standard deviation of $y = \log_e x$. Expressed in the notation that we are presently using, the mean value μ_t of the normally distributed $\log_e X_t$ is given by

$$\mu = \log_e \alpha_t - \frac{\sigma_t^2}{2}$$

α_t being the expected value of the lognormally distributed $\overline{X}_{it}$ (Aitchison and Brown 1957: 8–9). An unweighted arithmetic mean of the N_t observed values of $\overline{X}_{it}$, that is,

$$\sum_{1}^{N_t} \overline{X}_{it} \Big/ N_t$$

would serve as an estimator of α_t. Also, this unweighted mean would be identical in value to the weighted mean $\overline{X}_t$ if the variable $\overline{X}_{it}$ and the weight n_{it} are uncorrelated – that is, if a subpopulation's unemployment rate is independent of its size. Inasmuch as this seems in fact to be the case, and inasmuch as the value of σ_t seems nearly stable over time at something in the neighborhood of .348, we have as an approximation

$$\mu_t \doteq \log_e \overline{X}_t - \frac{(.348)^2}{2}$$

so that for a given value of the national unemployment rate $\overline{X}_t$, the distribution function is determined that describes the variation at that time among the N_t subpopulation unemployment rates $\overline{X}_{it}$.

The imagined periodic census enumerations of which we have been speaking would provide data upon the location and employment status of each member of the population. Hence, for each of our subpopulations, a value for $\overline{X}_{it}$ could be computed for each of the census dates. Although not based upon census enumerations, but rather upon what are generally looked upon as meager and otherwise suspect samples, estimations of the respective unemployment rates of 150 urban centers (major labor market areas) are made available several times each year by the Bureau of Employment Security of the U.S. Department of Labor. We have taken the 146 of these that lie within the 48 contiguous continental states and the District of Columbia; and the statements that we have just made – about $\overline{X}_{it}$ being approximately lognormally distributed, σ_t having a value that is nearly stable over time, and the independence of $\overline{X}_{it}$ and n_{it} – are based upon a study of some 51 frequency distributions, one for each of the reporting months over the period 1960–8.[3] The methods used were the simplest and least time-consuming that could be found and consist mainly of the graphic methods outlined on pages 31–4 of the book by Aitchison and Brown (1957). The data for each month were formed into a cumulative relative frequency distribution and plotted on logarithmic probability paper. This type of graph paper is explained in the foregoing reference. It is so scaled that a lognormal distribution function plots upon it as a straight line whose slope is determined by the standard deviation σ of the logarithms of the variable. With this slope, the position of the line on the graph is determined by the value of μ, the line passing through a point whose coordinates are .5 on the vertical scale and the value of the antilog of μ on the horizontal scale. If the plotting of the observed cumulative relative frequency distribution traced out an approximately straight line, this was taken as an indication that a lognormal distribution approximately described the variation of the $\overline{X}_{it}$ values at that time; and what would appear to be a best-fitting straight line was drawn in by eye. The values of μ_t, σ_t, and the "fitted" relative frequencies were then estimated from this straight line. Had a more elaborate method of fitting been used, or had this same graphic method been applied independently by someone else, the results, of course, would have been somewhat different; but at this stage of our study, at which the main focus is upon clarifying what the basic descriptive problems of our subject field really are, and considering the dubious quality of the data, I should think that such differences would not be large enough to matter.

The values of the σ_t terms so obtained from the 51 observed distributions showed no appreciable trend; and about three-fourths of them lay between .325 and .385. The mean of these estimated σ_t values was .348, and I shall assume on this basis that σ_t was approximately stable over that time at this value.[4]

The graphs of Figure 5.1 demonstrate the extent of the confor-

[3] All data are from monthly issues of *Area Labor Market Trends* (U.S. Department of Labor).

[4] It is the standard deviation σ_t of the logarithms of $\overline{X}_{it}$ that is assumed to be stable. The standard deviation of $\overline{X}_{it}$ varies directly with the mean value of $\overline{X}_{it}$. The variance of a lognormally distributed variable is given by $\alpha^2(e^{\sigma^2} - 1)$. See Aitchison and Brown (1957: 8–9).

Table 5.1. *Percentage distributions of cities for various national unemployment rates*

Unemployment rates in cities (%)	$\overline{X}_t = 2.0$	$\overline{X}_t = 3.0$	$\overline{X}_t = 4.0$	$\overline{X}_t = 5.0$	$\overline{X}_t = 6.0$	$\overline{X}_t = 7.0$
< 1.95	54.0	15.0	3.0	.6	.2	—
1.95–2.95	36.0	40.9	21.6	8.5	3.2	1.7
2.95–3.95	8.2	27.4	31.3	21.4	12.6	5.6
3.95–4.95	1.5	11.3	22.3	25.5	20.1	13.3
4.95–5.95	.2	3.7	12.3	18.3	20.2	18.5
5.95–6.95	.1	1.2	5.5	12.3	16.0	16.9
6.95–7.95	—	.3	2.4	6.4	11.0	14.3
7.95–8.95	—	.1	1.0	3.5	7.1	10.7
8.95–9.95	—	—	.4	1.8	4.1	6.9
9.95–10.95	—	—	.2	.9	2.6	4.6
10.95–11.95	—	—	.1	.4	1.3	2.8
11.95–12.95	—	—	—	.2	.8	2.0
12.95–13.95	—	—	—	.1	.4	1.1
13.95–14.95	—	—	—	.1	.2	.7
> 14.95	—	—	—	—	.3	1.0

Note: $\overline{X}_t$ is in percent.

mance of this variation to the lognormal statistical law. The eight months for which observed and fitted distributions are shown were not selected for their goodness of fit, but rather in order to illustrate the shapes of the distributions for this spacing of values of the national unemployment rate $\overline{X}_t$.[5] Note that each of the fitted theoretical distributions has been determined upon the assumption that σ_t = .348 and that

$$\mu_t = \log_e \overline{X}_t - \frac{(.348)^2}{2}$$

There would have been a closer conformance of the fitted to the observed distributions had the σ_t and μ_t values been estimated from the data for the corresponding months.

The theoretical distributions of Figure 5.1 are shown numerically in Table 5.1; and in Figure 5.2 the cumulative form of these distributions is shown on the logarithmic probability paper of which we have spoken.

[5] The observed value of $\overline{X}_t$ that we used is that of the aggregate labor force in the 150 labor market areas. This is not the same as the "national unemployment rate" but it is nearly so.

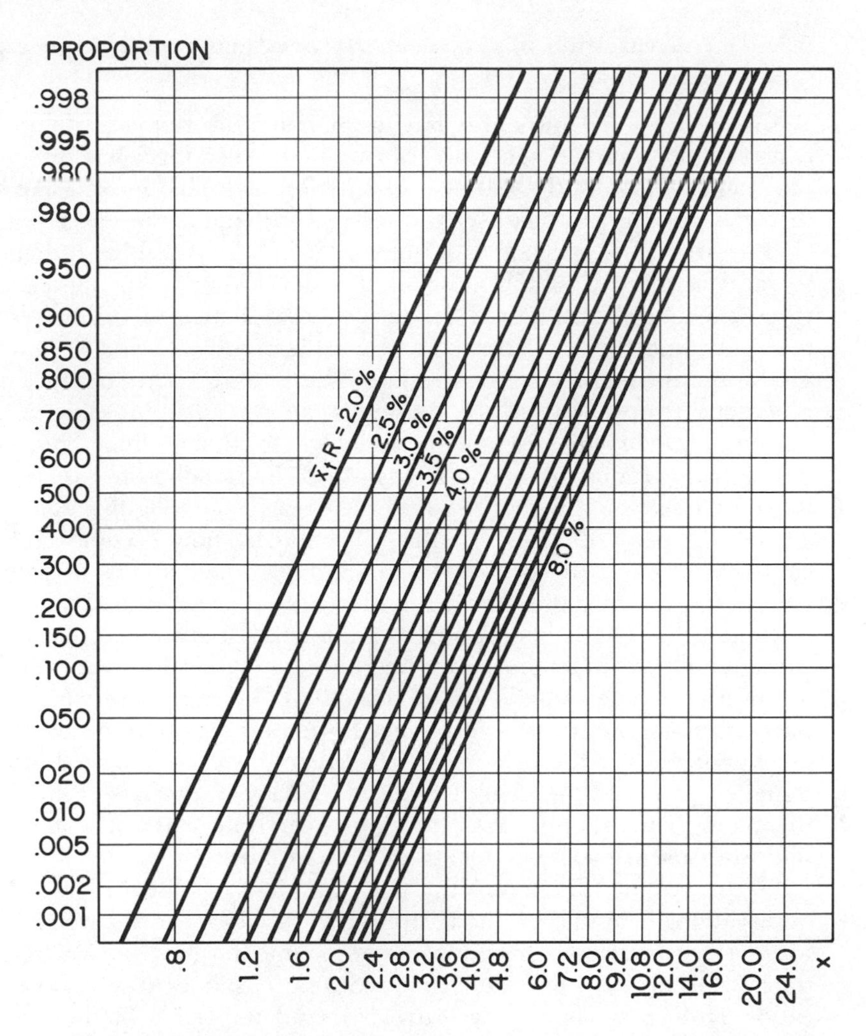

Figure 5.2. A set of logarithmic-normal distribution functions, with $\sigma = .348$ and mean values $\mu_t = \log_e \overline{X}_t - \frac{1}{2}\sigma^2$ varying as indicated, representing estimates of the proportion of urban areas having unemployment rates less than x when the national unemployment rate is $\overline{X}_t$. Each line corresponds to a national unemployment rate of $\overline{X}_t$, the $\overline{X}_t$ values being .5% apart and varying from 2.0% through 8.0%.

5.3 The variation of this property over geographic space and time

We have imagined ourselves having at hand the requisite data for constructing a model sequence of our maps showing what the employment aspect of the nation's population will have looked like in fact, developing as it actually did develop during some selected period of time. The specialist advisor in Exhibit A invited his audience to raise to mind a visualization of this development during a time when the population would be said to be in a state of full employment. Among these discussants, $\overline{X}_t$ is understood as being an index of the employment state of the population; and a state of full employment is the state that is indicated by an agreed-upon value of $\overline{X}_t$. At the time of the discussions recorded in that exhibit, and on through the 1960s and early 1970s, this critical value of $\overline{X}_t$ that was more or less generally agreed upon was set in the neighborhood of 3.5 or 4.0 percent. This specific value has by now become highly controversial; but the problem of assigning some value to this variable, for specifying that norm for which *full employment* is the name, is no less generally looked upon as "rationally discussable." We shall subsequently consider how that neighborhood of values was settled upon at that time – that is, by what method and mental process it in particular was hit upon – and how the matter has become by now unsettled; but for the present we shall take this earlier agreed-upon figure of about 4.0 percent and undertake a tentative description of the nation's population as it develops over time when it would be said in this sense to be in a state of full employment.

To this end, consider now the data for a pair of observation dates, observations having been made upon two variables for the area labor force of each urban center: its unemployment rate $\overline{X}_{it}$ at an initial time 0 and also at some later time t. Suppose that a two-way classification table were formed (Figure 5.3) and that each of these 146 subpopulations were recorded as a tally in the cell of the table corresponding to the two class intervals in which its unemployment rate at the two observation dates respectively fall. The extreme left-hand column of the table shows the class intervals covering the range of variation of the 146 observations upon the variable $\overline{X}_{i0}$ at the initial time 0; and the topmost horizontal row shows the class intervals for the range of variation of $\overline{X}_{it}$ at the later time t. In the right-hand marginal column, the frequency distribution of the 146 area unemployment rates at the initial time 0 is given; and in the lowermost marginal row there is shown the frequency distribution of these

% at time t / % at time 0	under 1.95	1.95 to 2.95	2.95 to 3.95	3.95 to 4.95	4.95 to 5.95	5.95 to 6.95	6.95 to 7.95	7.95 to 8.95	over 8.95	# of Cities	% of Cities
under 1.95										4	3.0
1.95 to 2.95										31	21.5
2.95 to 3.95										46	31.3
3.95 to 4.95										32	22.3
4.95 to 5.95										18	12.3
5.95 to 6.95										8	5.5
6.95 to 7.95										4	2.4
7.95 to 8.95										2	1.0
over 8.95										1	0.7
# of Cities	4	31	46	32	18	8	4	2	1	146	
% of Cities	3.0	21.5	31.3	22.3	12.3	5.5	2.4	1.0	0.7		100

Figure 5.3

rates at the later time t. In accordance with what has been said in the preceding section, we have anticipated these entries. If the value of the national unemployment rate $\overline{X}_t$ is the same at time t as at time 0, we will have been led to expect that these two marginal distributions would be much the same; and the entries that we have made are those shown in Table 5.1 under $\overline{X}_t = 4.0$.

In each of several of the rows of cells in the body of the table there will be a conditional distribution – the distribution of the unemployment rates at time t of urban concentrations whose rates were the same at time 0. And in each of several of the columns of cells there will similarly be a conditional distribution – describing the variation among the employment states of urban concentrations at time 0 whose states at time t are the same. It is the body of the table – the entries in the cells of its rows and columns – with which we shall now concern ourselves; and the task is an extension of the one undertaken in the preceding section: We shall seek by simple methods to find a rule for anticipating the entries in the cells of the table for any given value of t – thereby describing (the employment state of the whole being *full*) what typically or normally happens, during an interval of time of this length, to the employment states of those urban centers whose states were initially the same.

We shall first submit certain of our considerations, then briefly

0 \ t	under 1.95	1.95 to 2.95	2.95 to 3.95	3.95 to 4.95	4.95 to 5.95	5.95 to 6.95	6.95 to 7.95	7.95 to 8.95	over 8.95	No.	%
under 1.95	••••									4	3.0
1.95 to 2.95		•••••••••••••••••••••••••••••••								31	21.5
2.95 to 3.95			••							46	31.3
3.95 to 4.95				••••••••••••••••••••••••••••••••						32	21.3
4.95 to 5.95					••••••••••••••••••					18	12.3
5.95 to 6.95						••••••••				8	5.5
6.95 to 7.95							••••			4	2.4
7.95 to 8.95								••		2	1.0
over 8.95									•	1	0.7
No.	4	31	46	32	18	8	4	2	1	146	
%	3.0	21.5	31.1	22.3	12.3	5.5	2.4	1.0	0.7		100

0 \ t	under 1.95	1.95 to 2.95	2.95 to 3.95	3.95 to 4.95	4.95 to 5.95	5.95 to 6.95	6.95 to 7.95	7.95 to 8.95	over 8.95	No.	%
under 1.95		•	•	•	•					4	3
1.95 to 2.95	•	•••••••	•••••••••••	••••••	••••	••	•			31	21
2.95 to 3.95	•	•••••••••	••••••••••••••	••••••••••	••••••	•••	••	•	•	46	31
3.95 to 4.95	•	••••••	•••••••••••	•••••••	••••	••	•	•		32	21
4.95 to 5.95	•	••••	••••••	••••	••	•				18	12
5.95 to 6.95		••	•••	••	•					8	5
6.95 to 7.95		•	••	•						4	2
7.95 to 8.95			•	•						2	1
over 8.95			•							1	0
No.	4	31	46	32	18	8	4	2	1	146	
%	3.0	21.5	31.1	22.3	12.3	5.5	2.4	1.0	0.7		10

Figure 5.4

what rule these lead us to propose, and finally the empirical basis for a specification of this rule.

For a t sufficiently small, all of the tallies would of course be contained within the downward-sloping diagonal line of cells – as illustrated in the accompanying tabular form on the left (Figure 5.4). For example, the 46 area labor forces with rates at time 0 that fall in the interval having 3.45 as its midvalue are likely to be the same 46 labor forces whose rates fall in that interval an hour or a day or so later. As t becomes progressively larger – 6, 12, 18, 24 months and longer – the 46 tallies will come to be distributed among the cells of this horizontal row; and for a t sufficiently large – 10 or 15 or 20 years or so – the variation among these 46 observations upon $\overline{X}_{it}$ will become similar in magnitude and form to the variation among the 146 observations as a whole – or so one might surmise. $\overline{X}_{i0}$ and $\overline{X}_{it}$ would be correlated to a degree near to unity for a sufficiently small value of t and to a degree near to zero for a large enough value of t – so that after this long enough passage of time these 46 observations upon $\overline{X}_{it}$ are, as it were, a randomly drawn sample from the 146 as a whole.

The two tabular forms in Figure 5.4 illustrate these two limiting cases. In the one on the right, representing the case of the very long lapse of time, the marginal distributions and all the conditional distributions (at least this was the intent) have been made the same in form and shape – i.e., lognormal in form, with .348 as the value of σ_t and

$$\log_e .04 - \frac{(.348)^2}{2}$$

as the value of μ. It is a case of a bivariate frequency function of uncorrelated lognormally distributed variables having identical mean values and variances.

These two limiting cases corresponding to the extremities of the value of t, the very brief and the very long, are, of course, hypothetical: It is hardly conceivable that observations could be made so short a time as a day after the initial observations; nor is it conceivable that this stable state of the population, indicated by the constant value of $\overline{X}_t = 4.0$ percent, would be sustained over so long a time as the 10 or 15 years or so. But there are periods of time covering several years during the whole of which the bimonthly or monthly reported values of $\overline{X}_t$ did in fact remain within a close neighborhood of 4.0 percent. From 1966 through 1969, some four years, the value of $\overline{X}_t$ reported by the public agency responsible for this classifying and counting ranged narrowly within or about the vicinity of 3.5 or 4.0 percent. And the rule that we shall tentatively submit for constructing such tabular forms for intermediate values of t is based upon what these data seem to show: that the conditional distributions – describing the variation among the employment states at time t of area labor forces whose employment states at time 0 were approximately the same – are lognormal in form, with values of μ and σ that depend upon the length of time t. The value of μ for any of the conditional distributions at time 0 is given approximately by the logarithm of the midvalue of the class interval involved, the value of σ at this initial time being nearly zero – so that when plotted on the lognormal probability paper mentioned earlier, the cumulative conditional distribution at this initial time, as this rule would have it, would be shown as a nearly vertical straight line passing through a point whose coordinates are .5 on the vertical scale and the midvalue of the class interval on the horizontal scale. As t becomes larger, this straight line, in accordance with our rule, revolves clockwise, its slope becoming less steep, indicating a growing value of the parameter σ, a spreading out of the tallies in the row of cells involved – until, in the course of time, the value of this σ of the conditional distribution tends in the limit to the value .348, and the slope of the line to the corresponding slope of the line describing the marginal distribution. Along with this clockwise revolving of the line toward this limiting slope, the level of it shifts with the passage of time – its coordinate on the horizontal scale moves toward and tends to that of the marginal distribution, that is, the value of the antilog of

$$\log_e .04 - \frac{(.348)^2}{2}$$

And if we can now find a way of determining, for any value of t, the size of the σ that sets the slope of the line, and the size of the conditional mean value μ that fixes its coordinate on the horizontal scale, we will have completed the specification of our rule for anticipating the tallies in the tabular forms for the intermediate values of t–thereby describing the variation of and among the employment states of area labor forces during a time when the population as a whole is said to be in a state of full employment.

5.4 A description of this variation over a time of full employment

The empirical basis for our provisional statement of the rule consists of work done by students in fulfilling term assignments in an academic course of instruction. Using the data mentioned earlier–the monthly observations, during the four-year period from 1966 through 1969, upon the 146 area unemployment rates $\overline{X}_{it}$–students independently prepared a series of tabular forms for intermediate values of t similar to the hypothetical forms shown earlier for the two extremities in time. These were done for time lapses of 2 months, 6 months, 12 months, 18 months, and by 6-month increments up to 42 months. Figures 5.5 and 5.6 are illustrative of what this step showed.[6]

Next, the conditional distributions, for each of a succession of increasing values of t, were then studied by the same simple graphic method outlined in Section 5.2. Cumulative distributions were formed for the main class intervals, and these were plotted on log-normal probability graph paper. As was the case for the marginal distributions, each of these seemed to trace out an approximately straight line. These lines were drawn in by eye, and from them the values of the conditional μ and σ terms and relative frequencies were estimated. Figures 5.7, 5.8, 5.9, and 5.10–some of the data for which are graphically shown in Figure 5.5–illustrate what the results of this second step looked like.[7]

[6] Figure 5.5 is the work of John F. Cushman and Barry Love, and Figure 5.6 was prepared by Elizabeth W. Wogan. The other students whose reports I have drawn upon in this section are James L. Butkiewicz and Geoffrey Rockliffe-King.

[7] Figures 5.7 through 5.10 are from the reports of John F. Cushman and Barry Love.

Table 5.2 *Estimates of σ_t for selected values of t*

t (years)	σ_t graphically estimated from observations	σ_t calculated from formula ($\sigma_t \simeq .19 + .15 \log t$)
1/6	.095	.073
.5	.132	.145
1.0	.148	.190
1.5	.231	.216
2.0	.239	.235
2.5	.255	.250
3.0	.262	.262
3.5	.270	.272
.		.
.		.
.		.
10+		.348

The lines so drawn seeming approximately parallel, thereby indicating an equivalence among the variances of the conditional distributions,[8] we assumed this to be a characteristic of the development being described: that the σ_t for one conditional distribution is the same in value as for any other. The values of σ_t, thus graphically estimated from the data, are shown in Figure 5.11 plotted against time t.[9] A freehand line has been drawn through the plots of these values so as to represent roughly what we suppose to be the dependence of σ_t upon the length of time t elapsed. When the values of σ_t are plotted against the logarithms of t, there is a convenient suggestion of linearity; and this affords a simple formula for describing this dependence. With the base of the logarithms being 10, and t being expressed in years, the formula is this: $\sigma_t = .19 + .15 \log t$. The comparison in Table 5.2 indicates the extent to which this formula would have anticipated the values of σ_t as these were estimated from the data.

Figure 5.12 is intended as a visual aid for one's comprehension of the property mentioned earlier:[10] the clockwise rotation, as time progresses, of the straight line representing any one of the conditional distributions. The lines shown have been drawn with slopes corre-

[8] This property of joint frequency functions is called homoscedasticity in old-fashioned textbooks.

[9] Figure 5.11 is from the reports of John F. Cushman and Barry Love.

[10] Figure 5.12 is from the reports of John F. Cushman and Barry Love.

MARCH 1966 (t+0 months)

	under 1.95	1.95 to 2.95	2.95 to 3.95	3.95 to 4.95	4.95 to 5.95	5.95 to 6.95	6.95 to 7.95	7.95 to 8.95	over 8.95	Total	Cum. Total
under 1.95										8	8
1.95 to 2.95										49	57
2.95 to 3.95										40	97
3.95 to 4.95										30	127
4.95 to 5.95										7	134
5.95 to 6.95										8	142
6.95 to 7.95										1	143
7.95 to 8.95										3	146
over 8.95										0	146
Total	8	49	40	30	7	8	1	3	0		
Cum Tot.	8	57	97	127	134	142	143	146	146		

MARCH 1967 (t+12 months)

	under 1.95	1.95 to 2.95	2.95 to 3.95	3.95 to 4.95	4.95 to 5.95	5.95 to 6.95	6.95 to 7.95	7.95 to 8.95	over 8.95	Total
under 1.95										8
1.95 to 2.95										49
2.95 to 3.95										40
3.95 to 4.95										30
4.95 to 5.95										7
5.95 to 6.95										8
6.95 to 7.95										1
7.95 to 8.95										3
over 8.95										0
Total	6	44	43	30	14	4	2	1	2	
Cum Tot.	6	50	93	123	137	141	143	144	146	

MARCH 1968 (t+24 months)

	under 1.95	1.95 to 2.95	2.95 to 3.95	3.95 to 4.95	4.95 to 5.95	5.95 to 6.95	6.95 to 7.95	7.95 to 8.95	over 8.95	Total	Cum. Total
under 1.95										8	8
1.95 to 2.95										49	57
2.95 to 3.95										40	97
3.95 to 4.95										30	127
4.95 to 5.95										7	134
5.95 to 6.95										8	142
6.95 to 7.95										1	143
7.95 to 8.95										3	146
over 8.95										0	146
Total	10	37	52	28	11	4	2	1	1		
Cum Tot.	10	47	99	127	138	142	144	145	146		

MARCH 1969 (t+36 months)

	under 1.95	1.95 to 2.95	2.95 to 3.95	3.95 to 4.95	4.95 to 5.95	5.95 to 6.95	6.95 to 7.95	7.95 to 8.95	over 8.95	Total
under 1.95										8
1.95 to 2.95										49
2.95 to 3.95										40
3.95 to 4.95										30
4.95 to 5.95										7
5.95 to 6.95										8
6.95 to 7.95										1
7.95 to 8.95										3
over 8.95										0
Total	11	52	38	24	13	5	1	1	1	
Cum Tot.	11	63	101	125	138	143	144	145	146	

Figure 5.5. Bivariate frequency diagrams showing variations of urban area unemployment rates during times of national full employment.

JULY 1966 (t+0 months)

	under 1.95	1.95 to 2.95	2.95 to 3.95	3.95 to 4.95	4.95 to 5.95	5.95 to 6.95	6.95 to 7.95	7.95 to 8.95	over 8.95	Total	Cum. Total
under 1.95										4	4
95 to 2.95										28	32
95 to 3.95										51	83
95 to 4.95										36	119
95 to 5.95										15	134
95 to 6.95										6	140
95 to 7.95										3	143
95 to 8.95										1	144
over 8.95										1	145
Total	4	28	51	36	15	6	3	1	1		
um Tot.	4	32	83	119	134	140	143	144	145		

JULY 1967 (t+12 months)

	under 1.95	1.95 to 2.95	2.95 to 3.95	3.95 to 4.95	4.95 to 5.95	5.95 to 6.95	6.95 to 7.95	7.95 to 8.95	over 8.95	Total	Cum. Total
under 1.95										4	4
1.95 to 2.95										28	32
2.95 to 3.95										51	83
3.95 to 4.95										36	119
4.95 to 5.95										15	134
5.95 to 6.95										6	140
6.95 to 7.95										3	143
7.95 to 8.95										1	144
over 8.95										1	145
Total	2	22	52	36	18	5	5	2	3		
Cum Tot.	2	24	76	112	130	135	140	142	145		

JULY 1968 (t+24 months)

	under 1.95	1.95 to 2.95	2.95 to 3.95	3.95 to 4.95	4.95 to 5.95	5.95 to 6.95	6.95 to 7.95	7.95 to 8.95	over 8.95	Total	Cum. Total
under 1.95										4	4
.95 to 2.95										28	32
.95 to 3.95										51	83
.95 to 4.95										36	119
.95 to 5.95										15	134
.95 to 6.95										6	140
.95 to 7.95										3	143
.95 to 8.95										1	144
over 8.95										1	145
Total	3	31	52	31	19	4	3	1	1		
um Tot.	3	34	86	117	136	140	143	144	145		

JANUARY 1969 (t+30 months)

	under 1.95	1.95 to 2.95	2.95 to 3.95	3.95 to 4.95	4.95 to 5.95	5.95 to 6.95	6.95 to 7.95	7.95 to 8.95	over 8.95	Total	Cum. Total
under 1.95										4	4
1.95 to 2.95										28	32
2.95 to 3.95										51	83
3.95 to 4.95										36	119
4.95 to 5.95										15	134
5.95 to 6.95										6	140
6.95 to 7.95										3	143
7.95 to 8.95										1	144
over 8.95										1	145
Total	11	48	40	25	11	5	3	1	1		
Cum Tot.	11	59	99	124	135	140	143	144	145		

Figure 5.6. A second observation upon the subject of Figure 5.5.

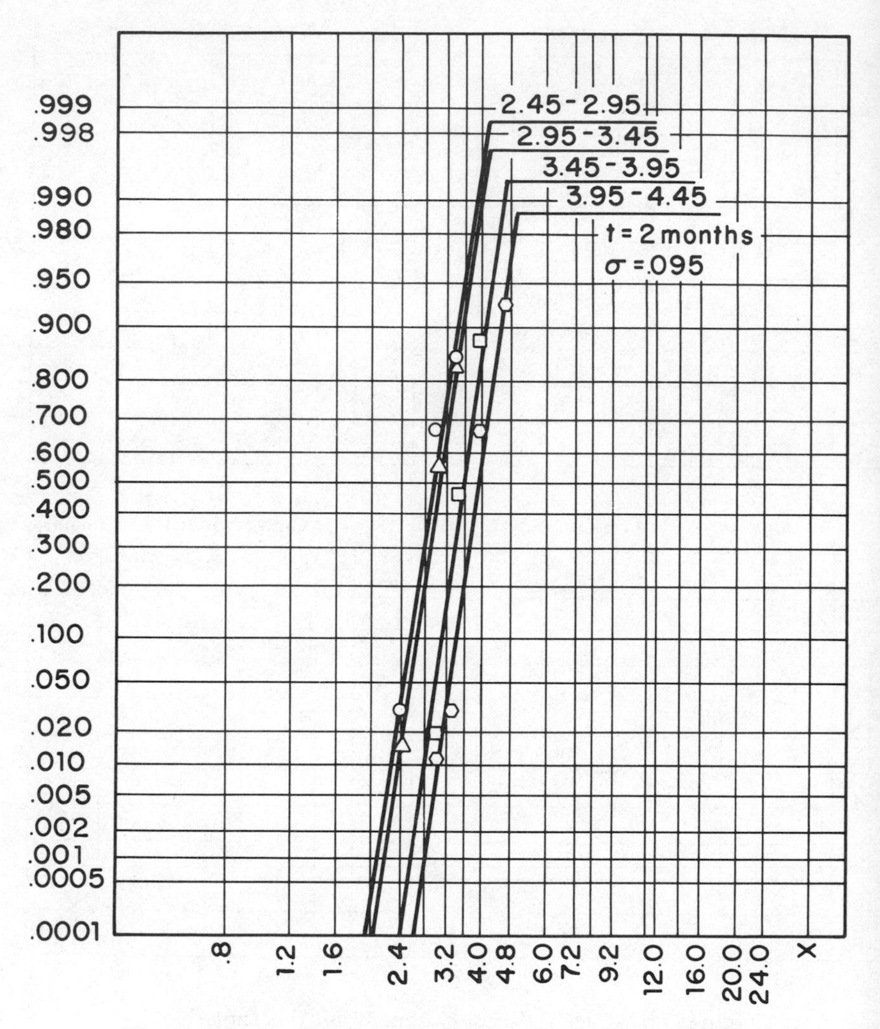

Figure 5.7. Conditional cumulative distributions showing, at $t = 2$ months, the variations of unemployment rates of urban areas whose rates at $t = 0$ were the same.

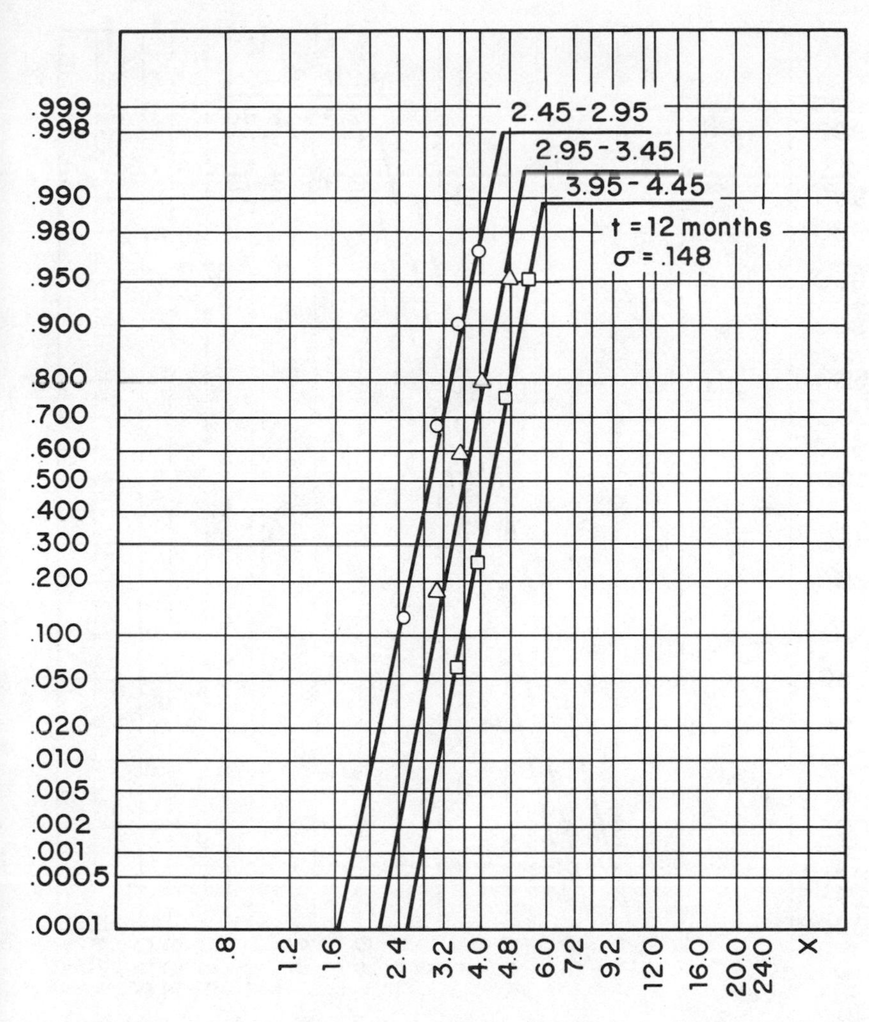

Figure 5.8. Conditional cumulative distributions showing, at $t = 12$ months, the variations of unemployment rates of urban areas whose rates at $t = 0$ were the same.

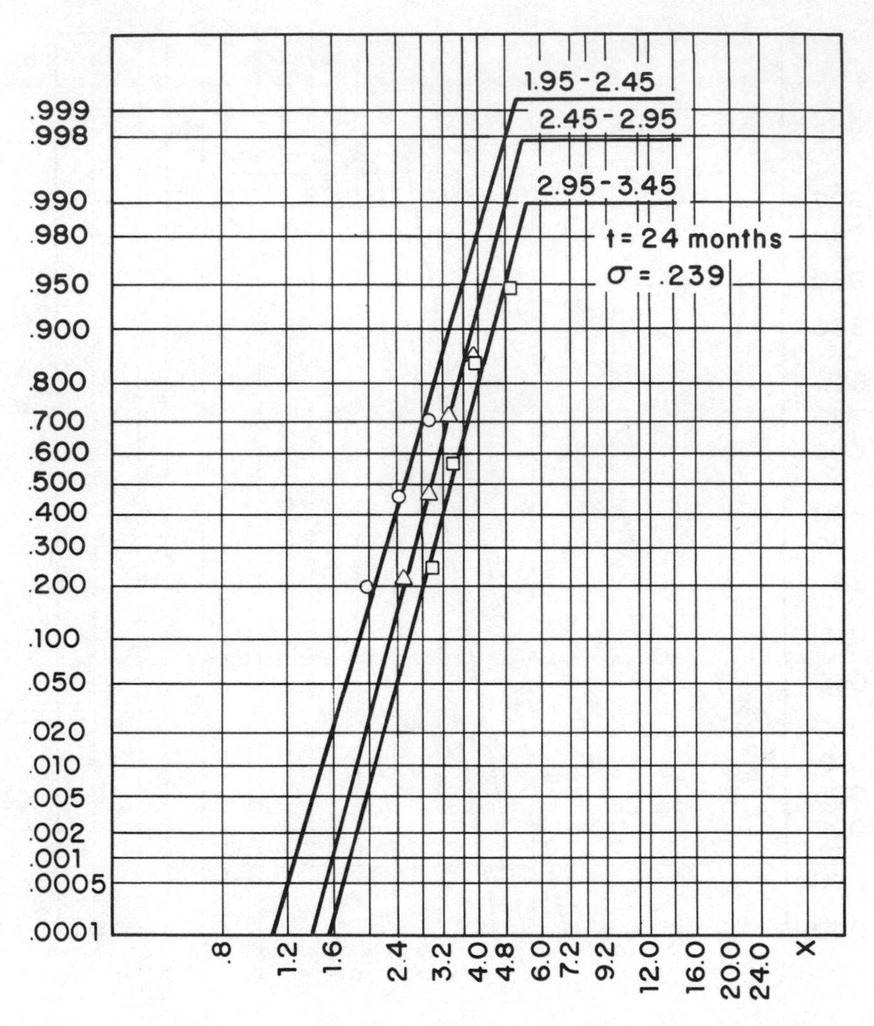

Figure 5.9. Conditional cumulative distributions showing, at $t = 24$ months, the variations of unemployment rates of urban areas whose rates at $t = 0$ were the same.

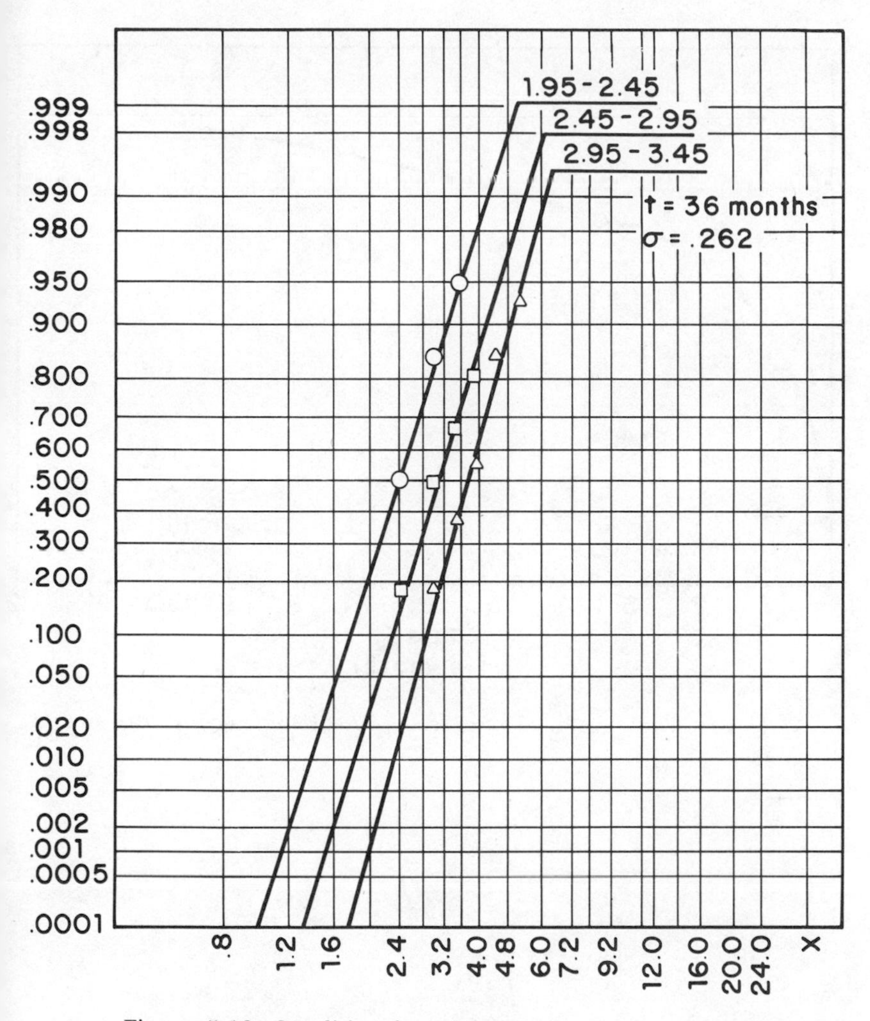

Figure 5.10. Conditional cumulative distributions showing, at t = 36 months, the variations of unemployment rates of urban areas whose rates at t = 0 were the same.

PLOT OF CONDITIONAL DISTRIBUTIONS AGAINST TIME

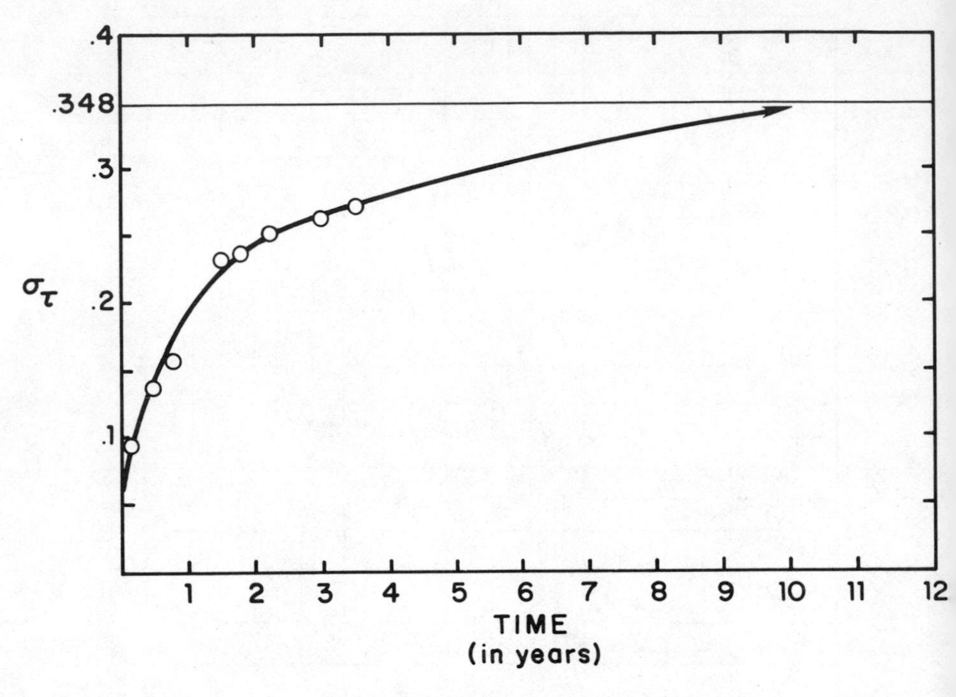

Figure 5.11. Estimated values of σ_t plotted against the time t elapsed.

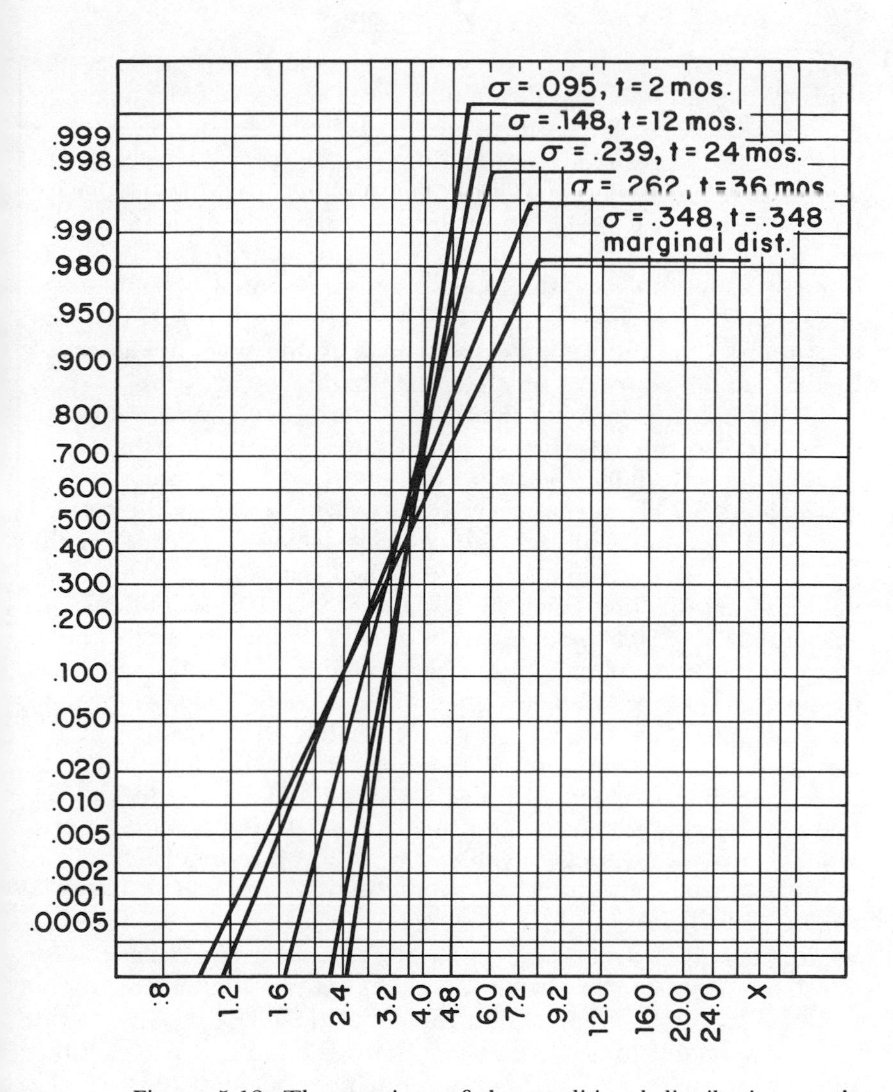

Figure 5.12. The rotations of the conditional distributions as the time elapsed increases.

sponding to the σ values that were estimated from the data – the values listed in the middle column of Table 5.2. One might as readily draw these lines with slopes corresponding to the σ values listed in the right-hand column – that is, to the values that were determined, in accordance with the formula, by the respective lengths of time t elapsed. It would look much the same, and each line would then be labeled, not by the value of σ_t, but only by the value of t; and thus we would have visually presented a rough gauge of the rapidity of the rotation – that is, of the rate of the spreading-out process whereby the left-hand tabular form shown in Figure 5.4 becomes in the course of time the right-hand tabular form.

For one's drawing any of these lines, there is, of course, required, in addition to this information upon the slope, the coordinates of some point through which the line is to pass. The point that is convenient for this purpose has .5 as the coordinate on the vertical scale and the value of the antilog of $\mu = \log_e \alpha - \sigma^2/2$ on the horizontal scale, α denoting, as before, the mean value of $\overline{X}_{it}$ itself. In determining the line representing the marginal distributions, we substituted $\overline{X}_t = .04$ for α and .348 for σ. For determining a line to represent any of the conditional distributions for the briefest lapse of time, that is, for a value of t that is near zero, the value of σ would be nearly zero and that of α approximately the midvalue of the class-interval involved. The line representing any of these conditional distributions for a t that is very large would coincide with the line representing the marginal distributions. Having obtained a provisional rule for assigning a value of σ_t for any intermediate value of t, we had hoped by the same simple graphic method to obtain a similar rule for assigning values to μ_t. For each of the observed conditional distributions and for each of the successive values of t for which these were constructed, a value of μ_t was estimated graphically; and we had thought that these would show a tendency, with increasing values of t, to converge toward the value of that parameter for the marginal distributions. But no evident pattern of this kind emerged. The variations over time of these estimated values of μ_t appeared as simply random.

The period of time was too brief, I think, for this tendency to show itself; for surely there is some value of t so large that $\overline{X}_{it}$ will have become by then very nearly independent of $\overline{X}_{i0}$. One student undertook the reaching of a judgment upon how long a time this would be.[11] There was no longer period than the one we had studied

[11] This task was undertaken by Geoffrey Rockliffe-King.

during the whole of which the national rate $\overline{X}_t$ remained approximately constant. But ignoring the source of disturbance that large variations of $\overline{X}_t$ would seem likely to be, he studied the serial correlation between these two variables $\overline{X}_{i0}$ and $\overline{X}_{it}$. We had proceeded upon the surmise that this correlation would be close to unity for small values of t and would decline and tend to zero as the value of t is increased. It does in fact, of course, begin with a value close to unity; and it declines regularly and smoothly with an increase of t, reaching a value of about .25 in about 10 years. But to an extent of time t as large as 15 years, this correlation showed no further tendency to become smaller.

This "stickiness" of the correlation coefficient at some such value would seem to indicate real differences among different parts of this population structure with respect to whatever qualities these are that area unemployment rates measure. Certain of these qualities readily come to mind. If the members of a labor force are classified – by age, by sex, by marital status, by educational and skill attributes, and the like – and unemployment rates computed for the respective classes, one is not surprised to find a systematic variation, the rates for some classes typically being relatively high and for others typically low. The unemployment rate $\overline{X}_{it}$ of the labor force of the ith urban center at any moment is itself a weighted mean of the unemployment rates of these respective classes of this area labor force. The proportionate composition or mix of an urban center's labor force with respect to these different classes of its members varies from area to area and changes but slowly over time. And thus, for values of t smaller than is required for an appreciable change of this proportionate composition of an urban center's labor force, one might plausibly expect from this source some dependence of $\overline{X}_{it}$ upon $\overline{X}_{i0}$.

Then, too, and I should think with more bearing, there is the reality that underlies the notion of a "depressed area." If the members of a labor force are classified by current or else most recent industrial occupation, and unemployment rates then computed for these respective industry classes, one is not surprised to find, no more than in the other case, a systematic variation, the rates for some predictable classes being consistently high relative to the rates for others. An industry, that is, a product class of firms, and the labor force associated with it, apparently does in fact pass through a characteristic and regular life cycle covering many years.[12] New in-

[12] Of the accounts of it of which I am aware, the most instructive to me is the one given in the study by A. F. Burns published many years ago (Burns 1934).

dustries emerge randomly in time, the initial appearances occurring at certain places. Each has a growth and spreading-out phase, in the course of which a maximum size is reached – and during which the unemployment rate that would be calculated for it would tend to be relatively low. There then follows a declining phase that ends with its virtual demise – and during which the unemployment rate that would be calculated for it would tend to be relatively high. This emergence–growth–decline–demise of industries is continually in process – so that there is always this mix of industry classes of the labor force with characteristically different unemployment rates; and the labor forces of urban centers differ quite substantially in their proportionate compositions of these classes.[13] An urban center's unemployment rate $\overline{X}_{it}$ is, again, a weighted mean of the unemployment rates of the respective classes of its labor force. And thus for values of t larger than those for which we have studied the data, one might plausibly expect an appreciable dependence of $\overline{X}_{it}$ upon $\overline{X}_{i0}$.

But whatever the mode of classifying the members of the labor force of an urban center, the mix or proportionate composition of these classes is itself a random variable over time – so that however large the value of that t might be, there surely must be some elapsed time long enough for this correlation to have effectively vanished – that is, for the left-hand tabular form in Figure 5.4 to have been transformed into the right-hand tabular form. The student's calculations led him to think this value of t to be in excess of 15 years. But the period from which his data came was not one during which $\overline{X}_t$ remained nearly constant at a value near .04. And for the illustrative purpose of a tentative statement of our rule, we shall roughly put this number of years at something on the order of 10 – which would be about the time that our formula for calculating σ_t would have its value approach that of this other parameter of the marginal distribution function.

On this basis, then, I shall propose the simplest way of which I can think for assigning values to μ_t for the intermediate values of t. Let $\overline{X}'_0$ be the midvalue of the class interval corresponding to some one of the horizontal rows of cells, the prime indicating some particular one among the several; and suppose it to be the mean value of the unemployment rates of those urban centers whose rates fell within that interval at the initial time 0. In accordance with our remarks immediately preceding, we would have $\mu'_0 = \log_e \overline{X}'_0$ and $\mu'_{10} = \log_e .04 + (.348)^2/2$. The value of μ'_t passing from μ'_0 to μ'_{10} over the

[13] See, e.g., R. Vining (1946*a;* 1946*b;* 1949).

course of 10 years, we shall suppose that one-tenth of this passage is effected each year – so that

$$\mu_t' = \mu_0' + \frac{\mu_{10}' - \mu_0'}{10} \cdot t$$

And this completes our tentative statement of a rule for anticipating the entries in any of the horizontal rows of cells of our tabular forms for the intermediate values of t: The straight line from which these entries would be read has a slope determined by the value of σ_t, which in turn is determined by the value of t; and it passes through a point whose coordinates are .5 on the vertical scale and the value of the antilog of μ_t' on the horizontal scale, which again is given by the value of t.

5.5 Toward a theory of the outcome of an economic system's working

I am sensitive enough to what I imagine the reader may be feeling about the poorness of the data and the primitiveness of our method whereby these specific values have been assigned to the various coefficients. But as I see the priorities of our inquiry, such concern at this time for numerical accuracy and elegance of technique can easily be overdone – to the point of becoming a distraction. I am much influenced by what I take to be the sense of Polanyi's remark to the effect that what is ordinarily called *knowledge* comes down essentially to being *knowledge of a problem* (Polanyi 1961: 466); and, accordingly, the really important thing presently, I think, is this descriptive problem itself, taken as being illustrative of a fundamental type. There can be no doubt that to any independent observer individuals do in fact vary in their employment states, as they do in their income states or wealth states or in their states of health – each over time and among themselves at any moment. This is the case however stable (or whatever is happening to) the employment state of the nation's population as a whole. And there can be no doubt that to any independent observer the constituent subpopulations, the urban concentrations in their rural environs, vary in their employment states – each over time and among themselves at any moment. Different observers, if left alone, will see different variations – there certainly will be differences in their respective classifications of the actual individuals. And thus, no numerical record of measurements made upon this variation, formed as such records are and must be formed – by clerical interviewers and enumerators classifying and counting individuals in accordance with instructions that some official committee will have authored – can convey an exact impression of just what an independent observer would have seen for himself. We must come to understand that there is no true and exact number of members of the labor force at any moment, and no true and exact number of such members who are unemployed at the time of the observation. There are not even true and exact numbers of members of these classes corresponding to a specific set of classification and counting instructions. Such classes of real things cannot conceivably be so exhaustively specified and defined – the case of biological species is not an exception to this – so that independent applications of the instructions would not result in differences of classifications and counts.[14] Moreover, however $\overline{X}_{it}$ be defined, its value is of no interest in itself; it is a proxy variable for something else that an observer "really" has in mind when reacting to observations made upon its variation. A specific value of it has different meanings at different places,[15] and at different times at the same places.[16] In this respect – this variation of its meaning over time at any place and from place to place at any time – it resembles, superficially at least, a linguistic sequence of sounds of which a word consists.

But a given set of classification and enumeration instructions – say the ones currently applied periodically by agents of the present Census Bureau – together with the procedures for selecting and training the clerical force of interviewers and enumerators, does define upon a population of really existent elements the random variables $\overline{X}_{it}$ and $\overline{X}_t$ – in the literal sense that an application of such instructions, procedures, and apparatus is a trial of a random experiment that does assign values to the variables n_{it} and $\Sigma_1^{n_{it}} X_{jt}$, there being N_t of each of these, which in turn determine the values of $\overline{X}_{it}$ and $\overline{X}_t$. And sequences of these observed values do in fact convey sense and meaning to persons in the act of deliberating upon how well or ill an economic system is working.

However more appropriate the classification and counting instructions might be made, and however more effectively interviewers and enumerators might be trained to consistently apply them, the variable $\overline{X}_{it}$ so defined would surely be found to have properties that are

[14] For a discussion of practical and philosophic difficulties inherent in the concept of a class of real things, see the references to classes in Polanyi (1958).
See also Williams (1978). These are disparaging remarks about the conventional standards of "goodness" of data. The familiar standard errors that typically accompany data esteemed as "good" are apparently radically unreliable as measures of reliability.

[15] See Bornstein, Haveman, and Bruton (1978).

[16] See Feldstein (1978*a;* 1978*b*).

generally similar, in a sense that I shall try to make clear, to the ones that we have described. And for illuminating the meaning that responsible observers read into observations upon this variable – and preliminary to further thought upon how the variable might better be defined and how a description of it might be made more cogent and comprehensive, and specifically in accordance with the understandings set forth in the Appendix at the end of Chapter 2 – I think the most useful next step in extending our description of the variable would be that of finding a laboratory model of a statistical mechanism to serve the purpose discussed in that Appendix: a mechanism which, when set in operation, would generate N_t series of values of $\overline{X}_{it}$ having statistical properties that are on the same general order of the ones illustrated by our rule. It is not a task that I am properly prepared to undertake, but I shall venture these remarks upon how I think a start might be made upon it – and, also, upon an important use to which it might then be put.

The variable $\overline{X}_{it}$ is a ratio of two variables, and the sought-for probabilistic model would be such as will assign a value to each for each value of t. The denominator n_{it} is a variable of the kind discussed in Section 4.5 and the Appendix to Chapter 4 – that is n_{it} is a measure of the size of a population that is developing over time in much the same way as are those for which P_{it} and M_{it} are measures of size (see the Appendix to Section 4.5). Its value changes from one moment to the next as a result of "births" (young persons coming of age and newly entering the labor force, as well as others, e.g., married women, initially entering at a later age due to altered circumstances), of "deaths" (present members of this ith labor force either dying literally or else retiring from the labor force as a result of altered circumstances, e.g., health or age), of immigrations (present members of labor force of other areas transferring to become members of this ith one), and of emigrations (present members of this ith one transferring to become members of labor forces of other areas). But so, too, is the numerator $\Sigma_1^{n_{it}} X_{jt}$ this kind of variable – it, too, is a measure of the size of a population that becomes larger or lesser as a result of "births" (employed members of the ith labor force becoming unemployed), of "deaths" (unemployed members of the ith labor force becoming employed), of immigration (persons entering the ith force as unemployed members), and of emigration (unemployed members of this ith labor force becoming members of labor forces of other areas). There would be thus already at hand a statistical model with which students might make a start with their experimentation – a compounding of two such models as were called in that section by the name Yule–Simon (see Section 4.5). It would be such as would generate a collection of N_t subpopulations, the *i*th of which at time *t* having n_{it} members, the *j*th of these having a value 0 or else 1 for X_{jt} – there thus being for each *t* and *i* a value of the ratio

$$\bar{X}_{it} = \sum_{1}^{n_{it}} X_{jt} \Big/ n_{it}$$

I may well be mistaken in this, but my feeling is that persons are legion who are now able to cope with the technical mathematical and computational tasks that would be encountered in implementing and analyzing a stochastic model like this one. The difficult problem, it seems, is that of comprehending why anyone would wish to do this – of understanding the comprehensive conceptual scheme into which these technical operations fit. Once this were understood, and a general interest in and curiosity about these technical problems were formed, there would be no lack of persons who would know how to make headway in an analysis of this random variable $\bar{X}_{it}$ so defined. The numerator and denominator each being a standard textbook case of a stochastic process about which much is already known, a sufficiently specialized applied mathematician, making sufficiently simplifying assumptions about the respective values of the relevant rates (of "births," "deaths," immigration, and emigration), might even almost immediately be prepared to say interesting things about the properties of this ratio $\bar{X}_{it}$.

But even so, I should think a more rewarding and informative way of proceeding would be by Monte Carlo methods. I have in mind now something generally similar to the applications of these methods cited in Section 4.5. Initially, of course, there would be the baldly unrealistically simplifying assumptions – say that for each of the subareas, i.e., for each value of *i*, the immigration and emigration rates are mutually offsetting and perhaps also the transitions that individuals make, from membership to nonmembership and from nonmembership to membership, occur randomly in time at rates that are unchanged over time and the same among the N_t areas. But with practice and experience, clever persons would soon hit upon how to do with less unrealistic assumptions about these rates – allowing them to vary among subareas, for example, in accordance with probability laws having some semblance of plausibility and that over the course of time might be made more realistically complex. The fundamental physical reality consists of the transitions that individuals make – into and out of the *i*th labor force, and into and out of its unemployed part. The values of n_{it} and $\Sigma_1^{n_{it}} X_{jt}$, and thus of $\overline{X}_{it}$ and $\overline{X}_t$, are simple resultants of a summing of the counts of the occurrences of these events. And the trick would be to find some approximately realistic assumption about the rates at which these transitions take place so that when the mechanism is set in operation, a numerical record of observations upon $\overline{X}_{it}$ will be experimentally generated, similar to the numerical record that we used as a source for the entries in our tabular forms, the one supposed to have been generated by the real mechanism that was at work during that observation period; and such that the properties of this experimentally generated variation of $\overline{X}_{it}$ are broadly similar to the ones described by some such rule as ours that purports to specify certain of the aspects of what took place in fact. I have been much impressed by how rudimentary and simplistic the initial versions of a probabilistic model of natural phenomena are[17] – and how rapidly, once the sense is grapsed of how the idea of it fits into a larger scheme, clever persons are able to develop the simple device into the intricate structure of which the mature theory of the phenomena consists. And I see no compelling grounds for not hoping that something similar would happen in the case at hand.

A modicum of success in the contriving of this mechanism would amount to a substantial extension of the description afforded by our rule – in that the working of it would show something considerable about what it is upon which the properties of the variables $\overline{X}_{it}$ and $\overline{X}_t$ depend; and in that a "running" of it would provide a way for legislators and their advisors to virtually look at a small-scale and somewhat more comprehensive version of what is being reacted to, thus facilitating their discussion of the reasonableness of one's experiencing an adverse reaction to the variation that is observed. The observation period for the numerical record that we used for the devising of this rule was an extended period of time during the whole of which the reported value of $\overline{X}_t$ ranged narrowly within or near 3.5 to 4.0 percent. Throughout the 1960s, this was a generally accepted criterion – this near-constancy of $\overline{X}_t$ at this value over an extended period – for one's identifying time spans of employment stability when the nation's population would appropriately be said to be in a state of full employment. This particular value, 4.0 percent,

[17] Among the interesting and instructive features of the truly fine textbooks now available in modern probability theory (e.g., Feller 1950; 1968; Cox and Miller 1965) are the many examples that are given of early elementary versions of probabilistic models that over the course of time have become the complex structures of the developed science of the subject.

will have been empirically determined, certainly not by any a priori argument, being the value of $\overline{X}_t$ that responsible discussants will have simply become used to seeing during the recurrent "good times" of employment opportunities. We interpreted the variable $\overline{X}_t$ literally for what it is: a measure of the density, at time *t*, of the unemployed members among all members of the nation's labor force; and also, as it no less literally is, an average of the N_t values of $\overline{X}_{it}$, each of these a measure of this density in one of the subareas into which the national area will have been partitioned. The mechanism in its working would show these densities – the global one being constant over time, along with the local ones constantly varying – as being completely dependent upon the aforementioned subarea rates – of "births," "deaths," immigration, and emigration, in the special senses of these terms there proposed. Whereas $\overline{X}_t$ is an average of the N_t values of $\overline{X}_{it}$, any of these latter is itself an average – of the n_{it} values of X_{jt}, each of these being either 0 or else 1 at time *t* and subject to transitions from one to the other that occur randomly in time.

As we are now viewing the matter, there would be two numerical records. The first would be the one formed by Census Bureau interviewers and enumerators, classifying individuals as either members of the labor force or not, and then, if a member, assigning to each the value 0 or else 1. The second would be generated by a laboratory running of the mechanism that we are now holding in prospect. At the start, with $t = 0$, all the n_{it} and X_{jt} terms would be set consistently with $\overline{X}_t = 4.0$ and with the variation of $\overline{X}_{it}$ being described as some such rule as ours would describe it. From that time on, the n_{it} and X_{jt} terms would vary, their values at time *t* being assigned by the outcome of the chance processes – a combination of rates having been found so that this generated variation of the $\overline{X}_{it}$ values would look like that depicted in our tabular forms. Individuals do in fact make transitions – in this case, as noted, into and out of the *i*th labor force, and into and out of the unemployed part of it. These events do actually and inevitably occur, however minimal and nearly constant the value of $\overline{X}_t$. The forming of the second numerical record of the outcome of this process differs from the forming of the first only in that the numbers are obtained by an alternative way of enumerating and summing up the resultants of these occurring events – this second way being based upon the fundamental assumption that the rates at which these transitions occur conform to probability laws that are stable during the span of time in question. In Section 1.6 we briefly discussed what that thing is for which *statistical mechanism* is a name in the natural science usage. For the case in that example, the mechanism is the matrix of transition probabilities. In the present case, and still in the natural science usage, the mechanism consists of these stable probability laws to which the transitions are assumed to conform.

Among many or most economists there seems to be a strong reluctance toward admitting that such statistical regularity and stability exist – that rates, in the form of frequency ratios, do in fact conform to stable probability laws, or that the frequency distributions that discussants talk about, of family incomes, firm sizes, urban growth rates, and the like, do in fact show a stability of form over time. But as we have argued all along, this reluctance is not consistent with one's taking for granted the possibility of *public policy*. To assume that a people's lot is subject to improvement by legislation designed and jointly chosen by its legislative agents – this lot being described by what these various numerical records show – is to imply that statistical regularities do in fact exist and whose forms are dependent upon the modifiable system of statutory law and administrative rule (see Section 1.4 and especially footnote 8 in Chapter 1). It is the intent of the legislative act to change the properties of the variation that is presently observed; and a contrast of what these properties are at present with what they are intended to become is a contrast of two forms of statistical regularity.

As I try to think about the matter, I do not feel clear at all about even what one would have in mind by "no regularity," that is, by an absence of form and pattern of the variation of a variable. What I almost immediately come upon for this concept of "no pattern" is the notion of randomness. But this will not do; for any particular instance of random variation is described and specified in terms of form and shape and pattern. That is what a distribution function of a random variable is: a description of it in terms of form and shape, telling one the relative frequency with which the values of the variable lie within any given range of its variation. Anyone who works with and studies the variation of a variable comes to form in mind conceptions of its typical value and of the expected frequencies with which its value falls within certain intervals. And it is only this that is meant by regularity and form and pattern.

Our description of the variable $\overline{X}_{it}$ in the present case is intended for no more than an illustrative start. The lognormal distribution was used for the most part as a matter of convenience. By its use, the entries in the tabular forms were calculated on the basis of values assigned to only five coefficients: μ_t, whose value was determined by assigning the value 4.0 to $\overline{X}_t$; σ, to which was assigned the value .348;

and the three to which we gave the values .19, .15, and .1, respectively. With these values having been roughly estimated from the data, the entries in the tabular forms were determined for any value of *t*. But it was noted at the time that I know of no basis for one's thinking that the variable's "true and exact" description is of lognormal form. Normal distributions provide approximations for limiting forms of quite a number of other distributions. And knowledge about the exact form of the distribution that describes this variable in question would come as a matter of course as students gain experience by working with such mechanisms as the one of which we have been speaking.

I am sure that inconsistencies can be found in the rule as I have presented it; and I am aware of a substantial incompleteness of it. By applying the rule, one can roughly trace out how the placements of the dots in the left-hand tabular form shown in Figure 5.4 become over the course of time the placements of the dots in the right-hand tabular form. Were more detail shown, each dot would be indexed in some way to indicate the particular subarea represented; and the horizontal spreading-out process comes by way of these indexed dots making transitions from cell to cell as time goes on. The right-hand form purports to show what the placements will look like when this process will have reached a state of equilibrium. The placement pattern in the left-hand form is unstable in an evident sense – by time *t* some dots will have moved out of the cells in which they were located at time 0, and no others will have moved in – for at this time there are no others. And the placement patterns that would be shown in the tabular forms for values of *t* between the times represented by these two extremes would similarly be unstable in a less definite but similar sense – more or else fewer would be making transitions out of each cell than would be making transitions into it. The right-hand form is supposed to depict the placement pattern when this process of transitions will have reached a state of equilibrium – in the accepted sense that the expected number of dots moving out of each cell from one moment to the next is the same as the expected number of dots moving in. But our description is incomplete in that we have presented nothing at all about these transition rates[18] – and no grounds for one's supposing that the transitions that would continue to occur would in fact be mutually compensating once the placement pattern of the right-hand form were reached.

[18] Unless, in my ignorance, I have implied something in setting .19 and .15 as the values of those two coefficients.

In regard to this latter omission, and as was noted at the end of Section 4.1, I think the concept of full employment, if understood to be a conceivably attainable stable state of a growing or otherwise developing national population of people, embodies a much too simplistic notion of stability. The concept as it appears in the actual discussions that take place is a more intricate and delicate one. *Full employment,* in the usage of these deliberations, is a name of a state that the population of people, as a principal component of the congeries of populations and processes of which the economy π_t consists, is observed from time to time to pass into, stay in for a while, and then pass out of. The length of time that it remains in that state, having made a passage into it, is a variable. Once it leaves that state, it stays out for a while before returning; and the extremity of its departure and the length of time the departure lasts are also variables. These three variables are presumed by discussants to have expected values that are dependent upon modifiable statutory law, but in ways that for the most part are yet a mystery. The *stability* that is involved as a subject of these discussions is a stability of the variations of these variables, that is, of the frequency functions that would be descriptive of them; and that which responsible and commonsensical discussants aspire to is a stability of these expected values – the first as large as can be come upon consistently with other desiderata, the other two as small. What our rule then purports to roughly specify are certain of the transitions and changes of states that are constantly taking place during a time when the population as a whole is in the state that is called by the name *full employment.*

CHAPTER 6

Concluding remarks upon what an economic system is, and the problem of specifying norms of the outcome of its working

6.1 What an economic system is

We earlier expressed the feeling that if there is to be a science pertaining to the economic system – a cumulation of knowledge about how a thing of this kind works and what happens to the outcome of its working when changes are deliberately made or otherwise occur in it – then surely it is of the very first importance that some specific understanding be reached among its students regarding what this working thing really is (see Sections 1.7 and 2.4). And now, with illustrations drawn from what has been presented in the preceding chapters, I shall sum up my tentative views upon this matter.

The outcome of the working of it – as anyone may see in recorded deliberations among persons responsible for its performance (see Sections 2.2, 3.6, 3.7, and 3.8) – is observed in the statistical properties of that vast congeries of populations and processes of events that we have denoted by π_t and called the economy (see Sections 1.4, 1.5, 2.3, and 2.4). The nation's population of people is a principal constituent of this congeries; and the properties of the variable $\overline{X}_{it}$ defined upon it (see Section 5.5) are illustrative of what discussants talk about when they talk about the *operating characteristics* of that working thing. So as to keep it distinct in one's thought, I have proposed that this latter be denoted by $\{\theta, S\}$ and the name *economic system* reserved exclusively for it. The S in this notation stands for the collection of statistical mechanisms that are presently operative – and the one of which we spoke at the end of the last chapter is illustrative of what a member of this collection is like. Were it the income state of the population that observers are reacting to – the distribution among its members of the jointly produced output – another variable would be involved, defined upon this same population. Were it the concentration of power or price instability or regional imbalance, the properties of variables defined upon other populations or processes of events would be the ones that are conveying the sense of the working of the system (see Sections 2.3 and 2.5). But the variation of any such variable would be generated by its corresponding statistical mechanism – and the S is the collection of these.

It is the statistical properties of variables defined upon π_t that convey the sense of performance. The variations of the values of these variables are generated by the statistical mechanisms of which S is the currently operative collection – this word *mechanism* being understood strictly in its natural science probabilistic usage. But it is only the system of statutory law and administrative rule, that is, "the rules of the game" – this is the θ in our notation – that is subject to direct alteration. The constituents of S, the statistical mechanisms that are in operation, can no more be directly determined than can the values of the variables whose variation these mechanisms generate. But the effect of newly enacted changes in θ, upon the properties of the variables that convey the sense of how well the system works, comes only through what these changes of the rules do to these mechanisms – that is, in the illustrative case at the end of the last chapter, to the matrices of transition probabilities.[1]

It thus follows, as we have earlier remarked, that the technical problems of public policy are of identically the same form as those posed in the theory of fair games (see Section 3.5). The primary task is that of designing changes in θ, that is, in the rules of the game, so as to effect predetermined alterations in the statistical properties of variables defined upon π_t – which, systematically done, calls for technical knowledge: not only of what the pertinent mechanisms are among those of which S consists, and of what these would be were they such as would generate variation the properties of which are those that are sought, but also of how to alter the θ so as to transform the S as it stands into the S as it would have to be. These are the same technical problems, on a stupendously difficult scale, as the ones posed for radically simple circumstances in the theory of fair games (see Sections 3.5 and 3.6): that of deducing from a set of rules a description of the outcome of its working; and that of transforming rules the properties of the outcome of whose working do not

[1] In this interpretation, the articles of Martin Feldstein (1978*a*; 1978*b*) would be understood as accounting for the rise of the minimal value of $\overline{X}_t$, from 4.0 to something on the order of 5.5 percent, in terms of the effect of changes of statutory law upon the pertinent transition rates.

In E. Parzen's *Modern Probability Theory and Its Applications* (1960) there is a simple problem that I have found useful in discussing with elementary students the sensitivity of this minimal value of $\overline{X}_t$ to certain kinds of changes of these transition rates – and also the apparent stability of this minimal value over the long period prior to the 1970s. See problem 5.1 (p. 136) in Parzen's text.

satisfy prescribed conditions into rules the properties of the outcome of whose working do.

It can be categorically stated, I think, that it is not possible for legislators, or for the authorities of a society whatever be its political form, to fix directly and specifically values of variables so defined upon π_t as to convey meaning to observers respecting how well the system works. What appears as a statutory fixing of the values of such variables is not simply that in fact – but, more important, to the extent that a control of its value is actually effected, the variable loses its meaning as *performance*. I shall try to illustrate the sense of this, first with a simple and familiar case.

Presently, the variation over time of the price of gold conveys to an observer some idea of the performance of the currently operating monetary system – perhaps not so very much of his comprehensive conception of this, but some; *performance* is the meaning that he sees in it. Were legislators now to enact a statute intended for the containment of the variation of the value of this variable within very narrow bounds, the monetary system being thus transformed into some version of a kind known by the name *gold standard,* this price which would hence be observed to be nearly constant over time would no longer tell an observer anything at all about how well or ill this altered system works. The near-nil variation of the price of gold would then be a detail in a description of the system $\{\theta, S\}$ and no longer a feature of the properties of π_t that convey a sense of performance. In passing, I think it should be remarked here, and more said about it at some other time and place, that the statute would not have merely *decreed* a fixed value of this price – that is, of this variable defined upon a stipulated class of transactions. It is in this connection that it is essential that a student of legislation keep in mind the distinction between, on the one hand, numbers as observed values of variables and, on the other, the reality upon which the variables will have been defined. A price is a number, an observed value of a variable defined upon an event, the transaction that really does occur in time and geographic space (see Section 2.3). Legislators cannot simply assign a value to this variable. What they do is to devise some subsidiary "game" for a created agency to play, and perhaps otherwise change the conditions and rules of the main game presently being played by the citizenry at large, intending that the outcome of this play be such as to alter in some predetermined way the properties of the variation of this variable – in this case, rendering it almost nil about its intended expected value. The agency is to stand ready to buy and also to sell the commodity at a fixed stipulated price. To be prepared to buy, it must have at hand the requisite money; and to be in a position to sell, it must have on hand the gold with which to part. But if its strategy for the playing of the subsidiary game is successful, the resulting near-constancy of this price over time would convey to an observer nothing whatsoever respecting the performance of the system so constituted. How well or ill it works would then be observed in the properties of other variables defined upon π_t.

Among these would be some measure of the growth rate of the aggregate size of one or another quasi-population which observers refer to as the nation's *stock of money*. The content of this variable's meaning as performance, during the time when the price of gold is being kept nearly constant, is of course derivative – from what connections its variation is supposed to have with the variation of other variables more directly indicative of the circumstances of a people's well-being: measures of the money values of the things people buy and sell, of the incidence of unemployment, of the frequency of personal and business failures. But from such attributed connections there is conveyed to an observer, as he attends to what is happening to this that he sees as the nation's stock of money, a sense of the aggregate size and growth rate of this quasi-population being about right or else not.

Suppose now that the legislators enact a statute intended for a fixing of this growth rate at some value that they will have been led to believe is the right one (see Exhibit B at the end of Chapter 2). Note again that the statute would not simply decree an assigned value for this variable. This is not within the realm of possibility. As in the case of the price of gold, the statute would set forth the rules of a new subsidiary "game" that the agent is to play, with actions authorized and conditions imposed, the objective of the play now being to keep within narrow bounds the variation of this variable that measures the rate of growth of a specifically stipulated quasi-population. The agency would thus be obliged to choose, within the constraints of rules set forth, a strategy for doing this; but supposing it to be successful, the resulting near-nil variation of the value of this variable would no longer tell an observer anything at all about how well the new system so constituted works. It would be a detail in a specification of the system itself and not a feature of its performance. During the tenure of the gold standard system, an observed stability of the value of this variable would have acquired an aura of something beneficent, indicative of a state of things referred to as *monetary stability*. But this meaning of it will have come from conjectured associations; and when the system would have been altered so as to effectively impose some semblance of stability over time of this observed rate of growth, it would then be in the properties of the variation of the variables that had been the subject of these conjectures that the performance of the new system would be observed.

But now come to the case of a statute the intent of which is a fixing at some stipulated value a variable so defined as to measure the degree to which the population in unemployed, or as to measure the minimum of the wages received among those that are employed at any moment. All that has been said respecting the other cases would hold for any such case at this. The statute would not simply decree that the defined variable have the assigned value. This is not what a statute does nor possibly can do, whatever the political form of the society. As in the other cases, the statute would set forth new "rules of the game," with actions authorized and conditions imposed – and with the fallible intent that strategies freely chosen by the players within the newly imposed constraints will in fact result in near-nil variation of the variable's value about some stipulated expected value. But even were this the outcome, it would no longer convey to an observer the meaning of performance that it heretofore had conveyed. The imposed steadiness of the value of the variable would be a detail of the altered system $\{\theta, S\}$ and not a feature of the properties of π_t in terms of which its working is observed. One may see the sense of this in recorded discussions of how well or poorly minimum wage legislation works.

There is a certain atmosphere of inefficacy about legislative action that is directed to specific economic reform. It comes across to one in his observing the many things that are apparently not changed much, if at all, by legislation specifically designed to change them – income distribution, concentration of power, monetary stability, employment stability, regional imbalance, and the like. And it seems at least as evident in the experiences of the so-called socialist states as in states more like our own. I am inclined to account for it in terms of the massive bombardment of crucial statistical mechanisms that is going on constantly and from all sides, from natural developments – technological but also institutional – as well as from deliberate legislative acts, actions intended to affect some of them always affecting others in unanticipated ways, the whole mass of effects tending to be mutually compensating on the whole – except occasionally when there seems by happenchance a persistent overweighting, such as what has apparently occurred to increase for the present the "full employment" value of the unemployment rate and the "price stability" value of the inflation rate.

Earlier we quoted a remark by Schumpeter that looks to me to be a very pertinent one – to the effect that students of our subject seem not "to have realized that the hunt for, and the interpretation of, invariants" of the kind set forth in the previous chapter, and for which such probabilistic models as mentioned there would be intended as something approaching an elucidation, "might lay the foundations of an entirely novel type of theory" (1949: 155–6). This idea of a new kind of theory that crossed his mind – new, that is, to the generality of economists, and newly to be conceived of as a subject field of economics – is the idea, I think, of the special kind of statistical economics of which we have been speaking (see Sections 1.6, 1.7, 1.8, 2.4, 2.5 and its Appendix, 4.5 and its Appendix, and 5.5) – the kind that Wesley Mitchell and his early associates made a promising start upon that has not been followed through (see Sections 2.3 and 2.5 and its Appendix).

6.2 Knightian principles of empirical inquiry in the social studies

In this final section I shall sum up the principles to which I have tried to conform in the descriptive work that has been presented – the Knightian principles, as I regard them, of empirical inquiry in the social studies. And for this, let the descriptive rule, set forth at the end of Section 5.4, serve illustratively as a tentative specification of a norm of an aspect of the economy of this nation as it existed over a particular span of time; and consider once again Knight's statement quoted earlier in Chapter 3:

> The ... propositions and definitions of economics are neither observed nor inferred from observation in anything like the sense of the generalizations of the positive natural sciences ... and yet they are in no real sense arbitrary. They state "facts," truths about "reality" ... or else they are really "false." Economics [deals] with knowledge and truth of a different category from that of the natural sciences, truth which is related to sense observation – and ultimately even to logic – in a very different way from that arrived at by the methodology of natural science. But it is still knowledge about reality [1956*a:* 154–5].

In what we have done so far, in defining and observing and formulating statements of purported fact, we have glossed over this difference that Knight put such stress upon. Ours are statements about the statistical properties of a nation's population of people in geographic space and time as this real thing was observed over an extended period when it was generally said to be in a state of full employment. And I shall now review certain of the steps in our method and try to see just where Knight's point comes to bear.

We have proceeded from the beginning in accordance with what we took as an eminently sensible suggestion by Knight: By studying actual cases of the practice of our profession, we have sought to find out what that science would be – what the technical and scientific problems are in a strict demarcation of its problem field – were there a science that is specifically and directly applicable in this actual professional practice. The cases at hand for study consist of records of the discourse and deliberations that occur when persons are in the act of critically reviewing the performance of the nation's economic system for whose working they are jointly responsible. There is a working thing, on the one hand, and there is the outcome of this thing's working, on the other; and in a typical such case, some one or several of the deliberators will have experienced adverse reactions toward what he or they think they observe in this outcome. And we have put as the initial task, calling for technical expertness on the part of a specialist advisor, that of identifying and specifying what in particular it is that is conveying to these responsible persons the sense of performance and inducing in them the feeling of disapprobation that they are in fact experiencing.

It is a demonstrable matter of fact, I think, that this particularity, when identified in any instance of these deliberations, invariably turns out to be some statistical property of a population of real elements, dispersed over the national area and developing over time, or else a process of events that really are occurring in space and time. We have illustrated the substance of this observation in Sections 1.3, 1.4, 1.5, 2.2, 2.3, 2.4, 2.5, 3.6, 3.7, and 4.1 and the Appendix to Chapter 4. And there would seem here to be several related facts of crucial importance in a conceptualization of what our science is about.

First, if the statistical properties in question are to be understood as conveying to an observer a sense of performance, and inducing in him a feeling of disapprobation, they must in some definable sense be stable statistical properties – else the discourse itself is not intelligible. It is not sensible that a group of persons should seek for ways of changing the property, and see in it a performance feature of an operating economic system, unless that property would in some sense remain the same were actions not taken to effect a change in it. Second, the stable statistical properties to which the responsible persons are reacting are not themselves subject to direct alteration (see footnote 8 in Chapter 1). It is only the system of statutory law and administrative rule that is subject to immediate and direct modification; and hence it must be supposed that there is some functional dependence of the statistical properties that convey the sense of performance upon the system of statutory law and rule that is subject to choice – else, again, the discourse and deliberations are not intelligible. And the initial task of the specialist advisor was thus extended to include this problem of determining what the statistical mechanisms are that are generating the variations of the values of the variables in which the statistical properties in question are manifested and what the dependencies of these mechanisms are upon the system of law and rule that is subject to direct modification.

This would be the first of two descriptive problems that are inherently involved in the group's pursuit of its deliberations: describing what the properties to which its members are reacting look like and are in fact and what the mechanisms are upon which these properties depend. Knight's remarks quoted earlier were evidently not intended to apply to what would come of a specialist's efforts upon this first descriptive problem. Rather, his view of what applies here is the ordinary one:

> An intelligent approach to economic problems must obviously begin with understanding the situation which it is proposed to change . . . The task of positive science is . . . to ascertain and describe the course of events in the absence of interference and the consequences of courses of possible actions in changing it . . . The methodology . . . is not essentially different from that of the natural sciences [1947: 327, 218, 243].

The elements of the population whose properties are being described and analyzed are no less "externally real" than those of any population of particles – each at any moment in some distinguishable state and from moment to moment subject to changes of state. The real mass of individuals either does or does not manifest the stable statistical properties to which the responsible persons think they are reacting; the supposed regularity of form of variation either is or is not generated by some particular statistical mechanism.

Proceeding now from these circumstances that pose this initial descriptive task, we come next to a third related fact to be noted in the deliberations: The participants who are reacting adversely to an observed state of a developing population are seeing in this real state of things an *aberrancy* – not a "disease" but truly and literally an aberration. This sensation of recognition, and the consequent act whereby the observed state is classified as aberrant, is subject to error – else the discussion among the participants is devoid of sense. It is the truth or falsity of the classifying of the real state of things as an aberrancy that is the principal subject of the deliberations (see Section 3.6) – the pursuit of which inherently involves the participants in efforts to reach mutual understandings upon what the norm is that the observed state is an aberration from. And we have put this as a second descriptive task calling for technical expertness on the part of a specialist advisor: that of identifying and tentatively specifying what this norm is – of finding out and describing what the population or process would look like as it develops over time and space were its properties such as would not induce the adverse reactions that are in fact being experienced.

These norms have names – at least some of them do – names that have become familiar and conventional parts of the speech in which the discussions are conducted. And Knight's remarks quoted at the outset of this section do directly apply to what would come of a specialist's efforts to specify what those norms are to which these names are given. The circumstances of the deliberations require of a discussant that he explain how others are to recognize the aberrancy that he will have noted; and it is in his trying to demonstrate why these others should also so classify the state of things he sees that the notion of a norm appears. And the truth or falsity of his conception of this norm is not of the same category of error and truth as the one involved in the practice of the natural sciences. The norm against which the observed state is to be compared is not the kind of norm of structure and functioning that can be learned about and specified by scientific studies of economic systems and how they work, treated exclusively as external reality. The normal state of things as this is understood in the natural science context of a sociobiologist's study of a society[2] is a state of things that may be reacted adversely to in Knight's social science context of a free society[3] – that is, a society possessed of a legislature whose members suppose the properties of such states to be dependent upon the laws that are subject to their choice. This, I think, is the substance, so far as it bears upon our present inquiry, of what Knight cited as "the factual root of the whole social problem"[4] – the insufficiency of the real

[2] See Edward O. Wilson, *Sociobiology: The New Synthesis* (1975), especially chap. 2, "Elementary Concepts of Sociobiology."

[3] For the special and restricted meanings of Knight's usage of the terms *free society* and *social,* see Section 2.1.

[4] See Section 3.2. It is this difference between the realities respectively studied in the natural and social (i.e., juridical) sciences that I take to be the "basic fact" that Knight thought Polanyi was ignoring in his discussion of the social and moral character of the natural sciences.

thing itself as a source of data for specifying the norm implied in this adverse reaction. Whereas the economy π_t is as externally real as any reality studied in the natural sciences – a vast congeries of populations and processes of events whose statistical properties convey to responsible observers a sense of how well or ill the economic system $\{\theta, S\}$ is working – the norms of its various aspects are not attributes strictly of the physical thing itself, but rather of the provisional consensuses that are continually being sought in deliberations about that thing among persons acting as agents in the choosing of the law.

This, then, is the condition of our descriptive problem: that the norm that is to be identified and described is something that none but the discussants themselves can directly sense and authenticate – like the clarity of image that an eye doctor strives to attain in the fitting of lenses to a patient's eyes, or the clarity of meaning of a sequence of sounds that a linguistic scientist seeks to determine and express. And in forming a tentative description of the state of a nation's population for which *full employment* is the name, we have conformed with this condition in the only way that has occurred to us to try: to find a span of time over the course of which the population was generally said by responsible discussants to have been approximately in that state; and then to specify and describe certain of the details of what this existent thing really did look like in its spatially oriented parts as it really did develop over that particular interval of time. It is understood, of course, that the thing thus described is subject to continuing review – that the norm itself changes over time and that the particularities of it that may be newly disclosed to responsible observers may well induce adverse reactions not previously experienced.

The true and simple prototype of the theory of our subject is the theory of fair games (see Section 3.4), with its focus upon the choice of rules of a game, and definitely not the more recently appearing theory of strategic behavior, with its focus upon the choice of strategic rules as means to private ends. Knight put as "the more crucial problem of a democratic society" that of "reaching agreement upon cultural norms" – to serve as guides "to the *direction* of change" to be sought through modifications of the law (1956*d*: 28). The norms of which we have been speaking are concrete instances of these; and finding and describing valid forms of such norms is conceptually much the same as finding and specifying valid criteria of the fairness of a game (see Sections 3.5 and 3.6). And it seems to me fitting that I close the present exploratory study of this descriptive problem with an extended quotation from Knight's early expression of this fair game theory analogy:

It is useful to think of social life as a game, and consider its peculiar features. It is played by groups, or teams – in this case an indefinite number . . . It goes on continuously, generation after generation, with "players" constantly dropping out and being replaced . . .

The first characteristic of play, as of all social activity . . . is that freedom is conditioned and limited by "law," in several meanings of the word . . . In the pure ideal form of play all the "laws" are taken for granted; the moment they give rise to any problem, the nature of the activity and of the association is fundamentally changed. Law, in the inclusive sense, is the essence of any social group, and the acceptance of the laws is a condition of membership. In free and progressive society, every social problem centers in differences as to what the law is or ought to be and takes the form of interpreting, enforcing, and eventually changing the constitution and laws. In free association, this is done by "discussion" . . . Discussion is an activity not directed to any concrete end but to the solution of the problem, necessarily unknown in advance. A social problem always combines conflict of interest with differences of opinion about what is right. Further, the differences must be associated with a common interest, the interest in perpetuating the group – in play, "the game" – while improving its character. It follows that freedom in social relations has three forms or components. First, every system of law allows some latitude for literal freedom of action by individuals and groups. Second, social freedom requires equal participation in the activities of lawmaking – or this is a condition of full membership in a group. Finally, since complete unanimity is not usually to be had, complete freedom implies the right and power to leave the group . . . and join other groupings at will. In principle, any group is "political" to the extent that its members do not have this third form of freedom . . .

In play, not much literal enforcement is possible without destroying the play spirit . . . The satisfaction of the individual interest in winning and of the group interest in having a good game are completely interdependent.

All problems of social ethics are like those of play in that they have the two components of obeying the rules and improving the rules, in the interest of a better "game" . . . It is a vitally important fact that capacity to play intelligently, from the standpoint of winning, is much more highly and more commonly developed among human beings than is the capacity to improve the rules or invent better games . . .

Perhaps the most important ethical principle of secular liberalism . . . that is to be learned from the consideration of play has to do with competitive self-assertion. As a matter of course, every party in a game must "play his own hand" to the best of his ability; otherwise, there is no game . . . Further, rigorous equality in the distribution of the results is self-contradictory . . . The ethical ideal is a "fair" and interesting game. Sportsmanship is a large part of liberal ethics. The conception of fairness calls for a certain minimum of inequality in capacity among the players. This need is often met by classification of players, choice of the game, handicaps, etc. Such devices are obviously needful in connection with the larger social, economic, and political game, and the difficulty of working out and applying them is a major aspect of the whole problem. The moral attitude of liberalism, being defined by the notion of law, is primarily impersonal. It is a matter of respect for the rules, and of ideals for their improvement, rather than a feeling toward persons, and the two things are as often conflicting as harmonious [1947*a*: 383–4, 390–3].

References

Aitchison, J., and J. A. C. Brown. 1957. *The Lognormal Distribution*. Cambridge University Press.

Ashton, W. D. 1966. *Theory of Road Traffic Flow*. New York: Wiley.

Berry, B. J. L. 1959. *Chicago Area Transportation Study, Final Report, Vol. I, Survey Findings*. Chicago: Western Engraving and Embossing Co.

Berry, B. J. L., and F. E. Horton. 1970*a*. "The Urban Envelope: Patterns and Dynamics of Population Density." Chapter 9 in *Geographic Perspectives on Urban Systems*. Englewood Cliffs, N.J.: Prentice-Hall.

1970*b*. "Internal Structure: Physical Space." Chapter 12 in *Geographic Perspectives on Urban Systems*. Englewood Cliffs, N.J.: Prentice-Hall.

1970*c*. "The Distribution of City Sizes." Chapter 3 in *Geographic Perspectives on Urban Systems*. Englewood Cliffs, N.J.: Prentice-Hall.

1970*d*. "Urban Hierarchies and Spheres of Influence." Chapter 7 in *Geographic Perspectives on Urban Systems*. Englewood Cliffs, N.J.: Prentice-Hall.

Berry, B. J. L., and A. Pred. 1961. *Central Place Studies–A Bibliography of Theory and Applications*. Philadelphia: Regional Science Research Institute.

Bornstein, M., R. H. Haveman, and H. J. Bruton. 1978. "Unemployment in Comparative Perspective." *Papers and Proceedings of the American Economic Association* 68(2):38–57.

Bryce, J. 1901. *Studies in History and Jurisprudence, Vol. II*. New York: Oxford University Press.

Buchanan, J. M. 1967. "Politics and Science: Reflections on Knight's Critique of Polanyi." *Ethics* 77:303–10.

Burns, A. F. 1934. *Production Trends in the United States Since 1870*. New York: National Bureau of Economic Research.

Christaller, W. 1966. *The Central Places of Southern Germany*, translated by C. W. Baskin. Englewood Cliffs, N.J.: Prentice-Hall.

Clark, C. 1951. "Urban Population Densities." *Journal of the Royal Statistical Society*, Series A 14(4):490–6.

Cootner, P. H. (editor). 1964. *The Random Character of Stock Prices*. Cambridge, Mass.: M.I.T. Press.

Cox, D. R., and H. D. Miller. 1965. *The Theory of Stochastic Processes*. London: Methuen.

Cox, D. R., and W. L. Smith, 1961. *Queues*. London: Methuen.

Cramer, H. 1951. *Mathematical Methods of Statistics.* Princeton University Press.

Cramer, H., and M. R. Leadbetter. 1967. *Stationary and Related Stochastic Processes.* New York: Wiley.

Dacey, M. F. 1968. "A Family of Density Functions for Lösch's Measurements on Town Distributions." In B. J. L. Berry and D. F. Marble (eds.), *Spatial Analysis,* pp. 168–71, Englewood Cliffs, N.J.: Prentice-Hall.

Dicey, A. V. 1914. *Law and Public Opinion in England,* 2nd ed. London: Macmillan.

Feldstein, M. 1978*a.* "The Private and Social Costs of Unemployment." *Papers and Proceedings of the American Economic Association* 68(2):155–8.

1978*b.* "The Effect of Unemployment Insurance on Temporary Layoff Unemployment." *American Economic Review* 68:834–46.

Feller, W. 1950. *An Introduction to Probability and Its Applications, Vol. 1,* 1st ed. New York: Wiley.

1968. *An Introduction to Probability and Its Applications, Vol. 1,* 3rd ed. New York: Wiley.

Haight, F. A. 1963. *Mathematical Theories of Traffic Flow.* New York: Academic.

Haran, E. G. P., and D. R. Vining, Jr. 1973*a.* "A Modified Yule-Simon Model Allowing for Inter-City Migration and Accounting for the Observed Form of the Size Distribution of Cities." *Journal of Regional Science* 13:421–37.

1973*b.* "On the Implications of a Stationary Urban Population for the Size Distribution of Cities." *Geographical Analysis* 5:296–398.

Hicks, J. R. 1946. *Value and Capital,* 2nd ed. London: Oxford University Press.

Hutchison, T. W. 1938. *The Significance and Basic Postulates of Economic Theory.* London: Macmillan.

Ijiri, Y., and H. A. Simon. 1964. "Business Firm Growth and Size." *American Economic Review* 54:77–89.

1971. "Effects of Mergers and Acquisitions on Business Firm Concentration." *Journal of Political Economy* 79:314–22.

1977. *Skew Distributions and the Sizes of Business Firms.* Amsterdam: North Holland.

Keynes, J. M. 1931. "The Great Slump of 1930." In *Essays in Persuasion.* London: Rupert Hart-Davis.

1939. "Professor Tinbergen's Method." *Economic Journal* 49:558–68.

1940. "Comment on Professor Tinbergen's Reply." *Economic Journal* 50:154–6.

1971. "Activities" In Elizabeth Johnson (ed.), *The Collected Writings of J. M. Keynes. Vols. XV–XXVII.* Cambridge University Press.

King, L. J. 1968. "A Quantitative Expression of the Pattern of Urban Settlements in Selected Areas of the United States." In B. J. L. Berry and

D. F. Marble (eds.), *Spatial Analysis,* pp. 159–67. Englewood Cliffs, N.J.: Prentice-Hall.

Knight, F. H. 1936. "Economic Theory and the National State." In *The Ethics of Competition,* 2nd ed., pp. 277–359. London: George Allen & Unwin.

1947*a*. "The Sickness of Liberal Society." In *Freedom and Reform: Essays in Economics and Social Philosophy,* pp. 370–402. New York: Harper & Bros.

1947*b*. "Science, Philosophy, and Social Procedure." In *Freedom and Reform: Essays in Economics and Social Philosophy,* pp. 205–24. New York: Harper & Bros.

1947*c*. "The Meaning of Democracy: Its Politico-Economic Structure and Ideals." In *Freedom and Reform: Essays in Economics and Social Philosophy,* pp. 184–204. New York: Harper & Bros.

1947*d*. "Religion and Ethics in Modern Civilization." In *Freedom and Reform: Essays in Economic and Social Philosophy,* pp. 163–83. New York: Harper & Bros.

1947*e*. "Freedom as Fact and Criterion." In *Freedom and Reform: Essays in Economics and Social Philosophy,* pp. 1–18. New York: Harper & Bros.

1949. "Virtue and Knowledge: The View of Professor Polanyi." *Ethics* 59:271–84.

1956*a*. " 'What Is Truth' in Economics?" In *On the History and Method of Economics,* pp. 151–78. University of Chicago Press.

1956*b*. "Free Society: Its Basic Nature and Problem." In *On the History and Method of Economics,* pp. 282–9. University of Chicago Press.

1956*c*. "Salvation by Science." In *On the History and Method of Economics,* pp. 227–47. University of Chicago Press.

1956*d*. "Science, Society, and the Modes of Law." In L. D. White (ed.), *The State of the Social Sciences,* pp. 9–28. University of Chicago Press.

Koopmans, T. C. 1947. "Measurement without Theory." *Review of Economics and Statistics* 29:161–72.

1949. "Methodological Issues in Quantitative Economics: A Reply." *Review of Economics and Statistics* 31:86–91.

1977. "Concepts of Optimality and Their Uses." *American Economic Review* 67:261–74.

Koopmans, T. C., and J. M. Montias. 1971. "On the Description and Comparison of Economic Systems." In A. Eckstein (ed.), *Comparison of Economic Systems: Theoretical and Methodological Approaches.* Berkeley: University of California Press.

Lösch, A. 1954. *The Economics of Location,* translated by W. W. Woglom. New Haven: Yale University Press.

Luce, R. D., and H. Raiffa. 1957. *Games and Decisions: Introduction and Critical Survey.* New York: Wiley.

Machlup, F., et al. 1964. *International Monetary Arrangements: The Problem of Choice–Report on the Deliberations of an International Study Group of 32 Economists.* Princeton, N.J.: Princeton University Press.

Mandelbrot, B. 1963. "New Methods in Statistical Economics." *Journal of Political Economy* 71:421–40.

Marshall, A. 1926. *Official Papers.* London: Macmillan.

Matui, I. 1968. "Statistical Study of the Distribution of Scattered Villages in Two Regions of the Tonami Plain." In B. J. L. Berry and D. F. Marble (eds.), *Spatial Analysis,* pp. 149–58. Englewood Cliffs, N.J.: Prentice-Hall.

Mills, F. C. 1927. *The Behavior of Prices.* New York: National Bureau of Economic Research.

Mitchell, W. C. 1927. *Business Cycles: The Problem and Its Setting.* New York: National Bureau of Economic Research.

National Monetary Commission. 1912. *Report of the National Monetary Commission.* Washington, D.C.: U.S. Government Printing Office.

Neyman, J. 1950. *First Course in Probability and Statistics.* New York: Henry Holt.

Parzen, E. 1960. *Modern Probability Theory and Its Applications.* New York: Wiley.

1962. *Stochastic Processes.* San Francisco: Holden-Day.

Polanyi, M. 1946. *Science, Faith, and Society.* London: Oxford University Press.

1958. *Personal Knowledge.* University of Chicago Press.

1961. "Knowing and Being." *Mind* 70(N.S.): 458–70.

Popper, K. 1971. *The Open Society and Its Enemies, Vol. 1,* 5th ed. Princeton, N.J.: Princeton University Press.

Raiffa, H., and R. Schlaifer. 1961. *Applied Statistical Decision Theory.* Boston: Harvard Business School.

Ricardo, David. 1952. "Speeches and Evidence." In P. Sraffa (ed.), *Works of David Ricardo, Vol. V.* Cambridge University Press.

Savage, L. B. 1954. *The Foundations of Statistics.* New York: Wiley.

Schrödinger, E. 1944. "The Statistical Law in Nature." *Nature* 153:704–5.

Schultz, T. W. 1950. "Reflections on Poverty Within Agriculture." *Journal of Political Economy* 58:1–15.

1953*a*. "Divergencies in Economic Development Related to Location." Chapter 9 in *The Economic Organization of Agriculture.* New York: McGraw-Hill.

1953*b*. "Income Disparity Among Communities." Chapter 10 in *The Economic Organization of Agriculture.* New York: McGraw-Hill.

Schumpeter, J. A. 1949. "Vilfredo Pareto (1848–1923)." *Quarterly Journal of Economics* 63:147–73.

Sherratt, G. G. 1960. "A Model for General Urban Growth." In C. W. Churchman and M. Verhultz (eds.), *Management Sciences – Models and Techniques, Proceedings of the 6th International Meeting of the Institute of Management Sciences, Vol. 2,* pp. 147–59. New York: Pergamon.

Simon, H. A. 1957. "On a Class of Skew Distribution Functions." Chapter 9 in *Models of Man.* New York: Wiley.

Simon, H. A., and C. P. Bonini. 1958. "The Size Distribution of Business Firms." *American Economic Review* 48: 606–17.

Simon, H. A., and T. A. Van Wormer. 1963. "Some Monte Carlo Estimates of the Yule Distributions." *Behavioral Science* 8:203–10.

Smith, A. 1976. *An Inquiry into the Nature and Causes of the Wealth of Nations, Vol. 1,* Glasgow edition, R. H. Campbell and A. S. Skinner (eds.). Oxford: Clarendon Press.

Stewart, J. Q. 1947. "Empirical Mathematical Rules Concerning the Distribution and Equilibrium of Population." *Geographical Review* 37:461–85.

1948. "Demographic Gravitation: Evidence and Applications." *Sociometry* 11:31–58.

1953. "Urban Population Densities." *Geographical Review* 43:575–6.

Stewart, J. Q., and W. Warntz. 1968. "The Physics of Population Distribution." In B. J. L. Berry and D. F. Marble (eds.), *Spatial Analysis – A Reader in Statistical Geography,* pp. 130–46. Englewood Cliffs, N.J.: Prentice-Hall.

Tinbergen, J. 1940. "On a Method of Statistical Research: A Reply." *Economic Journal* 50:141–54.

Veblen, T. 1904. *The Theory of Business Enterprise.* New York: Scribner.

Viner, J. 1929. "Review of F. C. Mills' *The Behavior of Prices.*" *Quarterly Journal of Economics* 43:337–352.

Viner, J., W. C. Mitchell, et al. 1940. *Critiques of Research in the Social Sciences: II – An Appraisal of F. C. Mills' The Behavior of Prices.* New York: Social Science Research Council, Bulletin 45.

Vining, D. R., Jr. 1974. "On the Sources of Instability in the Rank-Size Rule: Some Simple Tests of Gibrat's Law." *Geographical Analysis* 6:313–29.

1976. "Autocorrelated Growth Rates and the Pareto Law: A Further Analysis." *Journal of Political Economy* 84:369–80.

Vining, R. 1946*a*. "Location of Industry and Regional Patterns of Business Cycle Behavior." *Econometrica* 14:37–68.

1946*b*. "The Region as a Concept in Business Cycle Analysis." *Econometrica* 14:201–18.

1949. "The Region as an Economic Entity and Certain Variations to be Observed in the Study of Systems of Regions." *Papers and Proceedings of the American Economic Association* 39:89–104.

1953. "Delimitations of Economic Areas: Statistical Conceptions in the Study of the Spatial Structure of a Human Economy." *Journal of the American Statistical Association* 48:44–64.

1955. "A Description of Certain Spatial Aspects of an Economic System." *Economic Development and Cultural Change* 3:147–95.

1964. "An Outline of a Stochastic Model for the Study of the Spatial Structure and Development of a Human Population System." *Papers of the Regional Science Association* 13:15–40.

1969. "On Two Foundation Concepts of the Theory of Political Economy." *Journal of Political Economy* 77:199–218.

von Neumann, J., and O. Morgenstern. 1953. *Theory of Games and Economic Behavior,* 3rd ed. Princeton, N.J.: Princeton University Press.

Wald, A. 1950. *Statistical Decision Functions*. New York: Wiley.

Warburg, P. M. 1930. *The Federal Reserve System–Its Origin and Growth, Part I*. New York: Macmillan.

Williams, W. H. 1978. "How Bad Can 'Good' Data Really Be." *American Statistician* 32:61–5.

Wilson, E. O. 1975. *Sociobiology: The New Synthesis*, 2nd printing. Cambridge, Mass.: Harvard University Press.

Yule, G. U. 1924. "A Mathematical Theory of Evolution, Based on the Conclusions of Dr. J. C. Willis." *Philosophical Transactions of the Royal Society of London*, Series B, 213:21–87.

Index